D1556734

The Unforgettable Tests

ENGLAND v AUSTRALIA 2005

The Unforgettable Tests

ENGLAND v AUSTRALIA 2005

JONATHAN RICE

Foreword by Mike Gatting

Published in 2005 by Methuen

Copyright © 2005 Jonathan Rice

Foreword copyright © 2005 Mike Gatting
Photographs copyright © 2005 Patrick Eagar
Use of the image of the Ashes Urn on the front cover of this
publication is by kind permission of Marylebone Cricket Club

Methuen & Co. Limited
11-12 Buckingham Gate, London SW1E 6LB
Registered number 5278590

www.methuen.co.uk

A CIP catalogue record for this book
is available from the British Library

ISBN 0 413 77528 3

Typeset and designed by Louise Millar

Printed and bound in Great Britain by The Bath Press

10 9 8 7 6 5 4 3 2 1

For my friends Robert and Ann Chadwick,
Michael Clinch and the Radish Club,
and Bill and José Russell, whose company made those
hours watching the Tests even more enjoyable.

Foreword
By Mike Gatting OBE

What a summer it was! At the beginning of the year, England had reasonable hopes of giving the all-conquering Australians a good run for their money, but few people really gave England much of a chance of regaining the Ashes. For eighteen years I have held the increasingly unwelcome title of 'Last England Captain To Win The Ashes', and I confess that I had no real expectations of passing it on to Michael Vaughan.

But by mid-September, the title belonged well and truly to our current captain, and all England celebrated. The highlights for me were not so much the England performances from a statistical point of view, although of course they were good enough to win the little urn back; it was the way that both teams played. As President of the Lord's Taverners, I want to see cricket spreading back into schools and into the hearts of Britain's young people, and it was the spirit that every player showed – English and Australian – that made the game so appealing to so many people. Images of Freddie Flintoff (incidentally, 2005's President of the Young Lord's Taverners) consoling Brett Lee at the end of the Edgbaston Test, or of Shane Warne running the length of the Oval pitch to congratulate Kevin Pietersen on his match-saving innings will linger in my memory longer even than Andrew Strauss diving full length to his left to catch Adam Gilchrist, or Glenn McGrath's brilliant spell of bowling on the first afternoon of the Lord's Test. Whether anything will ever be able to help me forget the experience of meeting three Dame Edna Everage lookalikes at Trent Bridge is another question.

The 2005 Ashes series produced more than just great cricket and great sportsmanship. It also produced great excitement in every match, so that the final destiny of the Ashes was undecided until about teatime on the final day of the final Test. At lunchtime I feared we had blown it, and was too nervous to eat much: by teatime, my appetite was on its way back. The summer also produced new heroes – for England, men like Flintoff, Vaughan, Hoggard and Giles, the King of Spain, and for Australia Brett Lee. Suddenly they were household names, knocking Rooney and Beckham and the rest off the back pages for weeks on end. Cricket has made a comeback, and it is up to us all to build on this regained popularity and make sure that young boys and girls take part in schools and clubs (and on beaches and in parks) all around the country.

This book is rightly called 'The Unforgettable Tests'. Few of us have ever watched or played in a series of such sustained brilliance, and we can hardly expect to be lucky enough to do so again. Jonathan Rice's book captures the whole summer brilliantly, from the crushed expectations of the Lord's Test to the near hysteria of the final day at the Oval. Read, enjoy and don't forget!

Acknowledgements

I have many people to thank for their help, guidance and wisdom in putting this book together. Peter Tummons and his team at Methuen come at the top of the list, but mention must also be made of my wife Jan, Robert Chadwick, Michael Clinch, Bill Russell, José Russell, Alex Rice, Chessie Bent, Tim Whittome, Andy Rossdale, Hugh Wilson, Chris Old, Tim Rice, Chester McKaige and Dave and Tiddy Ebsworth, who gave me the opportunity to finish the manuscript on the Scilly Isles.

Introduction

Another summer, another Test series. But of course the Test series of the late summer of 2005 was not like any other series in recent memory. For the first time since Mike Gatting's team won the Ashes in Australia, there was a real chance that the rapidly improving England side could slug it out on reasonably even terms against the ageing Australians. This is the story of whether, and how, it happened.

Four years ago I wrote a book about the previous home Ashes series, entitled 'The Fight For The Ashes'. Unfortunately, with the honourable exception of Mark Butcher's brilliant and match-winning innings at Headingley in the Fourth Test of that summer, England did not put up much of a fight. 'Roll Over And Play Dead For The Ashes' might have been a better title. Sales were as good as the fight had been.

In retrospect, the highlight of the series for England was when Jimmy Ormond, on his Test debut at the Oval, won the sledging battle against Mark Waugh, as follows:

MARK WAUGH: (who has just dismissed an Ormond ball to the boundary with contemptuous ease) You aren't good enough for Test cricket.

ORMOND: Maybe not, but at least I'm the best cricketer in my family.

In Australia, a couple of years later, there were the first signs of an England improvement, although the idea that we might be the best Test team in the world by 2007, the stated aim of the England and Wales Cricket Board (ECB), still seemed as optimistic as a successful Conservative challenge in the 2005 election. That did not happen. In Australia, a few players began to feel at home in an Ashes Test arena, most notably Michael Vaughan, whose batting was of the very highest quality in a losing cause. But with no Flintoff on that tour (missing through injury) and with an old guard that was changing quite quickly, it was still very difficult to assess how well England might fare against Australia now. Only five of the players who had won the Fifth Test for England at Sydney two and a half years earlier were in the frame for this series – Trescothick, Vaughan, Key, Harmison and Hoggard. Ten of the fourteen players who had played for Australia during that series were picked to tour England in 2005. Clearly one of the confrontations of the summer would be the fundamental one of age versus youth, experience against callowness. Little did we realise what an epic confrontation it would be.

I have not spent the summer in the press boxes of the Test grounds, hunched over my laptop trying to beat deadlines. I have gone to the Tests as a paying spectator, trying to get the viewpoint of the man in the crowd, or in the queue for the beers or the gents (very often one queue led directly to the other). I did not record too many exclusive interviews with the main participants in the series, although I did mingle with several former Test players from both sides who expressed views about the series and the teams which I have tried to incorporate into the book. I also enjoyed hearing some of the very informed and stupendously uninformed opinions of some of the people in the crowd. I have thus been able to give my car a vigorous workout up and down the motorways to Manchester, Birmingham, Nottingham and London, not to mention Southampton, Canterbury and various other county grounds, in order to witness as much as I could of the Ashes summer. I very much hope the book catches the mood of the year and the tension of the Test series. Heroes were discovered, villains unmasked, and the fate of the Ashes was decided, as we had hoped, only in the Fifth Test at a completely sold-out Oval.

If all Test series could be as closely fought as this summer's, we would have no nerves left. The life expectancy of cricket fans, ripped apart by stress, would plummet, but we would die happy. Of course, not every series can be as gripping as this one, and nor should we expect that. We can only hope that a good proportion of the new followers of the game who have seen the light during 2005 will stick with it through dour and gritty draws against other sides in years to come. Even more importantly, how much will this summer contribute to an upsurge in the playing of the game? Will schools start to embrace cricket again? Will being Freddie Flintoff have a greater cachet than being Wayne Rooney? I surely hope so. Cricket is unique in providing not only a game of team versus team (the most important element) but also within that framework, duels between players and struggles to achieve individual and team landmarks. All cricket is interesting, every ball can change the match. Whether you are watching or playing, cricket is a permanent fascination, a multi-layered exercise of delights, and if 2005 has made this game popular again, then we must all be happy.

Oh, and the regaining of the Ashes is a reason for celebration too.

1

Start Me Up

An Ashes series is a milestone in cricket history. They come around on a regular basis every two years (or so – the regularity of the contests is subject to the whims of the International Cricket Council's scheduling as much as the next New Zealand v. Bangladesh series) and they give both nations a chance to see how good they really are. No victory, not even against the West Indians with Lara, or against the Indians with their stellar batting line-up of Tendulkar, Laxman, Dravid, Sehwag and Ganguly, gives as much satisfaction to Brits and Aussies as a win against their oldest cricketing rivals. The expectations are higher, the rewards greater and the downsides deeper than with any other cricket matches. The Ashes are what counts.

After the thumping England took in 2001, and the slightly less humiliating 2002/03 series, there was some hope that the summer of 2005 would bring some slight relief for England supporters who had been mocked mercilessly by the Aussies since 1989, when the Australians regained the Ashes on what was Steve Waugh's first tour. 2005 was to be Australia's first Ashes series since Waugh's retirement, and even though they were still ranked as the best in the world, and by some distance, who knows what a Waugh-less Australian side might be able to do? Or, more to the point, what a newly revived England might be able to do to a Waugh-less Australian team. There was nobody now to score centuries at will, with the greatest possible sense of timing and theatre, as Steve Waugh did at Sydney in his final Ashes series. There was nobody likely to hit a century on one leg, as Steve Waugh did in 2001, when by rights he should not even have been playing. And there was nobody leading Australia with quite the same sense of ruthless determination as Steve Waugh did. Surely the power in world cricket was shifting, but would it shift far enough for England to have a chance against these still mighty Australians? The summer of 2005 would reveal all.

However, if the Australians thought that the Ashes series was an event scheduled just for 2005, the great British public had other ideas. The home summer of 2004 proved to be the most successful, in terms of results, in English cricket history, with seven Tests played against New Zealand and the West Indies, and seven Tests won. Significant performances came from almost every player at one time or another – with the exception of poor old Mark Butcher, who injured himself in a succession of increasingly bizarre ways as the summer progressed, and he missed out on almost the entire season. Still, the likes of Andrew Strauss, Robert Key and Ian Bell used his absence to cement their places in the team, while Marcus Trescothick and Michael Vaughan both achieved the feat of two separate centuries in a Test. Geraint Jones scored his maiden Test hundred and Freddie Flintoff ended the summer with a reputation almost as high as Ian

Botham's at his peak, and with the International Cricket Council (ICC) laurels as one-day Cricketer of the Year. Add to these successes the resurrection of Ashley Giles as a potent left-arm spinner and the establishment of Steve Harmison as the best bowler in the world, according to the official ratings, and there did genuinely seem to be room for optimism in the England camp.

But still, England had not been tested against the Aussies, the world champions in every form of cricket. In the County Championship, Australians not quite good enough to make the national side were outperforming most Englishmen (quick bowler Andy Bichel even scored three centuries, for Heaven's sake) so the England squad were aware of the urgent need to find out how good they were. On 21 September 2004, the day of the autumn equinox, they got their chance. In the semi-finals of the slightly superfluous ICC Trophy, a competition the purpose of which nobody could quite divine, England faced Australia at Edgbaston. It was a one-day game, certainly, and no real yardstick for the Test matches to follow nine months later, but it was a serious match, and it was against the men in the baggy green, who had not been beaten by England in a one-day international (ODI) since 1999.

To judge by the reaction of some of the next morning's newspapers, the fate of the Ashes was decided in Birmingham that rather chilly September day. 'Victorious Vaughan on the right path to glory' trumpeted the *Daily Telegraph*, and other papers were as enthusiastic in their reception. But in reality, the game was no more than a straw in the wind – a harbinger of something maybe, but exactly what was more difficult to tell. 'The victory should have longer term benefits for the Ashes tussle next summer', wrote Derek Pringle, while Richard Hobson in *The Times* was rather more cautious when he noted that, 'there was enough in their manner to justify thoughts of 2005.' England did, in truth, win very convincingly, by six wickets with 21 balls to spare, but whether this one-off encounter would do anything other than strengthen Australian resolve was a question that would have to wait several months for an answer. At least England won without Flintoff making much of a contribution, showing on that day they were a complete team rather than a one-man band. However, with a long winter ahead, spent mainly in South Africa, there were clearly going to be major challenges to be overcome, even before the Australians were due to arrive in July. The fact that England went on four days later to lose a final, against the West Indies, that they should certainly have won made no difference. Even the cautious Michael Atherton described England's semi-final victory as a morale-boosting win for England.

However, all this was to reckon without Australia's almost sadistic ability to move ahead of the chasing pack whenever they felt the need. There was no evidence that they returned to Australia with their tails between their legs: they set off promptly for India, where – even without captain Ricky Ponting who had broken a finger in the England match – they beat India on Indian soil in a four-Test series. This was the one achievement that had eluded Steve Waugh as captain, and it was (at least for the Aussies) the hardest won victory of them all. Glenn McGrath came back to full fitness and bowled even better than before, and the Australians discovered a new star in Michael Clarke, who by November had become only the third Australian (and the first for about seventy years) to score centuries on both his home and away Test debuts.

By Christmas they had also made mincemeat of New Zealand at home, while England, ever able to slip two steps down for every one step climbed, were plunged into controversy in Zimbabwe.

However, they emerged from the brief one-day series there with their cricketing reputations largely intact, and while Australia took on Pakistan – and thrashed them mercilessly – the England touring party moved on to South Africa for a sterner examination of their achievements. By the turn of the year, Andrew Strauss had confirmed his reputation as England's wunderkind, becoming the first English player since Ranjitsinhji a hundred years earlier to score centuries on Test debut both home and away, emulating Michael Clarke's feat for Australia. His hundred in the First Test at Port Elizabeth led the way to another easy victory, by seven wickets, a record eighth Test win in a row against allcomers. If the Ashes were not already at Lord's anyway, safely in the permanent custody of Marylebone Cricket Club, then some optimistic souls would have wanted us to book the flight to bring them back straight away.

But then, just when it all looked too good to be England, the wheels began to wobble and the all-conquering side of 2004 began to look vulnerable. The Second Test in Durban was drawn after England had trailed massively on first innings. In the end, only bad light stopped an almost certain English victory, but the match was a close run thing all the way. It was also the first Test match that Andrew Strauss had played in and not been on the winning side. The Third Test, at England's nemesis ground of Newlands in Capetown, proved their undoing. Whether it was their New Year celebrations or the rigours of back-to-back Tests, or more prosaically Michael Vaughan's total inability to win the toss that was the root cause, the tourists were outplayed throughout the match, and they duly lost by 196 runs. This was England's first loss since Sri Lanka thirteen months earlier, Nobody on the England side scored a fifty, Mark Butcher failed a fitness test before the match began, and Flintoff picked up a side strain during the match. Perhaps even more depressingly, Steve Harmison, the world-number-one ranked bowler, had taken only seven wickets in the first three Tests, at an average of 61.71. The much vaunted England pace attack was not firing on all cylinders.

It was with far less spring in the step that England made their way to Johannesburg for the Fourth Test, and many commentators, as manic-depressive as ever, were already lamenting the prospect of yet another one-sided Ashes series.

However, once again, they were too hasty with their write-offs. The predictions moved from depressive to manic once again. Thanks to a brilliant 180 by Trescothick, and wholehearted bowling by the underrated Matthew Hoggard, who took twelve wickets in the match, England emerged from a frantic final day with a second victory in the series. All was not perfect, though, as several of the England team played well below their capabilities: Steve Harmison failed to take a single wicket, Thorpe made only 1 run in two innings totalling eleven balls, and Jimmy Anderson, brought in to provide an element of swing, took only two wickets, both with long-hops. Add to their efforts the frailty of Geraint Jones behind the stumps, and it was clear there was still significant room for progress before England would look good enough to challenge for the Ashes.

Even though the final Test of the South African tour, a rain-affected draw at Centurion Park, ensured that England won a series in South Africa for the first time in 40 years, there was still serious concern about Flintoff's fitness, Harmison's form and the quality of the fourth seamer, whoever he might be. Clearly England were not yet the finished article, despite winning four Test series in a row.

On the other hand, the Australians certainly seemed to be. They just kept on winning, match after match after match. Tests and ODIs, they all came the same to them. England managed to fumble any slight psychological advantage they might have built up in winning the Test series in South Africa by losing – and losing easily – the ODI series that followed. The 4–1 result, with one tied match and one washout, did not flatter the South Africans, who until then had been showing conspicuously poor form in one-day cricket. However, England uncovered one new hero: South African-born and raised Kevin 'KP' Pietersen, who hit three hundreds in the series, including the fastest ever hit for England. He scored more runs than Trescothick, Vaughan and Strauss combined. There were, inevitably, immediate loud cries for Pietersen to be included in the Test side, on the basis of his one-day form.

While there was little doubt of Pietersen's basic quality, the over-enthusiastic reception given to the new wonder boy only emphasised the reason why England have historically been so bad at one-day cricket: they treat it as an integral part of Test match and county cricket, rather than as the separate branch of the sport that it has become. Rugby enthusiasts would not assume that the best League players would make it to the top in Union, nor would athletics fans expect the same people to win both the one-hundred and two-hundred metre races every time. Tennis professionals perform quite differently on different surfaces, and though there are those who can excel at all forms of their chosen sport, it would seem to make sense to pick Test and one-day squads on the basis of the entirely different requirements of the two games. Flintoff may well be a selection certainty in both Test and one-day cricket, but what of Harmison – or Mark Butcher who has yet to make his one-day international debut? Australia's Michael Bevan was possibly the best one-day player the world has ever seen, but he had a modest record in the long format, and that limited the number of Tests he played. Similarly Andrew Symonds, with a mere two Test caps, is undoubtedly one of the best one-day players in the world today. Kevin Pietersen may well, in time, prove to be up there with Ponting and Warne as a player who can win any kind of cricket match, but a great one-day series does not prove a player is ready for Test cricket. But Pietersen has style (if not taste when it comes to hair colour) and the right mental approach to cricket at the top – such confidence in his own ability that it trips over into arrogance and a tigerish determination that brings out the best of him in a crisis – so most people were expecting a prompt Test debut for him in England, whether or not his early county form justified it.

The new season in England finally got underway a day late – rain washed out all possibility of play all around the country on the official start day, 8 April – but not before *Wisden Cricketers' Almanack* announced that for the first time since 1960, all five of their Cricketers of the Year were Englishmen. The five honoured were Marcus Trescothick, Andrew Strauss, Steve

Harmison, Ashley Giles and Rob Key, after a year in which the editor felt that the big story was the rise of England. Admittedly he also chose an Australian, Shane Warne, as the 'Leading Cricketer Of The Year', and by tradition nobody can be named a Cricketer of the Year more than once. All the same this affirmation in the cricketers' bible showed that, for the first time in almost two decades, England were being given a reasonable chance in the forthcoming Ashes series by the entire cricketing establishment. Great expectations indeed. By this time, the Tests were already all sell-outs, proving that English cricket fans are either optimists or good losers.

In early April, the first part of the waiting game ended, when Australia's selectors announced their squads for the Ashes series and the one-day internationals. There were no real surprises. Darren Lehmann, who had been dropped from Australia's most recent tour to New Zealand, was left out of the sixteen-man Ashes party, while Shaun Tait, a 22-year-old fast bowler who had suffered through a terrible summer with Durham in 2004, followed by a wonderful domestic season as the leading wicket-taker in the Pura Cup, was included. Otherwise, there was a familiar look to the touring party.

The full Test squad, announced on 5 April, was:

Ricky Ponting (Tasmania, captain) aged 30 and just 51 days younger than his counterpart Michael Vaughan. Since his debut at the end of 1995, he has been a regular member of the side, and generally regarded as their best batsman. A Test average of 56.50 coming into the Ashes series, along with 22 Test hundreds, vouch for his unquestioned batting ability. He used to be equally renowned for his skill at getting into trouble off the field as for his brilliance on it, but maturity comes with age and he was the obvious successor to Steve Waugh. His captaincy style is friendlier, but the Australians are still world champions under his leadership. He bears more than a passing resemblance to a young George W. Bush, which can be disconcerting.

Adam Gilchrist (Western Australia, vice-captain) is now 33 years old. One of three men in this party who would probably be picked for an all-time Australia XI (along with McGrath and Warne), he is a very great wicketkeeper–batsman, whose ability to turn a game round with the speed and ferocity of his batting has confounded all his opponents at one time or another. He came quite late into the Test side, taking over from Ian Healy at the end of 1999, aged 28, but since then he has scored almost 4,500 Test runs at an average of 55.64 and at a strike-rate of 83 runs per 100 balls, almost half as fast again as any of his free-hitting team-mates. His fifteen Test centuries are easily a record for a number seven batsman, and even though his wicket-keeping is sometimes less than perfect, his place in the side is rock solid.

Michael Clarke (New South Wales) is, at 24 years of age, by far the youngest regular Test player in the squad. Apart from centuries on Test debut both home and away, he had a season at Hampshire in 2004, when he did not rewrite the record books. He first played for Australia's Test side in October 2004, since when he has earned eleven further caps. His occasional left-arm spin (occasional in its appearance not in its spin) earned him the remarkable analysis of six for 9 against India, but after twelve Tests he has scored 669 runs at 41 runs per innings, and taken eight wickets, a slightly disappointing return after those initial centuries and his immense promise.

Jason Gillespie (South Australia) celebrated his 30th birthday in April 2005. In some parts of the world, this might be considered an advanced age for a Test match opening bowler, but as he is five years younger than Glenn McGrath and three years younger than Michael Kasprowicz, he still counts as part of Australian fast bowling's youth policy. Apart from being the first Test cricketer with some Aboriginal blood in him (his great-grandfather was a full-blooded Aborigine) he is also the most injury prone of Australia's fast bowling attack, having played 66 Tests, but missed a further 40 through injury – including a broken leg when he collided with Steve Waugh going for a catch. Somehow it was inevitable that Gillespie would come off worst.

Brad Haddin (New South Wales), aged 27, was chosen as reserve wicketkeeper for the tour, and had yet to play in a Test match. He is a former Australia Under-19 captain and good wicket-keeper and batsman, with a best first-class score of 154. He also has a handful of one-day international caps since his initial selection in his first season of top level cricket in 2001, but being Adam Gilchrist's understudy is a thankless task. If Gilchrist were to be injured, Haddin would have a daunting standard to meet.

Matthew Hayden (Queensland), a 33-year-old veteran of 67 Tests, held the record for the highest individual Test score when he made 380 against Zimbabwe at Perth towards the end of 2003, before Brian Lara took it back six months later. This is the highest score ever made by an Australian in Tests, but despite his Test average of 53, Hayden has a reputation as an unsubtle powerhouse at the top of the order. Signs of a dip in form over recent months caused concern, but Australia brought only two recognised opening batsmen to England, so his place in the side seemed secure.

Brad Hodge (Victoria) is already 30 years old but has yet to make his Test debut. He found his way to the edge of the Test side by virtue of several successful seasons as a batsman in English county cricket, including winning the Twenty20 title with Leicestershire in 2004, the year after he hit his highest score – 302* for Leicestershire against Nottinghamshire. For 2005 he trans-ferred his allegiance to Lancashire, but has hardly been seen in the red rose colours. He would probably stroll into any other Test side, and may get his chance this summer if injury or loss of form strikes any of his fellow tourists.

Michael Kasprowicz (Queensland) is now 33 years old, but his fast-medium bowling is as reliable as ever. He has played only 33 Tests for Australia, as he has never been a first choice strike bowler, having to wait in line behind McGrath, Gillespie, Lee, Bichel and several others over the years, but his commitment to the baggy green has never been in doubt. Like his fellow quicks, he ought to be past his prime, but Father Time does not seem to have visited the Australian dressing-room in recent seasons.

Simon Katich (Western Australia) made his Test debut on the previous tour of England in 2001, when Steve Waugh was injured. He then had to wait a few years until a place opened up in the Australian side and he was given his chance. An elegant left-handed batsman and more than useful left-arm wrist-spinner, he has yet to prove he is definitely of Test class, but he averages almost 44 in his sixteen Tests, despite having only scored two hundreds. 2005 could be a make-or-break year for him.

Justin Langer (Western Australia) turned 34 in November 2004, but remains the mainstay of Australia's top-order batting. Forming a left-handed opening partnership with the bigger and more muscular Matt Hayden, Langer averages 46.52 in 88 Tests, beginning in 1993. It took him six years to become anything like a regular member of the side, and like Brad Hodge and Simon Katich, it was probably his English county performances that forced the selectors to take notice of him. Langer and Hayden now form the most successful opening partnership in world cricket, and are statistically one of the best opening duos of all time.

Brett Lee (New South Wales) vies with Pakistan's Shoaib Akhtar for the title of fastest bowler on earth. He has had a few injuries over the years (he is now 28 years old) but is still the most effective shock bowler in world cricket. Despite this, he had not, until this tour, played Test cricket under Ricky Ponting's captaincy, but was seen as the right type of bowler to trouble Marcus Trescothick and exploit his well-documented lack of foot movement at the top of the order. He is also a very useful tail-end batsman who will always be hard to dislodge.

Stuart MacGill (Western Australia) has had the misfortune to be Shane Warne's contemporary. In most other eras he would have been a first choice for the Test team, but when your rival is the best the world has ever seen, you have to take what you can get. They have several times bowled in tandem in Test cricket and on those occasions MacGill has not always been the less effective of the two. Whenever Warne has been injured or otherwise unavailable, MacGill has never let the team down. In 33 Tests, he has 160 wickets at 28.81. His wrist-spin can be more vicious than Warne's, but his control of line and length is not in the same class.

Glenn McGrath (New South Wales) would be a top choice for anybody's all-time Australian eleven. Imagine an opening attack of Lillee, Lindwall and McGrath: could any batsman make more than a handful of runs against them? In a team of old men, only Warne is older than McGrath, and at 35 it is assumed that his very best days are behind him. He came into the Ashes series with 499 wickets in 109 Tests, at the wonderful average of only 21.22, and was looking forward to making either Trescothick or Strauss victim number 500 at Lord's. In all first-class cricket he has yet to take 800 wickets, which shows how little other cricket the top Test players play in this era of perma-Tests.

Damien Martyn (Western Australia) is a very fine batsman. Like Langer he took a long while to nail down a place in the Test side, but by the start of the Ashes series had scored almost 4,000 Test runs in 56 matches, at an average of 51.25. He is one of four members of the side with a Test average above the 50 mark, while the other three in the top seven average over 40. A combined average of around 350 for the first seven wickets is a daunting prospect for any opposition to face.

Martyn is one of the right-handers (along with Ponting and Clarke) in the batting line-up: they remain outnumbered in Australia's top seven by four to three.

Shaun Tait (South Australia) is the baby of the squad at only 22 years of age. The fast bowler is best remembered in England for his disastrous season at Durham in 2004, when in only two games he bowled eighteen overs and conceded 176 runs without taking a wicket. Against Somerset, his analysis of nought for 113 in twelve overs included 21 no-balls. However, after his return to Adelaide he was a changed man and in the Pura Cup season of 2004/05, he was the nation's leading wicket-taker and fully earned his place on the Ashes tour. As understudy to the fast bowling attack, he was still uncapped at Test level and was not expected to feature in the Test series unless something disastrous happened to at least two of their front-line bowlers.

Shane Warne (Victoria) was also captain of Hampshire for 2005. The greatest spin bowler the world has ever seen, he has surrounded himself in controversy as often as in adulation and wickets. By the time the season began, he was the world's leading Test wicket-taker with a total of 583 to his name, and it seemed most likely that he would reach 600 on this tour. As a slip fielder he has always been among the best, and his batting is not to be ignored, as a maiden century for Hampshire against Kent at Canterbury early in the 2005 season was to prove. Simply the best.

As four years ago, they were coached by John Buchanan, who had in the intervening years shaved off his moustache, which meant that the resemblance to Ned Flanders from *The Simpsons* cartoons was not quite so pronounced. The Australians under Buchanan (or indeed under anybody) were a formidable side, no doubt, but they were all getting old together, and at some time it seemed likely that age would catch up with them. Together, their 'first eleven' had played 730 Tests, scored 33,963 Test runs and taken 1,494 Test wickets. This made them statistically by far the most experienced and successful side in Test history, but also one of the oldest touring teams ever assembled. Even with the retirement of the Waugh twins since 2001, they were an older squad than four years ago. Would this tell against them? English supporters had to hope it would.

At the same time, the selectors announced a fifteen-man ODI squad for the three-way matches with England and Bangladesh, scheduled to take place before the Test series. Andrew Symonds, Brad Hogg, Michael Hussey and Shane Watson were included, in place of Justin Langer, Stuart MacGill, Shaun Tait and Shane Warne from the Test squad. Warne had announced his retirement from one-day international cricket, but the others were simply a matter of picking one-day specialists (Hogg, Symonds and Watson) as well as the next Test batsman but one (Hussey) in place of a batsman, a quick bowler and a leg-spinner surplus to one-day requirements.

The ODI squad in full: R.T. Ponting (captain), M.J. Clarke, A.C. Gilchrist, J.N. Gillespie, B.J. Haddin, M.J. Hayden, G.B. Hogg, M.E.K. Hussey, M.S. Kasprowicz, S.M. Katich, B. Lee, G.D. McGrath, D.R. Martyn, A. Symonds and S.R. Watson.

On the England side, the key men were also lining up for the fray. It was assumed that most of the side that had performed so well in South Africa during the winter would be selected for the Ashes series, but first of all there was a two Test series against Bangladesh to be dealt with. Bangladesh may not be the absolute minnows of world cricket any more, since Zimbabwe shot themselves in the foot by inciting a walkout of most of their leading players, an event which led to several of the biggest Test defeats ever seen. Even so, Bangladesh are not a strong side. An easy workout against a squad completely inexperienced in English conditions may not be the best preparation for the series of the century, but that is what the calendar had come up with and that is what was going to happen. Duncan Fletcher was determined that he would not field anything but his strongest eleven against Bangladesh, and that no quarter would be given.

The main candidates for a place in that strongest England eleven, at the start of the summer, were:

Michael Vaughan (Yorkshire, captain), who celebrated his 30th birthday as the winter tours of 2004/05 got under way, has proved to be one of England's most successful captains of recent years, leading England through thirteen undefeated Tests in 2004. As a batsman, he reached the top of the world rankings in 2002, just before he was appointed captain of England, and since then his form has dipped. However, when in full flow, there is no better sight on a cricket field than a Michael Vaughan innings, with his trademark cover-drives, clips through mid-wicket and straight drives. Vaughan is also a useful off-spinner, but he has been very reluctant to use himself in that role in recent matches. In all, his 55 Tests before the Bangladesh series brought him over 4,000 runs, including thirteen hundreds, at an average of a little over 44.

Marcus Trescothick (Somerset), Vaughan's vice-captain on the winter tours, is much maligned as a batsman who does not use his feet to get to the pitch of the ball, which, according to cricket theory, means that he is very vulnerable at the start of his innings. This may not be the best qualification for an opening batsman, but Trescothick, who was born on Christmas Day 1975, uses his superb eye and very quick hands to overcome any perceived problems in the footwork department. In 59 Tests, he has scored 4,430 runs, including ten hundreds and a top score of 219, at an average of 45. The Australians think they have him all worked out, but the Trescothick of 2005 is a far better player than the man who failed to impose himself on the two previous Ashes series he has played in. He is also a very safe pair of hands at first slip.

James Anderson (Lancashire), only 22 years old, has already played twelve Tests but his fast bowling, which was so exciting when he first broke into Test cricket, seems to have taken a few steps back in recent months. 35 Test wickets at 36 runs each are not the statistics of a world-class bowler. No longer a first choice in the England attack, he needs to take wickets for Lancashire to force his way back into the side. Still, he has proved capable of match-turning spells, and must surely come again soon.

Gareth Batty (Worcestershire), an exiled Yorkshireman, has played five times for England, but has taken only ten wickets at almost 69 runs each with his off-spin. The natural substitute if Giles is injured, he adds something with his batting and brilliant fielding, all of which make him more a part of the one-day squad than the Test side. The days when England had off-spinners like Jim Laker to call on – and groundsmen who would tailor-make their wickets for them – are long gone. Off-spinning in Tests these days is a thankless task.

Ian Bell (Warwickshire) missed out on the winter tours despite an encouraging Test debut against West Indies at the Oval in August 2004, but is clearly marked out as a talent for the future. The Cricket Writers' Club picked him as their young cricketer of the year in 2004, a year in which he helped Warwickshire to the County Championship. He began the 2005 season by scoring 480 first-class runs before the end of April – a record. He was then just a few days past his 23rd birthday. He also bowls useful medium-pace 'dibbly-dobbers', and would have been in the mix with Rob Key, Graham Thorpe, and Kevin Pietersen for the final two middle-order batting slots.

Mark Butcher (Surrey), England's hero at Headingley four years ago when he made a match-winning 173 not out, has had a terrible time of it in the past two years. Every sort of freak accident, beginning with whiplash when somebody drove into his car while he was on his way to the Oval in 2004, meant that he played only four county games for Surrey that season. He then pulled a thigh muscle while doing some tidying up at home, and followed that up by injuring his wrist while weightlifting during the winter tour of South Africa. He was still sidelined at the start of 2005. England would love to have him fit again, though whether he could force his way back into the side at the age of almost 33 is questionable.

Paul Collingwood (Durham) is England's one-day specialist batsman, bowler and fielder. Twenty-nine in May 2005, he has only played two Tests, but has 70 one-day international caps. A strong lobby has been pushing for his selection in the Test side, but the emergence of Bell and Pietersen, in particular, makes it unlikely that he will play unless injury ravages the England middle order. He is centrally contracted with England, but was expected to score many more county runs than international runs during the 2005 season.

Andrew Flintoff (Lancashire) is at 27 the peak of his powers. When he was first selected for Test cricket, in 1998, he was still only 20 years old and was chosen for his promise rather than his achievement. Up to the day of his debut, he had not even taken ten first-class wickets, but by the start of 2005 it was his fast bowling which was considered even more potent than his equally explosive batting. With 110 Test wickets (and fewer than 200 in all first-class cricket) and 2,239 runs in his 45 Tests, he was beginning to be acknowledged as the world's leading all-rounder. Due to injury, he had never played a Test against the Australians before 2005, and although most of the Australians knew all about him from county cricket, they were not entirely confident of how to counter his aggressive style.

Ashley Giles (Warwickshire), at 32 the oldest regular member of England's team, is a left-arm spin bowler who turned from being an economy item into a match-winner in 2004. Much maligned as a 'wheelie bin' and 'The King Of Spain' (after a misprint on his benefit mugs), Giles has had the last laugh on his critics, improving his control over flight, spin, line and length to the extent that his Test figures are actually better than those of his immediate predecessor, Phil Tufnell, who many would have thought the more gifted bowler. He took 22 wickets at 23.13 against West Indies in 2004, including his own version of the ball of the century to dismiss Brian Lara at Lord's. A useful batsman who has three first-class hundreds to his name, he has many times helped stave off an England late-order collapse.

Stephen Harmison (Durham) is, at 26, perhaps the most intimidating bowler in the world today. He was briefly ranked the number one Test bowler after his brilliance in West Indies in 2003/04, but homesickness has been a problem when he has toured in the past. A gentle man in his personal life, he is truly frightening to face from 22 yards, as batsmen all over the world are discovering. His figures of 111 wickets in 28 Tests at 28 runs apiece are not earth-shattering, but as the spearhead of an ever-improving England pace attack, Harmison has always bowled his heart out.

Matthew Hoggard (Yorkshire) is now 28 years old and is a veteran of 38 Tests, in one of which, against West Indies in Barbados in March 2004, he took a hat-trick to set up an England victory in what had been until that moment a closely fought game. Often underappreciated as the slowest of England's four fast bowlers, he is the man who gets the swing. If the ball is not swinging, Hoggard can get hit all over the ground, but on his day, he is extremely good. His record of 143 wickets at over 30 reflects the slow start he made to his career, but his average seems to be falling with every series. As a batsman, he makes a dogged nightwatchman.

Geraint Jones (Kent) is the man currently in possession of England's wicketkeeping gloves. The arguments continue to rage over whether the best 'keeper (generally thought to be Chris Read of Nottinghamshire) or the best batsman/'keeper should play for England. Jones is certainly a better batsman than Read, with one century in his thirteen Tests, and an average over 30, but his wicketkeeping continues to attract strong criticism. There are others challenging for the position, notably James Foster and Matt Prior, so the incredibly friendly 29-year-old Papua New Guinea / Aussie / Welsh / Man of Kent has his work cut out to retain his place in the face of all his rivals. Duncan Fletcher is on his side, though, and that counts for a lot.

Simon Jones (Glamorgan) is another Christmas Day baby, three years younger than Marcus Trescothick. He is the son of Jeff Jones, the former Glamorgan and England left-arm opening bowler whose career was cut short by injury, and after the terrible knee injury that young Simon sustained fielding in the Brisbane Test of 2002/03, it seemed that he would be a footnote to England's fast bowling history rather like his dad. But he has made a complete recovery, and his brilliance as a reverse swinger of the ball has made him a crucial part of England's team. In twelve Tests to the start of the summer, he had taken 36 wickets.

Rob Key (Kent) was the man in possession of one of the middle-order batting positions at the end of the South African tour, but had failed to impose himself on the opposition. In fifteen Tests he was only averaging 31, despite a double-hundred against West Indies at Lord's in 2004.

Brian Luckhurst, the England opener who died of oesophageal cancer early in 2005, said that if he had had half the talent that Key had, he would have played in 100 Tests, not the 21 he actually played. Still only 26, Key has the opportunity to cement his place in the side with a few good innings against Australia, who admired his performances on the 2002/03 Ashes tour.

Kevin Pietersen (Hampshire) had not played any Tests for England at the start of the summer, but had already made his mark in limited-overs matches. After eleven games, he had scored three hundreds in nine innings and was averaging 139.50. One of those centuries was the fastest ever scored by an English player in one-day internationals, taking him only 69 balls of mayhem in East London. As a South African with English parentage, he qualified as an England player only at the end of 2004, but at barely 25 has potentially a long career ahead of him. He was expected to make his Test debut during the summer but somebody would have to make way for him and his multi-coloured hairstyles.

Andrew Strauss (Middlesex), the wunderkind of 2004, came into the side by accident when Vaughan's injury left a gap to be filled, but there has been no accident about the way he has compiled his Test runs since then. In twelve Tests, he has 1,246 runs at almost 57 runs per innings, along with five centuries. With Trescothick he has formed a left-handed opening partnership that threatens to be one of England's best ever. The Australians were quoted as saying that they thought they had detected weaknesses in his game, but if they had, they did not tell the West Indians, New Zealanders and all the others Strauss put to the sword in his first year of Test cricket. At 28 he is a latecomer to the England side, but now is the front-runner to succeed Vaughan as England captain some day.

Graham Thorpe (Surrey), the old man of the side at 35, was closing in on his 100th Test cap at the start of the summer. England's most reliable batsman for many years, at least once he reached the crease, there was as ever a doubt about his motivation as the season began. A fully fit and motivated Thorpe is an asset to any side, and with him at number five there is a solidity in the line-up that a middle order of Pietersen, Flintoff and Geraint Jones might not supply. 6,636 runs at almost 44 are a good return for a Test career that has only just fallen short of greatness.

Chris Tremlett (Hampshire), the son and grandson of first-class cricketers, is a 6 foot 7 inch fast bowler of immense promise, still aged only 23. He has vaulted over Anderson in the England pecking order, and left those one-day specialists like Jon Lewis and Alex Wharf in his wake, but whether he will earn a full Test cap (or indeed a one-day cap) depends more on the fitness of the four quick bowlers ahead of him than on his own success in 2005. Having been earmarked as one for the future, he will surely play Test cricket soon.

These were the principal players in what promised to be a summer of great cricketing excitement. Bring on the Aussies! (Not forgetting the Bangladeshis first).

2

Come On

The Bangladeshis arrived to the cold spring climate of England, in every way underprepared for what awaited them. It was not the fault of the players themselves, who have made the most of the very few opportunities they have to share the cricketing limelight, but all the same, the squad that arrived in England looked as though they had simply turned up to give England some batting and bowling practice. They were smaller than their English opponents, younger (in one case not even out of school) and very cold. None of the players had ever played senior cricket in England before, and they were being asked to play a Test at Lord's within weeks of arriving in a climate and on wickets of which they had no experience. If it was proving impossible to beat anybody but Zimbabwe in Bangladesh, it would surely be unthinkable that they would win even one game against international opposition during a chilly early summer in England.

The First Test, at Lord's, was scheduled to start on 26 May and to last for five days. Few tickets had been sold beyond the second day, a pragmatic response from the general public that seemed all the more sensible when the England team was announced. The main issue seemed to be the make-up of the middle order – how much would England experiment just a few weeks before the start of an Ashes series? The answer was that they did not experiment at all, giving absolutely nobody a Test debut. Though not quite at full strength because of an injury to Ashley Giles, the England side did not contain Kevin Pietersen, but it did contain Graham Thorpe and Ian Bell. Early season form obviously counted for something because Bell edged out Rob Key, despite Key's good start to the summer. Bell had begun the summer as though he wanted to score all the runs in the world. Key could certainly consider himself unfortunate to be left out, but in the three Tests he played in South Africa after taking over from the injured Mark Butcher, he scored only one fifty, and finished with an average lower than all the other batsmen, and lower than Giles and Geraint Jones as well. When Duncan Fletcher came down to Canterbury in the first few weeks of the season, on a regular tour of all the counties, he made it clear to Key and to Kent that he would be playing against Bangladesh, but he was obviously overruled by his fellow selectors, David Graveney and Geoff Miller, and his place went to Ian Bell.

Pietersen missed out as well, partly because the claims of Bell and Thorpe were so strong, but also because he had a slightly slow start to his career with Hampshire. His first century for his new county came in the match against Glamorgan, just after the First Test team had been announced. So he had to wait, like Key, for another opportunity, and compile county runs in the meantime.

The first day of the First Test was not a warm one, and when England won the toss and put Bangladesh in to bat, it soon became clear that there would be little time to move away from the action to buy a beer. At least the queues for the beers were not likely to be particularly long, as Lord's itself was no more than half full. Vaughan was reported to have one eye on the football play-offs scheduled for the Sunday, for which he had tickets, and wanted to finish the match off quickly. The football season finishes ever later each summer, and the cricket season seems to start ever earlier, so that about six weeks of the cricket season overlap with football between mid-April and the end of May. By fixing the Australian Tests so late in the summer the ECB ensured that almost the complete series would clash with the start of the new football season, not to mention a friendly international or two, which meant that the England cricketers were under pressure to perform really well if they were to keep cricket on the back pages of the newspapers, and not have football monopolising the headlines yet again.

Against Bangladesh England did perform really well. The First Test was over almost before it started, with England needing fewer than 40 overs to roll over their hapless opponents. They then compiled a clinical and rapid 528 for three declared, with Trescothick gorging himself with 194 cheap runs, and Michael Vaughan taking 120 off this toothless attack, despite looking very out of form most of the time. This was his third successive century in Lord's Tests, equalling a very obscure record held by Jack Hobbs. Strauss was the only player to fail, making just 69, but Bell and Thorpe added over 100 together before Vaughan declared. Bangladesh's second innings was nine balls longer than their first, but only because of an eighth wicket stand of 58 between their wicketkeeper Khaled Mashud and their number ten Anwar Hossain Monir. Opening bat Javed Omar and Aftab Ahmed at number four were the only two players to reach double figures twice, although sixteen-year-old schoolboy Mushfiqur Rahim, the youngest ever Test cricketer at Lord's, made a promising 19 in the first-innings debacle. The wickets were shared around by England's bowlers, with six for Hoggard, five for Flintoff and four apiece for Harmison and Simon Jones. Gareth Batty neither batted, bowled nor held a catch, but at least he can say he has played in a Lord's Test, and while Giles was laid up, he did nothing to jeopardise his place for the Second Test. For the record, England won by an innings and 261 runs, a winning margin only once beaten at Lord's, when England beat India by an innings and 285 runs in 1974. I saw that game, when Chris Old and Geoff Arnold wiped out India for just 42 in their second innings, completing the job before lunch on the fourth day and ruining what should have been a glorious full day's cricket. This time, England completed the rout before lunch on the third day, and Michael Vaughan was able to use his tickets to the football match.

The Second Test, at Chester-le-Street, followed a similar storyline. England could hardly change a side that had won so convincingly, so Pietersen, Key and all the others with Test pretensions had to carry on round the county circuit, which was probably more of a challenge. England won the toss again and put Bangladesh in again. Once more they failed to last 40 overs, although they only missed that target by one ball. They totalled 104, which was four fewer than in their first innings at Lord's. The main destroyers were Steve Harmison, all thoughts of homesickness forgotten on his home ground, with five for 38, and Matthew Hoggard with three wickets in twelve overs for only 24 runs. One Harmison thunderbolt which yorked skipper Habibul Bashar and pulverised his stumps was particularly memorable. Geraint Jones took six catches behind the stumps in the first innings, and did not concede a bye in the entire game: not bad for a rotten wicketkeeper.

When England batted, their innings followed the same pattern as at Lord's. Trescothick, who clearly scared the wits out of the Bangladeshi bowlers, hit a run-a-ball 151, and Strauss failed again, this time quite seriously. His 8, caught plumb lbw by Mashrafe Mortaza, was the only single-figure score to be made by an English batsman in the entire Test series. I know it was only two Tests long, but has that ever happened before? Without checking through *Wisden* for what is after all a fairly unimportant record, I doubt it. Strauss looked very out of form, and had not scored any runs in county games either. The Golden Boy of 2004 needed to find his touch again or England were likely to be in serious trouble later in the summer. Trescothick and Vaughan, on the other hand, decided to pile on the runs, with the result that the score increased by 223 between tea and stumps on the first day, for the loss of Vaughan for 44 in 40 balls.

Ian Bell was promising to be the Golden Boy of 2005. Seizing the chance that a split selection panel had given him, he scored his maiden Test century, making 162 not out as he shared in a stand of 187 with Graham Thorpe, who made a comfortable 66 not out in his one hundredth Test. Bell's innings included 105 runs between the start of play and lunch on the second day, the first time this has been done by an Englishman since Les Ames, the first of a long line of Kentish wicketkeeper–batsmen, scored a hundred before lunch at the Oval against South Africa in 1935, seventy years before. When England declared at 447 for three, it meant that six of their players had not batted in the entire series (another obscure record, and without checking through *Wisden* etc., I doubt if that has ever happened before either). Records were created, broken and re-created with almost every ball that an English batsman faced, but it was all rather uninteresting. By the end of the match, Ian Bell had a Test batting average of 297, three times that of Bradman. It is unlikely that history will record him as being three times as good as the Don, but you never know. Hope springs eternal when the Ashes are at stake.

Bangladesh then failed to roll over and play dead in their second innings, making a gritty 316, built round good innings from Javed Omar and Aftab Ahmed. Hoggard finished them off in a flurry of wickets to snaffle the Man of the Match award, although Aftab Ahmed and Tapash Baisya added 60 for the ninth wicket to prolong the inevitable annihilation. The total of 316 was still 27 runs too few to get England to bat again, but at least their defiance meant that Gareth Batty got a bowl, and a wicket. The final analysis showed that England lost only six wickets in the whole series, and put on an average of 162 per wicket. Bangladesh lost forty wickets, at an average cost of just over 17. When one side outclasses the other by almost 10 to 1, it is hardly Test cricket, but as the old sports saying goes, you can only beat the opponent you are up against.

England v. Bangladesh

First Test Match, at Lord's, 26, 27, 28 May.
England won by an innings and 261 runs.
Bangladesh 108 (Javed Omar 22; Hoggard 4-42) and 159 (Khaled Mashud 44; S.P. Jones 3-29, Flintoff 3-44)
England 528 for 3 wickets declared (Trescothick 194, Vaughan 120; Mortaza 2-107)
Man of the Match: M.E. Trescothick

Second Test Match, at Chester-le-Street, 3, 4, 5 June.
England won by an innings and 27 runs.
Bangladesh 104 (Javed Omar 37; Harmison 5-38) and 316 (Khaled Mashud 82 not out, Javed Omar 71; Hoggard 5-73)
England 447 for 3 wickets declared (Bell 162 not out, Trescothick 151; Mortaza 2-91)
Man of the Match: M.J. Hoggard

It seems unlikely that the Australians, who arrived in England during the Second Test, were unduly worried by England's huge margin of victory. Ricky Ponting merely noted what was going on, but from their position of absolute supremacy the Australians saw no reason to be alarmed. Perhaps they missed something. Even though the Australians would have beaten Bangladesh with similar ease, there was a new dimension to England's players that marked them as a complete team. They played for each other and truly enjoyed each other's successes. They are not a team built round one or two superstars who carry the rest of the side along with them. There are several world-class players in the England team now, but everybody plays his part to the full. There is no obvious weak link in the side, however much the Australians would like to expose one. The Bangladesh series was not a complete waste of time. It built up England's confidence, team skills and kept up their habit of winning, a useful habit to be in when you come up against the world champions.

The next stage of the summer was to be the NatWest Series of one-day internationals, a three-way game of musical chairs between England, Australia and Bangladesh, followed by the NatWest Challenge, a two-way game of musical chairs between England and Australia. Why? Money.

The Test matches had been sold out virtually from the day the tickets went on sale in the autumn, and the ECB therefore used the NatWest Series as an opportunity to show how magnanimous they are: it is the only way those without Test match tickets will be able to see the Aussies playing serious cricket. The England v. Australia matches were sold out quickly, but the Bangladesh games were a harder sell, at least until the Australians found the perfect marketing ploy – they lost their first match against them.

In truth, the result was not quite as much a shock as it would have been a month earlier. The Australian tour, from a playing point of view, got off to the worst possible start. After an easy workout against a PCA Masters XI at Arundel, they moved up to Grace Road and brushed

Leicestershire aside in a one-day game, their winning margin being 95 runs. Not everybody had hit his top form, but enough of the parts of the machine were working for there to be no real alarms, and Australia seemed to be set along the steady path of success that was their due. And then on Monday, 13 June, the rot set in.

The Twenty20 is not a form of cricket that has yet really taken hold of Australia, but several of the Australians who took part in the game at the Rose Bowl had played Twenty20 in England. Andrew Symonds and Mike Hussey in particular were expert at the format. England's players had hardly any more experience as most of them were centrally contracted players who had not been released by England to play in the few games that had taken place since its launch in 2003. This was the first ever Twenty20 international played in England, and although a festival atmosphere prevailed at the Rose Bowl, everybody knew that beneath the joviality and the smiles there was the chance to strike the first psychological blow of the Ashes series. While Mike Gatting, the last England captain to win the Ashes, set off from the Rose Bowl with several doughty companions on the epic Ashes Walk, a fund raising trudge between all the county grounds of England, the first clash of the summer between England and Australia got under way. The Ashes Walk was organised by the Lord's Taverners to raise money for the 'Chance To Shine' project to bring cricket back to schools, particularly inner city schools, and by the time it reached Lord's in time for the First Test, (via Durham, Cardiff, Leicester, Old Trafford, Canterbury and all other county headquarters – not the most direct route ever taken from Southampton to St John's Wood) not only did Mike Gatting and many others have sore feet, but also the 'Chance To Shine' project was richer by a significant sum of money. It was in many ways typical of the cricket that was to be played throughout the summer: it was hard work, not always stylish, but done in the best of spirits and in a manner that made both the participants and the observers on the sidelines proud to have been a part of it. What's more, it raised the profile of cricket and brought it to many pages of the newspapers that are normally devoid of sporting achievements, just as the cricket was to do in the months ahead. For pure excitement the Ashes Walk perhaps never matched the Ashes Cricket, (unless you get your kicks on Route 66, the A249 or along Offa's Dyke) but in every other way it met the mood of the summer perfectly.

OK, so the Aussies do not know how to play Twenty20. They do not do it Down Under very much, but they had previously played a Twenty20 international, unlike England, so that was hardly an excuse for the complete mismatch that followed. Michael Vaughan won the toss and batted. In 20 overs, England rattled up 179 for eight, with Paul Collingwood's 46 off 28 balls just edging out Trescothick's 41 off 37 balls and Kevin Pietersen's 34 off just 18 balls as the best score of the innings. For the first time in the summer – but surely not the last – Jason Gillespie was targeted by the England batsmen, to the extent that his four overs went for 49 runs. Vaughan got a first-ball duck, giving his opposite number some simple catching practice, but most of the rest of the batsmen enjoyed themselves. The sell-out crowd certainly did.

When Australia came out to bat, it was energetic, but it was the energy of a headless chicken, undirected and doomed to sudden death. After fifteen balls, Australia had reached 23 without loss, and already some commentators were reaching for their thesauruses to find new words to describe Australia trouncing England once again. But then Gilchrist, having smacked three fours off Gough and Jon Lewis, mishit Gough to Kevin Pietersen and the first wicket fell. The batsmen had crossed, and next ball Hayden did virtually the same thing – c. Pietersen b. Gough. Jon Lewis' second over produced two more wickets, Michael Clarke being caught behind first ball and Andrew Symonds, the one Australian with a fine track record in Twenty20, caught yet again by Pietersen, also for a duck. It seemed at this time that Pietersen could catch a falling star and put it in his pocket: everything was working for him. When Hussey fell in Gough's next over, and Lewis removed two more in his third over, Australia were 31 for seven, and the match was over as a contest. Gillespie and Lee managed to put on 36 for the eighth wicket but after only 14.3 overs they were all out for 79. England's victory by 100 runs was a huge one. However much the Australians played it down, and it is certainly true that Twenty20 cricket and Test cricket have little in common except the bats and the stumps, there was no doubt that the England camp had discovered that the Australians are not invincible. It was a happy English squad that left the Rose Bowl that night,

For Australia, the preparations for the Ashes series went from bad to worse. The structure of the summer should have played into their hands. A later start to the tour meant that many of the tourists who were contracted as county overseas players, notably Hodge, Hussey, Kasprowicz, Katich, Symonds and Shane Warne, could get themselves used to English playing conditions again. Also, the late summer Tests ought to find wickets taking more spin than in the early summer, which would tend to help any side that contains the best wrist-spinner the world has ever seen. Then there was the fact that England gave themselves a schedule that involved unchallenging games against Bangladesh followed by a series of one-day internationals that would mean that the England regulars were unlikely to get any first-class cricket between the two Test series. Australians, on the other hand, had a few county fixtures to get themselves into the groove while the rest of England was involved in the county Twenty20 competition. Something has to be done about the ludicrous summer scheduling, which seems designed to put people off Test cricket, but that will have to wait until after 2005.

The Australians' next task was to get themselves into form, and into the mood, for the one-day internationals against both England and Bangladesh. They first of all went to Taunton, England's highest scoring ground, to play a fifty overs game against Somerset. Ricky Ponting won the toss and decided to bat. Against what is not the most feared county attack on the circuit, the Australians racked up a good score quickly. So confident were they of their form that both Hayden, on 76, and Ponting, on 80, retired themselves to give others some practice. Nobody made fewer than Katich's 12, and apart from Haddin, who only faced four balls, the next lowest score was Damien Martyn's 44. At 342 for five, the innings was closed.

Even the most jingoistic Englishman, who loves to see Australian cricketers humiliated, will have to admit that the two men who were the main cause of the downfall of Australia are not Somerset born and bred. Graeme Smith, captain of South Africa, and Sanath Jayasuriya, holder of Sri Lanka's record Test score, are hired guns. But it was Somerset who hired them, and it was on Somerset's behalf that they put on an opening stand of 197 in barely 25 overs to set up a remarkable victory. Both hit centuries, although it was left to lesser names like James Hildreth and Carl Gazzard to seal the win with three overs to spare. The Australian bowling was not successful. They were resting Gillespie (and Warne, having retired from one-day internationals, was playing for Hampshire) but even so, this international attack should have done better. Kasprowicz bowled eight overs for 89 runs, an analysis that went some way to keeping him out of the First Test team a month later. The press began to scent an upset of major proportions, and as only the English press can, immediately went into manic mode building up England's chances and their readers' hopes. The depressive mode would come later.

Australia's next match was against Bangladesh, at Sophia Gardens, Cardiff on 18 June. England had already coasted past the same opposition at the Oval two days earlier, so at last the Australians had a chance to get things back on track. A good stiff workout would not go amiss, but a victory was what was expected, and by this time very much needed. A victory was not what they got. In one of the biggest upsets in ODI history, the Bangladeshis restricted Australia to 249 for five in their fifty overs, and then reached 250 for five with four balls to spare. That is the simple statement of the result, but within those few words lie a multitude of achievements and emotions. The main guns of Australia's mighty cricketing machine were just not firing. Crisis would be too big a word for the state in which the tourists found themselves – and indeed the word was repeatedly denied, laughed off or just ignored by the Australians themselves, but the English press was loving it. Even before the match began, Andrew Symonds, on his day the linchpin of Australia's one-day side, was dropped for what turned out to be disciplinary reasons, celebrating Shane Watson's birthday too well but not too wisely. When the game began, Gilchrist lasted two balls. Ponting faced sixteen deliveries for a tortuous single, and only Hussey and Katich at the end, with an unbroken stand of 66 in 6.3 overs, managed to break out of the shackles that Bangladesh had imposed, with the complicity of the Australians themselves. Mohammad Rafique, who ended the Test series with one wicket for 257 runs, bowled his ten overs for a miserly 31 runs, and even top scorer Martyn, with 77 in 112 balls, hardly set Sophia Gardens alight.

It was Mohammad Ashraful who did that. The Australians cannot have imagined that 249 would not be enough, especially with all their big boys on duty. The Bangladeshi openers, Javed Omar and Nafees Iqbal, went along sedately enough, and though the fifty came up, for the loss of just one wicket, in the sixteenth over, Australia still seemed to be in charge. But from the moment that Javed was caught by Hayden in the 21st over, with the score at 72 for three, the balance began to tip in favour of the Bangladeshis. Their captain, Habibul Bashar, the only member of the side with any sort of a one-day reputation coming into the match, and Mohammad Ashraful put on 130 for the fourth wicket in 23 overs, and by then the game was almost won. The makeshift attack of Hogg, Clarke and Hussey, who had to share 20 overs between them, went for 114 runs and the game was lost. Even though Habibul was run out by

Gillespie, and Ashraful, almost immediately after completing a very rare Bangladeshi one-day century, was caught with another 23 runs to win, there were no further alarms as Bangladesh achieved by far their best one-day result of their short time at the top. There were no excuses from Australia, just a great deal of wide-eyed astonishment, as though they could not quite conceive of what had actually happened.

The next day, at Bristol, Australia lost again, this time to England, by three wickets. Ponting got a first-baller, Martyn lasted two balls and Harmison took five wickets for 33 in his ten overs. Matthew Hayden might consider himself unlucky, as his innings of 31 in 44 balls was ended by a catch by Collingwood at backward point that can rarely have been exceeded for athleticism and anticipation. Hayden, the strongest of the Australian batsmen, hit a ball from Harmison full in the meat of his bat, only to see Collingwood leap higher than he had any right to, and pluck the ball one-handed out of the sky. Four runs, or possibly six, were saved, and Hayden was back in the pavilion. None of the other batsmen could make such excuses. Only Mike Hussey, with 84, and to a lesser extent Michael Clarke, contributed much to an Australian total of 252 for nine, which England beat with fifteen balls to spare. It sounds easy enough, but in fact the Australian performance was much better than against Bangladesh the day before. It was Kevin Pietersen's 91 not out in 65 balls that won it for England. Michael Vaughan contributed 57 in almost 30 overs, but nobody else got to 20. Gillespie and Kasprowicz were very expensive once again (nineteen overs for 134 runs between them) and although, as the Australians were at pains to point out, there were positives to take out of the game (well, they would say that, wouldn't they?), the tour seemed at this stage to be heading towards disaster of major proportions. The tourists were a beatable side, as Somerset, Bangladesh and England had proved in six dreadful days for the Australians.

The Australian problem was not one of a lack of basic talent. On paper, the side was still the strongest in the world, but the big difference between the last time England and Australia had played each other over an extended series – in Australia in 2002/03 – was that now it was clear that Australia could be beaten. Until 2005, there seemed to be a reluctance on the part of the England players to believe in their hearts that they could beat Australia. Losing was in their comfort zone: winning was just too difficult. To be fair to England, probably every other team in the world over the past ten years or so has felt the same when faced with Australians in baggy greens, but however much they may have proclaimed that Australia are beatable, it was only in 2005 that they really began to believe it. The England team was beginning to feel that they really could beat everybody in the world. They did not necessarily believe that they would always beat everybody in the world, but there was now a strong feeling that matching even the Australians at full strength was possible, and indeed probable. A shift in the power of cricket seemed to be taking place. Whether or not England would finish the summer as the holders of the Ashes, a change in the order of things had started and it seemed unlikely to be reversed. The Australians were getting older together, like a contented married couple well past their ruby wedding anniversary, and one day quite soon they would no longer be a match for the much younger England team. That is what the Bangladeshis did for England at Sophia Gardens, and what they did for all Australia's cricketing rivals.

It was at this point that the status quo began to be restored. If mid-June was the nadir of the Australian summer, then July was probably their high point. During that month, as we shall see, they played four ODIs, of which two were won, one lost and one tied. They played two drawn games against county sides and won the First Test match at Lord's. But even this successful month was by no means a procession of triumph for the Australians, any more than it was a cycle of defeat for the English.

On 23 June, after a four-day rest, Australia met England once again, at Chester-le-Street, and this time Australia managed to record a victory. A comfortable 57 runs was the final margin, but once Martyn and Symonds got together, adding 142 in 24 overs, it was clear that the final target England would be asked to reach would be substantial. The Australian innings ended at 266 for five, and England replied in what can only be described as the Olde England style. Three wickets down for 6 runs after fewer than six overs was about as bad as it could get. 'Banger' Trescothick proved his nickname owed more to his love of sausages, rather than the ability to score quickly, by making a fifteen-ball duck, while his opening partner Andrew Strauss continued his worryingly poor form with 3 runs in thirteen balls. Paul Collingwood, often the touchstone of a brilliant England performance, followed his world-record-breaking match against Bangladesh two days earlier, when he had become the first man in ODI history to score a century and take six wickets in a match, by making nought, to follow a bowling analysis of 17 runs conceded in three overs for no wickets. Although Solanki and Flintoff, not to mention top scorer Darren Gough with 46 not out from 47 balls at the end of the innings, made the score respectable, England were never in the hunt.

Australia, relying rather heavily on their one-day specialists, Andrew Symonds, Mike Hussey and Brad Hogg, began to return to winning ways, so that by the time that both England and Australia duly reached the final of this rather odd tournament, there was no clear favourite. The Bangladeshis had managed no further surprises, although when the Australians came to Canterbury for their third encounter with them, billed rather optimistically as 'the decider', their performance was a winning one, but hardly a thrashing. Australia won the toss and put Bangladesh in, but Shariar Nafees and Khaled Mashud ensured that there would be a solid total for the Australians to chase. Once again, it was the non-Test player Andrew Symonds who bowled most economically, while Lee, Gillespie and Kasprowicz did little to stop the flow of runs. It was a curiously uncertain performance by Australia, and their batting was hardly more convincing. Adam Gilchrist, for once, made an impression but could not sustain it, and Ricky Ponting initially looked totally out of sorts, but he rode his luck and got himself back into some sort of rhythm with a carefully made 66 off 95 balls. It was left to the new boy Michael Clarke, who showed what a fine batsman he is destined to be in his innings of 80 not out, and the big-hitting Andrew Symonds, fresh from a couple of seasons at Canterbury playing for Kent, to win the game with eleven balls left.

The final of this series, played to another full house at Lord's, proved to be a much better match than had seemed likely. England won the toss and put Australia in. On a pitch that proved difficult for batting, only Mike Hussey got properly stuck into the England bowling, making 62 of the final 103 runs scored by Australia, in 81 balls. Nobody else made 30, and Steve Harmison began to show what a threat he might be to the Australians by taking three for 27, all three caught behind by Geraint Jones, in his ten overs. England should have been confident at the break.

Unfortunately for the home side, the Lord's hoodoo struck again. Within ten overs, five wickets had fallen to McGrath and Lee for just 33 runs, and the crowd, that had been cheering so loudly while Australia seemed to be making a pig's ear of their 50 overs, fell ominously quiet. At this stage, it all seemed to be over apart from the Man of the Match awards, but Collingwood and Geraint Jones had other plans. They added 116 runs for the sixth wicket in 34 overs and one ball, before Collingwood was smartly run out by – who else? – Andrew Symonds for 53. At this point a further 48 were needed off 39 balls with four wickets to fall, an equation for a tight finish. Giles and Gough, in particular, helped Jones get very close, but when Gough was run out on the last but one ball, England still needed 3 to win. The batsmen had crossed, so at least it meant that Giles was facing. Needing 3 or more win the game, he could only scramble 2 leg-byes, which brought them level. Even though England had lost one fewer wicket than Australia, under the rules of this competition the match was tied and the trophy was shared. England looked rather happier than Australia at the presentations, especially Jones the Gloves who took the Man of the Match award for his 71.

So – on to the Test matches, surely? Er . . . no. The NatWest Series was over, and the NatWest Trophy had been shared, but now it was time for the NatWest Challenge, a three-match ODI series featuring just England and Australia. Now do not ask why this series exists, and do not even attempt to ask the good people at NatWest to explain the reason why they feel the urge to sponsor two competitions. Just remember that another three games not only fills in time before the Ashes series gets under way, but also allows England's cricketers to have even less preparation for the Test matches. And then there are the extra newspapers the whole shenanigans help to sell. It must be good for cricket.

The NatWest Challenge was an anticlimax, despite the innovations of substitutes and 'power plays', with which the ICC in their wisdom had seen fit to complicate further an already complicated format. England won the first game, at Headingley, by nine wickets, and Marcus Trescothick at last scored a century against the Australians. England substituted Simon Jones and brought in Vikram Solanki after Jones had bowled his overs, but as Solanki neither batted nor took a catch (there was some confusion over whether he would have been allowed to bowl, but anyway, he did not), it really did not matter. Australia's Brad Hogg, who took over from Matt Hayden halfway through England's innings, became the first substitute to take a wicket in a one-day international, but one cannot imagine that being a particularly interesting quiz question in years to come. In the second match, at Lord's, Australia won by the equally convincing margin of seven wickets, with more than five overs to spare, a victory that was built around a five-wicket haul for Brett Lee and a century by Ricky Ponting, now beginning to reach his best form. Neither side bothered to use their substitutes. The final of this nail-biting series was at the Oval on 12 July. Australia won at a canter, thanks to Gilchrist's only innings of note so far, a completely dominating century which made sure that England's 228 for seven was not nearly enough. He reached his century in 81 balls and finished with 121 not out from 101 balls, including seventeen fours and two sixes. Harmison, who had taken three for 27 ten days earlier, finished with figures of 9.5-0-81-0. Only Flintoff, whose bowling was clearly a yard or two faster than the Australians had been expecting, and much more accurate than some of England's supporters had anticipated, bowled well, his nine overs going for just 34 runs. The only item of real interest about the match was that Simon Jones, picked in the starting eleven, was substituted before he had batted, when Geraint Jones was out in the 28th over, and thus took no part whatsoever in the match. Did he win an ODI cap for his trouble? The record books say he did. Anybody in the crowd could have matched Simon Jones' performance that day, and most of us would have given our eye teeth for an international cap. But we have to admit that it will never be, however daft and bizarre the new substitute rule.

Australia left the Oval feeling as though their tour, which had started so disastrously, was at least back on the rails, even if there were still plenty of metaphorical leaves on the lines. Would they prove to be the wrong sort of leaves? They moved up to Grace Road, Leicester, a ground which, despite its romantic name, would struggle to make the finals of a Most Beautiful Ground competition, and would still be hard pressed if such a contest were restricted to cricket grounds in Grace Road. Leicestershire, fielding the usual mix of second eleven players, first team players testing out a niggle and overseas cricketers with a point to prove, were dismissed for 217 in 55 overs, with Brett Lee taking the bowling honours with four wickets for 53 runs. Australia then reached 169 for two wickets in 34 overs by the end of the first day, and on the second day pushed on to make 582 for seven declared. Langer, who had not been in the ODI squad, Ponting and Martyn all hit centuries, and Hayden made 75. Ponting rather unsportingly declared at their overnight total, leaving Gillespie on 49 not out. Little did Gillespie realise that this particular hurt would not be the last of his troubles on the tour. Stuart Broad, a promising opening bowler and son of Chris Broad, took two wickets for 77 runs in 22 overs, possibly the first of many Australian scalps in a career that many good judges thought might be long and successful.

When the home side batted again on the third day, the Australian bowling attack failed to wrap up the game in the manner that they no doubt expected. It was a good batting track, even on the third day, and a double-hundred by a 27-year-old from Sydney by the name of Chris Rogers was certainly not in the script. His 209, the highest score by an Australian in tour matches so far this summer, helped Leicestershire reach 363 for five and secure a comfortable draw. Australia moved on to Lord's with the media pundits baying in their ears that they were no longer the great team they had once been. It was all to play for, the most open Ashes series for two decades.

3

You Can't Always Get What You Want

The First Test Match, Lord's

After all the preliminaries (during which time the County Championship had been pottering along, with Sussex, Kent and Nottinghamshire setting the pace), the table was finally set for the main course to be served. On the same day that Chris Rogers was proving that even Australians who nobody outside New South Wales and Leicestershire has ever heard of can make mountains of runs against the best bowling attack in the world, the England selectors announced their side for the First Test. It contained only one surprise, and even that had been telegraphed long in advance of the event. Kevin Pietersen replaced Graham Thorpe in the eleven that had so tidily beaten Bangladesh.

The debate about England's middle order had rumbled on all the previous winter and into the summer. The selectors and the watching public felt we had a very secure opening partnership in Trescothick and Strauss and a potentially brilliant number three in the captain Michael Vaughan. Flintoff was inked in at number six, and with the selectors making no secret of their intention to play the batsman/wicketkeeper Geraint Jones at seven, the only possible batting slots that could inspire debate were numbers four and five. Over recent seasons many a player has been given a chance to make a place in the middle order his own, but only Graham Thorpe and the now retired Nasser Hussain have ever looked permanent. Names like Adams, Crawley, Collingwood, Key and Ramprakash, not forgetting the greatest enigma of them all, Graeme Hick, have had long or short runs in England's middle order over the past decade or so, but nobody has held down the position for long. Even the injured Mark Butcher has not been a clear choice for most of his Test career. Remember Aftab Habib and Usman Afzaal, or Darren Maddy, Ed Smith and Ian Ward? Then consider Owais Shah, Jim Troughton and Vikram Solanki, all of whom have played one-day internationals without winning full Test caps – the list goes on and on.

As the Ashes series approached, it became clear that the middle-order places would be given to two of Thorpe, Bell and Pietersen. Thorpe and Bell were the men in possession, and they had done nothing wrong against Bangladesh – neither had even been dismissed – so the easy choice would be to pick them and stick to an unchanged side. But Pietersen had been the star of England's one-day squad since he qualified at the end of 2004, and even though there is clear evidence to the contrary in the shape of people like Paul Collingwood, Adam Hollioake, Michael Bevan and Andrew Symonds, success at ODI level is reckoned a natural stepping stone to the full Test side. Thorpe, now obviously moving towards the end of his career, has had his ups and downs, but the downs seemed to coincide with periods when his personal life was not going well. In 2005, this enigmatic sportsman was as contented as could be, and his experience against Australia was seen by many to be a necessary backbone in a young England side, short on knowledge of what it is like to take on the Australians in an Ashes Test. He had already retired from one-day internationals, so played for Surrey while the limited-overs festivities were going on, but then he blotted his copybook by announcing that he would not be available for the winter tours because he was taking up a coaching position with New South Wales. In truth, it was widely expected that Thorpe would announce his retirement from international cricket, so this was no real surprise, and the timing of the announcement was forced upon him by Australian regulations governing registered players for the coming season. All the same, it once again brought into question his motivation. At 36, and with the landmark one hundredth Test cap achieved, was he still hungry for Test success? And then his back let him down again, and he spent much of the months of June and July on the physio's bench rather than out in the middle.

There was no doubt that Ian Bell and Kevin Pietersen were hungry for Test success, but the question was, could they deliver it against the Australians? Did experience count for anything? In the end, the choice of Bell and Pietersen in the middle order confirmed that the selectors were taking the attacking option, which seemed to be the right thing to do if England were to have any chance of winning the Ashes. With Pietersen, Flintoff and Jones at five, six and seven, there would be little doubt that runs would come quickly if they came at all, but was it too flaky a middle order? Was it reasonable to ask Pietersen to sit out another Test when he had done all that had have been asked of him in his one-day career, and more? Should Ian Bell, with a Test batting average of 297 going into the Ashes series, be excluded?

It is difficult to surmise exactly what went on in the minds of the selectors as they made their decisions, but it would be reassuring to think that they realised that the only way England could win the Ashes this summer (as opposed to taking the soft options and waiting for McGrath and Warne to retire, and winning them in a couple of years' time) was to attack the Australians from the first ball of the first day's play in the First Test. Playing safe was no good. England might as well lose by the 5-0 score line that Glenn McGrath had predicted, as limp to a dull 1-0 or 2-1 defeat. That meant Pietersen and Bell, and no place for Thorpe. It also meant, whether by accident or design, that of England's top seven, only Trescothick and Vaughan had ever played in an Ashes Test before they came to Lord's. The Australians were fond of saying that they had worked Trescothick out, and that he would never make big runs against them, and though they had obviously not worked out Michael Vaughan quite so well, given his very high average of 63.30 against Australia, they felt he had got used to losing, and that was the way they meant to keep it. The rest of England's side, though, had not got used to losing. Apart from the New Year Test at Cape Town six months earlier, most of the England side just did not know what it was like to lose a Test match. The likes of Strauss, the Jones boys, Ian Bell and Harmison had enjoyed their Test careers because they were winners. For the first time in many years, the Australians were about to face a team who were much more used to victory than defeat. Of course, the same could be said about England. Since their last visit to Australia two and a half years before, they had not faced a team who really expected to beat England.

The teams were:

England: M.P. Vaughan (Yorkshire, captain), M.E. Trescothick (Somerset), A.J. Strauss (Middlesex), I.R. Bell (Warwickshire), K.P. Pietersen (Hampshire), A. Flintoff (Lancashire), G.O. Jones (Kent, wicketkeeper), A.F. Giles (Warwickshire), M.J. Hoggard (Yorkshire), S.J. Harmison (Durham) and S.P. Jones (Glamorgan). C.T. Tremlett (Hampshire) was the man left out of the final eleven.

Australia: R.T. Ponting (Tasmania, captain), M.L. Hayden (Queensland), J.L. Langer (Western Australia), D.R. Martyn (Western Australia), M.J. Clarke (New South Wales), S.M. Katich (New South Wales), A.C. Gilchrist (Western Australia, wicketkeeper), S.K. Warne (Victoria), B. Lee (New South Wales), J.N. Gillespie (South Australia) and G.D. McGrath (New South Wales).

These were the strongest elevens available. At this stage there were no fitness problems, unless you count poor Mark Butcher's long-term injury which was to prevent him from playing any first-class cricket until August, thus ruling him out of contention for the entire series.

The match certainly attracted public attention. For most of the newspapers, there was probably a high degree of *schadenfreude* in the reporting angles – build the England side up and then rejoice in the inevitable knocking down that would come when the first serious encounter with the world champions took place. But some of the more astute commentators had noticed that the hectic Test schedule would probably favour the young England squad rather than the ageing Australians. Matthew Hoggard was widely ridiculed when he said that it would be interesting to see how the Australians cope with back-to-back Tests, but events were to prove him rather more foresighted than his detractors. Still, at the start of the First Test, both teams were at full strength and full fitness, despite a small scare which revolved around Jason Gillespie's knees, which were reportedly rather sore. In the end, he overcame his soreness and was able to play.

The crowds were vast. Of course, the entire Ashes series was a sell-out but at Lord's there is the extra factor of the MCC members. If all 18,000 or so decided to turn up, as is their right, then the Pavilion would be full, the Allen Stand and the Warner Stand next door would be full, the Harris Garden would be full, and so would the Museum, the Library, all the offices and probably the entire Indoor School and the open spaces at the Nursery End would all be seething with humanity. Fortunately, not all the members did decide to come to the first day's play, but even so, the newly redecorated Pavilion was completely full well before the first ball was bowled. No seats were available beyond about 9.30 a.m., with some members taking up their posts as early as half past seven. The revamped balcony area on the top of the Pavilion, with its champagne bar and perfect view, was packed out, and champagne and beer sales broke all records. The Long Room had members standing five or six deep, to such an extent that it was not even silent in there. An excited hum was the background noise, broken regularly by earnest conversations assessing the chances of the sides.

The events of 7 July in London meant that bag searches were extremely thorough, so those who assumed that by turning up at 10 a.m. they would be in their seats with plenty of time for the first ball had a rude awakening. The queues snaked up and down the St. John's Wood Road, and from the tube station to the Grace Gates, as an army of searchers burrowed through picnic lunches, binoculars, umbrellas and newspapers in the cause of keeping out bombs, knives and Semtex. Nobody complained, and no offensive weapons were found.

As one member explained, getting seats for the Lord's Test is like a military operation. He regularly comes to the Test with a squad of four or five, and 'we send half our team to get seats in the Warner Stand, and the other half to Marble Arch Marks and Spencer for the food and drink. It's all in the planning. A bit like D-Day, or crossing the Rhine.' And only slightly less dangerous.

Australia won the toss, which was only to be expected. Michael Vaughan's luck with the coin in his 27 Tests as captain had been truly awful. By calling correctly Ponting added one more loss to Vaughan's tally and chose to bat first. It was not a difficult decision and he adhered to the old adage: nine times out of ten bat first; if the pitch favours the bowlers, think about it for a while, but still bat first. It may have been disproved too many times to be followed too faithfully, but a team is more likely to impose itself on the opposition at the start of a series by batting first. After a brief ceremony in which Pietersen was formally presented with his England cap, Langer and Hayden came out to bat, and the ball was handed not to Matthew Hoggard, as England usually did, but to Steve Harmison.

The first over set the tone for the match and for the series. Justin Langer, who had been left out of the Australian one-day squad, had elected to take strike, through whatever process he and Hayden share the opening responsibilities, and from the second ball of the series was probably regretting his decision. A slightly short ball from Harmison, who needed no time to warm up to a very hostile pace, hit Langer on the right elbow. The 'oooh' from the crowd told anybody who had not seen the blow that it was a nasty one, and even though Langer is, as the increasingly bizarre player biographies persist in telling us, a black belt at zendokai, he found it difficult not to show the pain. This was, as it turned out, the first of many times that morning when the Australian physio and the twelfth man, Michael Kasprowicz, had to walk through the Long Room to bring aid and succour to the besieged Australian batsmen. Each time they came past the members, there was a sympathetic buzz, which was rather drowned out by the happy chuckles at the sight of an Australian on the receiving end. The English smiles lasted all morning.

Play in the first session was punctuated by stoppages for injuries as pretty well all the Australian batsmen made involuntary contact with a quick delivery. Hayden and Ponting were both hit on the helmet, both trying to hook Harmison. Ponting's blow drew blood when the helmet grille smashed into his cheek, and it may be that the incident contributed to his early dismissal. The first man to go was Hayden, bowled by Hoggard, Matthew to Matthew, with the score at 35. A roar from the crowd marked the moment when Australia's most powerful and most prolific batsman over the past few seasons had to begin his walk back to the Pavilion. Hayden has endured a noticeable dip in form over the past eighteen months or so, and there was little sign from this rather tentative cameo that anything was likely to change in the near future. Langer, despite his bruises, struggled on, but Ponting, despite being dropped before he had scored by debutant Pietersen in the gully off the hardworking Hoggard, did not. He and Langer brought up the fifty, but at 55, Ponting was neatly taken by Strauss off the rampant Steve Harmison. He had been significantly unsettled when a ball from Harmison hit the side of his helmet, and the grille caused a big cut on his cheek. Blood and gore all over the place, more physios running in and out of the Long Room, and studied unconcern from the England players, who perhaps were taking the 'play hard' aspect of the series a little too literally. It would have done no harm to check that Ponting was not seriously hurt. As it was, he wore a plaster on his cheek as a badge of honour for most of the rest of the game.

When Langer was caught by Harmison off the fourth ball that Andrew Flintoff ever bowled in an Ashes series, and Martyn edged Simon Jones' first ball of the series to his namesake behind the stumps three balls later, Australia were suddenly stumbling at 66 for four. Langer's 40 was a brave innings, and pretty quickly put together – only 44 balls faced – but nobody else ever really mastered the pitch.

I like Langer. He famously almost came to blows with the Barmy Army during the 2002/03 series in Australia, complaining that their support was off-putting, too loud and not the way that spectators ought to behave. However, he soon realised that the Barmy Army was not an enemy he could easily deal with, and within a couple of days had apologised and grovelled before them at the MCG. But he is an intelligent cricketer, who makes the very best of his abilities, and best of all he looks like a throwback to the 1930s, a smallish dark man with a neat haircut hidden under his enormous baggy green cap. No earrings, studs or coloured hair for Justin Langer: he is a solid old-fashioned cricketer who just gets on with making runs. Since the previous tour, in 2001, he has raised his game considerably, and a Test batting average that was then under 40 is now around the 47 mark. His value to the Australian side is often underestimated, which is a mistake.

Langer was replaced by the new golden boy of Australian batting, Michael Clarke, whose first Test innings at Lord's was not a long drawn-out affair. It ended before lunch when he was leg before to Simon Jones for 11, but during his stay he hit two boundaries that showed his potential: the only problem with potential is that once you are a Test player, that's not enough. You have to deliver. The general view was that before the series was over, he would deliver.

Lunch was taken with Australia at 97 for five, after only 23 overs in the two-hour session. The buzz in the Pavilion, and all around the ground, was wonderful to be part of for every

English cricket supporter. Australia had won the toss, and were on the rack. The England pace quartet had all bowled well and had shared the wickets around. As a unit, they were formidable. We probably did not really notice the fielding, which ranged from the very fine to the lamentable. In the second innings, it would take on a far greater significance.

The over-rate in the pre-lunch session was truly feeble, but what with all the injuries and all the wickets that fell, none of the spectators would have felt short-changed. Over-rates are a subject of great contention in the cricket world, but most spectators would agree that as long as the cricket is exciting and there is no deliberate time wasting, the number of overs per session or per day is comparatively unimportant. By the end of a match, if a team can stave off defeat because there is no time to bowl a reasonable number of overs, clearly the over-rate takes on a greater significance, but in a five-day Test, it is rarely a serious issue, unless the weather has played a major role. Both sides can slow the game down, so to penalise only the fielding side is unfair. Some day somebody will come up with the answer, but as long as the umpires show the same sense of proportion that Steve Bucknor showed in Karachi in December 2000, when England were allowed to bat on for victory in the gloaming because Pakistan had wasted so much time in the hours leading up to dusk, the problem will never get out of hand.

After lunch, before a mass gathering of thousands of smiling Englishmen and a few hundred glowering Australians around the ground, England continued and indeed completed their demolition of the Australians. Adam Gilchrist, batting as though his reputation for fast scoring depended on this innings alone, hit 26 in eighteen balls before edging the nineteenth, from Flintoff, through to Jones the Gloves, who made no mistake. Although Harmison was the leading wicket-taker, the contribution of Flintoff in dismissing the dangerous left-handers Langer and Gilchrist, after both had got a start, should not be forgotten. Katich took the route to an undistinguished score of twenty-something that Gilchrist had decided against, grinding out 27 in 67 balls. All the same he proved his worth, resisting the England bowlers for longer than any of his team-mates. Harmison was the destroyer this time, as he had been when he bowled Warne for a belligerent 28. Australia had been 175 for six before Warne fell, but in the space of four overs Harmison took the final four wickets while only fifteen runs were added to the score. His first spell had resulted in several bruised batsmen, but only one wicket for 32 runs, but his second spell after lunch lasted only four overs and two balls, with which he took four wickets for 12 runs. Two caught behind (if you can count Katich's dismissal as caught behind: he hit a high swirler to about fly slip, where Jones ran to make the catch), one caught in the slip cordon, one bowled and one lbw was a tribute to his speed and accuracy. His first ever five-wicket haul at Lord's was well earned, and there was no doubt in the minds of all present at the ground that first blood was to England. For Australia to be all out for 190 before

Previous pages: After the one-day series, Pietersen had a good reputation as a fielder. This is the first of his dropped catches – five further chances were grassed over the series.

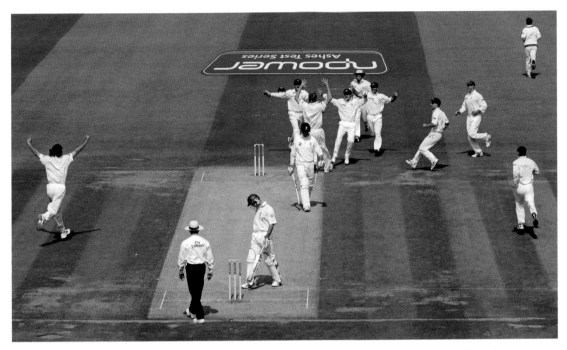

McGrath picked Trescothick as his 500th Test victim, and brought some golden boots along for the moment – his confidence was not misplaced.

tea on the first day, having won the toss and chosen to bat, represented a massive achievement by this England team. As they came back into the Pavilion, the Long Room was as full as it can ever have been. A pathway through the membership had to be roped off by the Pavilion attendants, but it did not stop the throng from cheering and applauding loudly as the England team came off the field. I think I even caught the word 'Huzzah!' which can hardly have been heard anywhere in the world since the Charge of the Light Brigade 150 years earlier, but which still emerges from the collective memory of MCC membership when circumstances require.

We read in the Book of Proverbs that 'Pride goeth before destruction, and an haughty spirit before a fall.' For 21,000 spectators, the truth of this ancient saying was about to be proved once again. Trescothick and Strauss strode out jauntily enough to begin the England innings, but whatever they had prepared for, it was not the greatest opening bowler of his generation bowling one of the greatest spells of his career. Glenn McGrath was simply brilliant. He came into the series needing just one more wicket to become the fourth bowler in history to take 500 Test wickets, following Courtney Walsh, Muttiah Muralitharan and McGrath's team-mate, Shane Warne. He had already lined up Marcus Trescothick to be the five hundredth, and Trescothick was quite calm about the idea – as long as he had scored a hundred first.

The openers took England safely into tea, at 10 for no wicket, and Englishmen ate their cucumber sandwiches and sipped Earl Grey tea safe in the knowledge that this was going to be England's day. However, after tea the landscape changed. Trescothick's hundred was not to be, but Pigeon's five hundred was. With McGrath's first ball after tea, Trescothick attempted an over-optimistic shot through midwicket off a precisely pitched delivery, just on a length outside off stump. He got an edge, and the ball flew to third slip, where Justin Langer held on to the catch. Trescothick had been very much more laborious than usual, and managed only one scoring stroke, a four, in seventeen balls. The acclaim for McGrath's five hundredth Test wicket came not only from his fellow Australians, but also from everybody in the ground. At this stage, nobody really thought that England were in trouble, and there was no harm in even a partisan English crowd acknowledging McGrath, the greatest Australian fast bowler most of them are ever likely to see. The applause all around the ground was long and heartfelt, and Glenn McGrath deserved it. His golden boots, specially designed and worn for the occasion, glowed with pride like their owner.

Four balls later, the applause was perhaps not quite so heartfelt when McGrath and his golden boots took their 501st wicket, getting Strauss caught in the slip cordon by Warne for an even more laborious 2 off 21 balls. It was a very good ball that got rid of him, but Strauss continued to look like a man seriously out of form. Form is temporary and class is permanent, but there was a danger that Strauss' loss of form might become permanent. He just did not look

After his batting heroics in the last series, Vaughan was the English batsman most feared by the Aussies. McGrath bowls him for 3 in the first innings.

like a man at ease with his batting. He did not look as though he wanted to be out in the middle. It must have made him feel even worse to walk back into the Pavilion for yet another low score, but he did not look even a poor relation, a third cousin twice removed, of the all-conquering batsman of the first nine months of his Test career.

Michael Vaughan, another England batsman who did not look really convincing in any of his innings in the first half of the season, struggled to cope with McGrath, and was soon undone by a ball that kept lower than it should have done when he played back. In retrospect it is easy to say that he should have played forward, but McGrath's length was so good that he put every batsman in two minds every ball. Forward or back? – a dilemma every bowler tries to implant in every batsman's mind. Suddenly England were 18 for three, and the three back in the Pavilion were the three around whom the England batting was expected to revolve all summer. But this was just the start of the disaster. Two overs later, Bell was also bowled by a ball he may also have thought kept a bit low. Well, it might have done, but Bell had failed to learn from what he saw from the other end when Vaughan went. At least his 6 was the top score to date. England at 19 for four were in deep trouble, a trouble which got deeper when Flintoff, Freddie the Fearless, Freddie the man who would dominate the Australians as he had dominated everybody else in the past two or three seasons, was out in his first Ashes innings for a fourth-ball duck.

At 21 for five, the game had gone. McGrath had all five wickets in eight overs and one ball of quite magical bowling. His pace, which is no longer super quick, varied just enough to induce mistimed shots. His length varied just enough to keep the batsmen undecided about where and when to transfer their weight from one foot to the other, and his direction varied just enough to force batsmen to risk following the occasional delivery that might cut back and bowl them, or go straight on and give a feathered catch to the 'keeper. It was, in the view of some people at Lord's who had seen a great deal of bowling over the years, the best spell of fast bowling they had ever seen. It is of course impossible to compare bowlers of different generations, but for sheer accuracy, persistence, movement and, above all, the psychological value to a team who looked to be under the cosh an hour before, this was one of the great spells of Test cricket. Any doubts about whether or not McGrath was too old at 35 were answered, for the time being at least, at Lord's after tea on the first afternoon of the First Test. It was not hard to believe that the real difference between the teams was Glenn McGrath. However good the rest of the Australians may be, it was the ability of Glenn McGrath to conjure a perfect spell of thirteen overs on the trot for just 21 runs and five wickets that separated the teams at the end of the first day. He easily topped Harmison's great figures of five for 43 in 11.2 overs, as if to show that the pretender to his crown has still a long way to go before he can be considered anything other than a good Test bowler. Greatness only comes when you can bowl a spell like McGrath did on Thursday, 21 July from the Pavilion End at Lord's.

At the other end, Brett Lee, playing his first Test match under Ricky Ponting's captaincy, in Ponting's fourteenth Test as captain, bowled quickly and well, but failed to take a wicket in his opening spell. He only allowed 10 runs in eight overs, and his economy kept the pressure on England. The batsmen were unable to break free from the shackles the two bowlers imposed on them, until the seventeenth over, just after Flintoff had gone, when Jason Gillespie was brought on at the Nursery End. Gillespie had come into the match with some doubt about his fitness, but with almost 250 Test wickets to his name, there was no doubt the Australians wanted him to be fit. However, on that first afternoon, Gillespie bowled more like his name-sake Dizzy than the usually so tidy, economical and hairy Jason. He was the only man that England felt they could take liberties with, Pietersen and Geraint Jones taking 30 off his eight overs. This was the only moment of the innings when England felt they might make the jail-break. After the highs of the first two sessions of the day, McGrath's spell caused normal service to be resumed – Australians on top, everybody else nowhere. All around the ground the England spectators were trying hard not to give space in their minds to the same old thought – same old Ashes series, same old result.

Kevin Pietersen, in his debut Test innings, got a huge welcome as he strode out to bat, but he cannot have wanted to take guard for the first time at 18 for three, especially as it rapidly deteriorated to 21 for five. Compare that to his captain, Michael Vaughan, who had taken guard in his first Test against South Africa at 2 for two, a score which rapidly deteriorated to 2 for four, so Vaughan might have been in a position to give advice from direct experience. Unfortunately he was already back in the Pavilion, the reason why Pietersen was out there in the first place. Pietersen's cricket is built around confidence, of which he has plenty, and talent, of which he has almost as much. His character was put to the test during the previous winter in South Africa, when he had to play for his adopted country in front of his homeland's spectators. He was given plenty of stick by the home crowds, but he still played superbly, dominating the South African bowlers throughout the one-day series. Whether he would have the patience to succeed in Test cricket was probably the only question that needed answering, and one thing seemed probable – it would not take long to find out.

Pietersen surprised us all. By the end of the day, he had faced 69 balls during a stay of 24 overs and four balls, but he had made only 28 runs. The important thing was that he, and nobody else who had faced the Australian bowlers that Thursday, was still not out. He had shown that he could knuckle down to play a Test match innings when the need arose, and was not just a slogger with a wonderful eye and a lot of bottom hand. In partnership with Geraint Jones, who made 30 off only 56 balls, Pietersen helped to steady the England ship, but their partnership of 58 for the sixth wicket, while acceptable if the fifth wicket had fallen at 300 or so, was hardly enough when the starting point was 21, even if the total they were aiming at was only 190. Jones was done by a good bouncer from the hard working Lee, which caught his gloves as he tried to fend it off, and gave a routine catch to Gilchrist. Still, Pietersen could not be blamed for England's troubles. If everybody had batted as well as he did (facing more of McGrath's bowling than any other top-order batsman), England would have been firmly in the driving seat.

When Jones went, Ashley Giles joined Pietersen with three or four overs to go to the end of the day's play. Giles decided that attack was the best form of defence. His batting style is slightly similar to that of John Emburey, although Emburey employed a wider range of strokes, mostly of his own devising. Both men know how to bat, and both can look either totally safe or seriously at sea. We never really had time to decide which mode Giles was batting in on this occasion, although it was probably the all at sea one. On what proved to be the final ball of the day, Lee's pace forced him back on to his stumps, rather more literally than he had probably intended. To be out hit wicket off the final ball of the day was unfortunate for Giles but a ghastly finish for England. Or at least we all thought he was out hit wicket when the mess his stumps were in was inspected. An official correction later made it clear he had been caught behind, so obviously the ball had nicked the edge of his bat and thumped into Gilchrist's gloves before he trod on the woodwork.

That it was the final ball was rather a surprise to the crowd, who thought that there were about a dozen overs more to come, but apparently the scheduling of *The Simpsons* at 6.00 p.m. on Channel Four was deemed to be more important than a paying public of around 30,000 who were being done out of an eighth of their money. The broadcasting of cricket, even in a summer when the game was clearly an audience winner, was a matter of contention from the first day.

The score of 92 for seven, even more than 92 for six, meant that the newspapers the next day would largely ignore the superb morning and afternoon sessions, which had left England in the driving seat, and concentrate only on the third session, which left England hanging out of the sidecar, possibly not even still on the right road. The reckless pace of the whole day is what remains in the memory, a real boneshaker of a day. Maybe only 282 runs were scored in 77 overs, but seventeen wickets fell. If this had been a county pitch, points may have been deducted. Yet it had been a great day's play, a worthy opening joust. The pitch was not a great one for batting, but it was a great one for cricket. Cricket is not a game exclusively for batsmen. The vast crowd left Lord's in a state of dejection, made all the worse because we could remember how great it all had seemed two hours earlier. Ho hum, another bloody Ashes summer ahead.

'McGrath sparks England free-fall' was the *Daily Telegraph* headline the next morning. Even after all the hype leading into the series, the general tone of the press on the Friday morning was 'I told you so.'

Day 1, Close of Play:
Australia 190 all out (Langer 40; Harmison 5-43).
England 92 for seven wickets (G.O. Jones 30, Pietersen 29 not out; McGrath 5-21).

On the second morning, the priority for the England tail was to stick with Pietersen long enough to restrict Australia's lead to as few runs as possible. They were still 98 behind as Hoggard accompanied Pietersen to the middle, and making 98 is a tall order for the final three wickets, especially as the remaining batsmen, apart from the debutant Pietersen, had a combined average of a little under 33. For by no means the first time in cricket, statistics did not lie. Matthew Hoggard, whose average was the lowest of the three at a smidgen under ten, tried his best to stick around, but he could only help the new boy add 9 runs, and bring the total just past 100, and his part in the partnership was, frankly, negligible. In the style of reporting that dominated the sports pages a hundred years ago, one would be forced to write, 'Hoggard failed to trouble the scorers'. Bill Frindall, BBC Radio's Test Match Special scorer would take issue with that statement. Ducks are an immense bother to scorers, even though the adding up of the runs, or producing the wagon wheel of his run-scoring strokes, is not very testing. You still have to write down 'c. Hayden b. Warne', which was Hoggard's fate, check to see how many ducks he has made previously in Test cricket (Courtney Walsh is way out on his own in this particular list), and see what damage that has done to his overall Test average. Scoring a duck is just as much trouble for the scorers as recording a century. The scorer probably raises more sweat in the process than the batsman does.

Hoggard faced sixteen balls for his duck, and when he trudged back to the Pavilion, he was replaced by the bowling hero of Australia's first innings, Steve Harmison, promoted from number eleven, according to the official scorecard, at the expense of Simon Jones. One has to assume that Harmy was pulling rank, because all those who saw Simon Jones' 44 on debut against India a few seasons before will continue to believe that he is a better bat than the Durham man. Still, Harmy it was, and he played admirably alongside the more swashbuckling Pietersen. It was a minor feature of this match, and was to become a major feature of the series, that the lower orders of both teams were forced to salvage a pretty hopeless situation bequeathed to them by the upper halves of the batting orders. They often succeeded. It would be going too far to say that England's lower order on this occasion salvaged the situation, but at least they turned the disaster of 21 for five into a total that was within range of the Australian's own modest score. The Australians put on 103 for their final five wickets, after the first five had made only 87; the England lower order made 134, over six times as many runs as the top five partnerships. Pietersen was clearly under instructions to make as many runs as he could, and he set about the Australian bowling with bottom-handed glee.

'KP' will always be a controversial cricketer, however many hundreds he may score for England, Hampshire or anybody else. It is not just his coloured hair and his cocky attitude. After all, he may well grow out of a liking for purple or white stripes in his hair (or he may one day grow out of hair), and confidence is a useful quality in a sportsman. His showmanship keeps him at the centre of public attention and media interest, and his South African background adds a little spice to his success with England. His problem is that at the moment he is not quite as good as he thinks he is, and until he has some real achievements under his belt – which probably will not be long in coming – there are people in Britain who will be willing him to fail. Curmudgeons they may be, old-school county members who sit in smoking rooms dozing beneath a copy of yesterday's *Times*, but they still make their feelings heard and felt in

A rare indignity for McGrath – Pietersen deposits him into the Pavilion.

world cricket. 'Love him or loathe him' may be the slogan for KP, but he needs to be careful that too many people do not loathe him. The profile of cricket in 2005 was raised spectacularly, and Pietersen had an important role to play in that process, but there was a view that if he did not translate his promise into actual achievement, the knives would be out. If you play your cricket as outlandishly as Pietersen does, and wants to continue doing, there is no problem as long as the ends justify the means. Those who live by the hair dye die by the hair dye.

Pietersen did play well on the second morning. He added 29 more runs in only 20 balls, playing in a much more aggressive vein than the previous evening. He was finally out to one of the best outfield catches seen at Lord's in some time. Pietersen had already hit Glenn McGrath, the destroyer of the previous day, for four, six and four in consecutive balls, the six hitting the middle tier of the renovated Pavilion, no doubt adding a few pounds of touch up work to the eight million already spent on the building. Aiming to hit his county team-mate Shane Warne equally hard, he hit a huge six into the hospitality boxes in the Grand Stand, but next ball slightly mistimed his shot. It still appeared to be safe as it flew towards the unprotected boundary in front of the Grand Stand, destined to be either a six, or a one-bounce four.

Damien Martyn had other ideas. Running along the boundary, he threw himself at full stretch to take a brilliant catch as he flew horizontally about two feet above the ground, and then, almost more astonishingly, held on to it as he hit the turf in what in airline circles would be described as a heavy landing. Pietersen was out, but it was hardly his fault. His 57 on debut was by some way the highest score of England's innings, and also the first indication of a way to counter McGrath and Warne. His attacking theories were adopted by the rest of the England side at Edgbaston and beyond, but at Lord's he was the only batsman who had any sort of real success against the deadly Australian duo.

When Pietersen left, the score was 122 for nine, and England were still 68 behind. Harmison and Simon Jones had to try to reduce the gap. Ponting immediately took Warne out of the attack and reintroduced Lee to partner McGrath, but this was what the tailenders wanted. Jones, determined to prove he is really a number ten, or even a number nine, played several wonderful forcing strokes, including 2, 4, 3 off consecutive balls from Brett Lee, so Ponting abandoned his idea of using two quick bowlers and brought back Warne for Lee. Harmison welcomed Warne with a shot that any top-order batsman would have been proud of, taking a couple of steps down the wicket, turning the ball into a full toss and smacking it back over mid-on for four. Warne looked bemused, and the 150 was up for England.

Enough of this merriment. At the other end, Ponting rested McGrath but rather than turn to his number two quick bowler, Gillespie (8-1-30-0, and surplus to requirements on the second morning), he gave the ball back to Lee, who came steaming in from the Pavilion End. One ball was enough. Harmison, aiming for another stylish boundary over mid-on, failed to connect properly with a full length ball, and could only spoon it to Martyn at mid-on, who took his second catch of the innings with rather less trouble than the first. England were all out for 155, a deficit of 35. They would rather have been ahead on first innings, but 35 runs are not much to make up, and after fewer than four sessions and only 90 overs, the game was half done. The weather forecast was set reasonably fair, so if England could make quick inroads into this formidable Australian batting line-up for a second time (they are only human after all, so why not?), then a victory was still very much a possibility.

Unfortunately, that was not quite the way it happened. Although the pace of the cricket was not quite as fast as the rate that all batsmen seemed to throw themselves off the Lord's ridge on Thursday, Australia still made steady progress in their attempt to put the game out of England's reach. There was still an hour to go before lunch, and Australia set about their task with a will. Langer and Hayden, who had only managed 35 together in the first innings, knew this would be the moment to emphasise Australia's superiority, and although they showed Harmison the respect due a five-wicket man, they played fast and loose with Hoggard. They probably would have played fast and loose with Flintoff, had they had the chance, but when he was brought into the attack, in only the sixth over, the first of many misunderstandings

Opposite: Clarke was on 21 when Pietersen dropped him – he made the most of his let-off, top-scoring with 91.

between Australian batsmen occurred. Langer called a single as the ball went out into the covers, where Kevin Pietersen and his hair were on duty. Pietersen swooped on the ball, transferred it quickly from left to right hand and threw the stumps down at the bowler's end with Langer run out by six inches. It was a fine piece of fielding, but unfortunately for KP, did not herald a brilliant performance from then on. At lunch, with Hayden and Ponting pressing on, the score was 47 for one wicket after twelve overs. Australia were piling on the pressure and England did not seem to have any answers.

The next two sessions of play were the low point of England's summer, although we did not know it at the time. The fact that no Australian managed to make a century in the match shows that even the low point was never as low as the 2001 low points, which came with monotonous regularity during almost every game of the series, but Australia were on top. At this stage in the series, everybody in the crowd at Lord's or watching the game on television would have had a feeling of déja vu: here we go again, another thrashing by the world champions. As far as the Lord's Test was concerned, they would not have been far wrong, but then England always lose at Lord's . . .

Hayden was the next man to go, when he dragged a ball from Flintoff on to his stumps. He had made 34 in 54 balls, a perfectly adequate score, but even though his dismissal had an element of bad luck about it, he now needed that elusive century even more than ever. Ponting and Martyn carried on untroubled. Martyn was probably lifted by the catch he had taken earlier in the day to get rid of Pietersen. Good fielding often spills over into good batting or bowling, and vice versa. Martyn, the unsung nugget in Australia's middle order, set out to build a big score. He and his skipper had moved the total to 100, and Ponting had taken his personal score to 42, giving him a career total of 7,001 Test runs, when Hoggard induced a false stroke and Ponting had his first lethal encounter with an England substitute when he cut uppishly and gave a straightforward catch to James Hildreth, the 20-year-old Somerset batsman who was fielding at point. England's liberal use of substitutes was to become a bigger issue for Ponting and all his side later in the summer. However, Ponting's exit did not in the event prove any sort of disadvantage to the Australians. Michael Clarke, who was in shaky form so far on the tour, came in to join Martyn, and between them they scored quickly and heavily, although not without alarms. Clarke hit his third delivery from Hoggard off his pads through midwicket for four, to set the tone.

In 35 overs, between early afternoon and about half an hour before the end of play, they built the highest partnership of the match, 155, at a rate of 4.5 runs an over. Martyn was the more circumspect, scoring his 65 in 138 balls, with only seven fours and a 5 (courtesy of a no-ball from Flintoff, which Pietersen's overthrow turned from a single into a 5, to bring up the 200 and the hundred partnership). Pietersen dropped Clarke, a fairly straightforward chance, when he was on 21. Clarke went on to hit 91 in only 106 balls, finding the boundary fifteen times in the process. He and Martyn were out in successive balls in the final over before tea. Three dropped catches by Pietersen in his first Test match is not good. Top scoring in both

Clarke came into the Lord's Test with a fast-growing reputation as a dashing batsman.

innings certainly goes a long way to atone, as does his good run-out of Langer, but as Clarke made 70 more runs after his let-off, you could say that Pietersen made only a net 51 runs in the match. Mind you, that was still more than any other individual Englishman in the game. However, whereas some players are worth their place for their fielding – Jonty Rhodes, Colin Bland and Roger Harper spring to mind – there are others whose top level career was cut short by their clumsy fielding. There was no danger that this was going to happen to Pietersen after one game, or even one series, but it was a part of his game that the debutant needed to address. He was not the only man to drop catches at Lord's, for Flintoff and Jones the Gloves were both guilty at different times, but with a safer pair of hands Pietersen would become indispensable to any World XI, not just to England.

It was at about this time that Graham Thorpe, left out of the team, chose to announce his retirement from all international cricket. This was not a real surprise as he had already signalled his firm intention to give up at the end of the summer, but the fact that he had been omitted from this side and had seen his replacement Pietersen bat better than anybody else in the side probably tipped the balance. It was a pity, because by the end of the series there were those who were wishing that a fully fit and motivated Thorpe could have been there to bring a little calmness to the frenetic finishes to the next three Tests, at least. But when did England last have a fully fit and motivated Thorpe? In 2004 he was motivated but not always fully fit; in the seasons before that he was often distracted by personal matters. Thorpe knew that the choice of Bell over him was final, and even if Bell was injured, Key or Joyce would be ahead of him in the pecking order. So he announced his retirement, at the hour of England's greatest need of the summer.

Clarke was finally undone by Matthew Hoggard. It was an unlucky way to get out, having a rush of blood and a big swing at a wide delivery, which then cannoned on to his boot and from there very slowly on to his stumps. The ball did not hit the stumps very hard, but the bails fell, and Clarke had to go. He had missed his chance of a hundred at Lord's on his Test debut there, but in many ways he was lucky to get anywhere near, after his let-off on 21. The Lord's crowd, even though they knew he had taken the game away from England, gave Clarke a generous standing ovation as he made his way back to the Pavilion.

Next ball, the first of a Harmison over, did for Martyn, who played back to a ball that seamed back into him, kept low, and trapped him leg before. No problems for the umpire, but just a few for Australia who were now 255 for five wickets. Enter Gilchrist, whose first innings had been disappointing to Australians and indeed to all lovers of a good Gilchrist innings, to join Katich who had yet to face a ball. At 255 for five, and with a match lead of almost 300, this situation was tailor-made for the incoming batsman – a solid lead that could be turned into something completely unattainable if he stuck around for twenty overs. He tucked his first ball away for a single and Katich hit a four from his first delivery. But at the end of the over, Vaughan showed his shrewdness as a captain and immediately brought Flintoff into the attack. Flintoff had removed Gilchrist in the first innings, and clearly it was part of England's plan that Freddie should bowl to the Australian wicketkeeper as much as possible. They thought they might have worked him out. Flintoff's first over was a maiden. From his second over, Gilchrist scored 3 runs, and from the first ball of Flintoff's third over to him, he leant back to one short of a length and a little wide, and cracked it backward of point for four. The crowd sat up. Clearly they were in for a big, brash Gilchrist innings.

But no. The next ball was on that nagging length that Flintoff has perfected, and the Aussie 'keeper, going for yet another expansive shot, played an inside edge on to his stumps. Gilchrist out for 10 off fourteen balls, and Australia, hardly in deep trouble, were 274 for six wickets. In the context of the series, this was a fascinating cameo. Flintoff had clearly worked with Duncan Fletcher and Troy Cooley, the bowling coach, on a definite plan for Gilchrist, and here it had worked. For the rest of the summer, Flintoff seemed to have the edge on Gilchrist. He was not always the one who took his wicket, but his control frustrated the usually free-scoring Aussie, and that made him more prone to rash shots against other bowlers. As a unit, the England bowlers were to bowl very well throughout the summer, but this little duel, in a losing cause for England, had a significance that was to last well beyond that evening at Lord's.

Shane Warne was the next man in, for what was certainly his final Test innings at Lord's. He received a huge ovation, but did not last long. He decided the best way of playing Harmison, who was bowling generally a full length, was to shuffle in front of his stumps and try to work him to leg. It was not a good plan. The very first ball Harmison bowled to him hit him on the pads in front of the stumps. Umpire Koertzen gave Warne the benefit of what little doubt there might have been, but it was a risky strategy. In the next over, he tried to turn a rather shorter delivery to leg, but only got a leading edge to give Giles a straightforward catch at gully. Australia were 279 for seven wickets, and England must have been thinking they were by no means out of it yet, even though Australia led by 314, the sort of total that few teams relish chasing in the fourth innings.

At this point it was hard to believe that there had only been two days' play. 624 runs had been scored and 27 wickets had fallen. There had been some good batting, some outstanding fielding and some really great bowling, especially from Harmison and McGrath. The world champions were finding themselves in some sort of a scrap, but they were not really troubled. They certainly would have slept far better than the Englishmen that night.

Day 2, Close of Play:

Australia 190 and 279 for seven wickets (Katich 10 not out).
England 155.

In many ways the third day's play showed how much England still had to learn about playing the Australians, and the subsequent Tests showed how quickly they had learned. There was probably a sense of gung ho optimism as the England side took the field, had their group hug and then set about the Australian tail. Yes, over 300 is lot to ask in a fourth innings, but knock over the final three wickets for fewer than fifty and it is a theoretical possibility, at least. Gilchrist and Warne had gone, along with all the batsmen except for the least feared of them all, Simon Katich, so there was no real resistance to come.

Brett Lee disabused any England player of those comfortable thoughts with the first ball of the day, a full length ball from Harmison which Lee had a heave at and hit to the third-man boundary. He spent much of the short time he was at the wicket having a heave, but with little success this time. He too would put in a few hours in the nets between Lord's and Edgbaston, sharpening his batting, but for the moment it was brutish, violent and short. His demise came when he fended a short ball from Harmison towards gully. Although it went pretty well straight to Ashley Giles fielding there, Lee was perhaps thinking of Giles' 'wheelie bin' reputation, and took on the run. Giles picked the ball up and his throw to the bowler's end hit middle stump and Lee was some way short despite a spectacular dive for safety. At least he had only run himself out, and had nobody else to blame. But if even Giles can do that sort of thing, what are these Pommies on? 289 for eight.

At this point it really should have been all over. Gillespie and McGrath, combined Test batting average 23, were what was left to help Katich, who had only reached 12 by this time, put on a few runs. Gillespie and McGrath, however, had not read the script. Gillespie's batting is not beautiful (well, if truth be known, he is not all that beautiful either) but in this case it was effective. In 26.4 overs before lunch, Australia added 93 runs for the loss of only two wickets. Nothing spectacular, but much more successful than they had any right to expect. By lunch, with a 400 lead, the game was well and truly gone from England. Only rain could save them.

Katich was the leading light in this flourishing tail. In one over from Flintoff, he hit three consecutive fours, two square cuts and a pull down to long leg, but for the most part he was happy to bat without any particular display of supremacy. He just kept the runs coming at a respectable rate. His team-mates in the Pavilion were loving it: they were getting a few more overs with their feet up and an impregnable position into the bargain. Katich is too often underrated in this team of all-stars, but he has his days, and this was to be one of them. When England took the new ball, as soon as they could, the Australian score was 317 for eight, and one ball later it was 321 for eight. Katich hooked the first ball from Harmison, which the big man had dug in short, chancelessly for four.

England's fielding was a shambles as Australia pressed on in the second innings – here 'keeper Jones drops Gillespie off bowler Jones.

Michael Vaughan is not a man to let the match drift, even when the situation looks hopeless. In the first eight overs of the new ball, he tried all four of his quick bowlers, but the only success they had – unless you take Mrs Gillespie's point of view – was when Dizzy was hit very hard in the box by Harmison. He went down, beard, long hair, helmet and all, and stayed down for a while. Suddenly, in sixteen overs, there was a fifty partnership to celebrate, as Gillespie gloved a ball from Simon Jones rather unintentionally for four to fine leg. They should not have got there, as Jones the Gloves had spilled a regulation catch from Gillespie off his namesake when the score was 333 – treble Nelson not quite working for England this time. But the ball after the 50 partnership was raised caused Gillespie's downfall. Simon Jones, who was bowling very well and getting a little reverse swing even with the new ball, bowled one that was simply too good for Gillespie, and as he played down the wrong line, so his off stump was neatly knocked back. 341 for nine, and the lead was now 376. We were into the realms of world records if England really thought they had a chance of winning. The crowd at Lord's, apart from the Australians, was subdued. All around the ground, the excitement that had been there on the first two days was very much more muted: this was what it was like to be on the wrong end of a drubbing and it hurt.

Glenn McGrath cannot bat. Everybody knows that. He holds the world record for most Test innings before a maiden Test fifty, but his top score, 61, is actually the third highest ever made by a number eleven in Test cricket. Not a lot of people know that, and certainly the England team did not want to be reminded of it. But that's roughly what McGrath did. First of all, Katich reached his half-century, taking the single he needed after Gillespie's departure by playing Flintoff down to long leg. From then until the lunch break, he and McGrath just kept the England bowlers out, hitting the few loose balls, but making sure that all Australia would enjoy the lunch interval, while all England, and especially those at Lord's crowding into the Harris Garden, would choke on their champagne and pâté. At lunch, the score was 372 for nine, with Katich on 66 and McGrath, he who cannot bat, on 10.

I suppose an optimist would say that the session between lunch and tea on the third day belonged to England. After all, they took the final wicket that had eluded them, and then reached tea without losing a wicket. So yes, in strictly cricketing terms, you could say that England had the edge in that session. It was a pity they could not edge more sessions at Lord's, because even at tea after this positive start to their innings, they were doomed to continue the run of draws and losses against Australia at Lord's which stretches back to 1934. Even in years when Australia has been totally outclassed by England, such as in Jim Laker's summer of 1956, Australia manage to win at Lord's. The world champions of 2005 just could not lose here.

Getting rid of the final wicket was not as straightforward as it ought to have been. Simon Jones, who had persevered in the face of an almost complete lack of help from his team-mates, suffered once again when Flintoff, of all people, put down a simple chance at second slip off McGrath when the score was 376 for nine. This was to prove not a particularly expensive drop in runs terms, but in morale terms it can have done little for England's confidence. That made seven catchable chances that had gone down in the match. Pietersen's personal score was three and Geraint Jones two, and it was Pietersen's dropping of Clarke that proved most costly. But the seven chances together probably cost England at least 100 runs, which could have meant chasing a difficult but possible 320 instead of a distant and impossible 420.

Australia took little benefit from Flintoff's error. Eight runs later, Katich's long innings ended when he decided he could not resist the temptation of a short ball from Harmison. He had a go at the Gilchrist uppercut shot, but only succeeded in finding the fielder at third man, who ran to make a good catch. It was Simon Jones, who must have been sorely tempted to point out to the rest of his side that that was the way to catch the ball. It was Harmison's third wicket of the innings, his eighth of the match, for 97 runs. He had certainly made his mark on the Australians.

After the game was over, England took comfort from the fact that their bowlers had dismissed Australia twice in the match. At the time, we all thought this was a piece of Alastair Campbell-like spin, because the point of the game is to take twenty wickets at a cheaper cost than your opponents do, and it was England's failure to fulfil the second part of that objective that lost them the match. But actually, this was a major achievement. Australia's batting line-up has been terrifying all opponents for a decade and more, and it is a rare match when they are all out twice. What it showed was that Australia's batting was vulnerable. The problem was that there was no sign that Australia's bowling was. After all, it was the attack led by McGrath and Warne, two of the greatest Australian bowlers of all time, who consistently set up their Test victories.

England set off on their daunting task with roughly 20 overs to go until tea. That would be the first landmark for Trescothick and Strauss to reach. The pair were clearly in no hurry – after all there were 250 plus overs to go in the match, so almost any old run-rate would get them there. McGrath and Lee were on the spot from the very beginning, and the two England left-handers were forced to be watchful: second nature for Strauss but against the grain for Trescothick. The Australians could attack hard. Time, history and, it seemed, talent, were all on their side. It was not until the sixth over of the match that England managed a boundary, when Strauss cover-drove Lee with easy timing. At the end of eight overs, England were 9 for no wicket. Trescothick did not hit a boundary until the 34th ball he faced, a delivery from Lee that he drove to the point boundary. That brought his score up to 6. It was a gritty period, and the England batsmen were being given very little leeway. You expect McGrath to be economical, even metronomically boring, but Lee ought to be good for a few loose deliveries, provided you can survive the 95 miles per hour exocets in between. The real release came only when Gillespie came into the attack after eleven overs. Lee's first five overs went for only 9 runs. Strauss pulled Gillespie's first ball for four.

Things eased to such an extent that the 50 came up with the last ball of the 19th over, but that was the cue for Ponting to toss the ball to Shane Warne. There is still something magical about Warne's bowling. He may be fatter than when he was last here on tour, he may be older and more prone to shoulder and back problems, but he can still do things with a ball that nobody else who bowls with a straight arm can do. Facing him is the ultimate test for a

Camera trickery – two images of Lee holding an athletic caught-and-bowled.

batsman, because he manages to combine his wide variety of deliveries – leg-breaks, googlies, sliders, top-spinners, you name it – with a nagging good length and total mastery over direction. There are not going to be a whole load of loose balls, which are the stock in trade of most leg-spinners, when Warne is bowling. For the spectator, whichever team you support, it is an experience to be relished. In his first over of this innings, he had two good shouts for leg before against Marcus Trescothick, who used his pads to play Warne's spin, a dangerous tactic for a left-hander. Aleem Dar turned both appeals down, and Trescothick, a calm character, hit the final ball of the over for four. In Warne's second over, the final one before tea, Warne seemed to have Trescothick absolutely plumb lbw, playing back to an off-spinner that hurried on to hit his pads, but once again the umpire was unmoved. England reached tea comparatively unscathed at 65 for no wicket.

We have to remember that two days earlier at tea, England had not lost a wicket. Australia were all out for 190, and England were 10 for no wicket. Everything in the garden was lovely.

Forty-eight hours later, the tables were turned, if not overturned. But if Strauss and Trescothick could carry on after tea, then there might be some hope. It could always rain for the final two days (the forecast was for sunshine and showers, but not for the floods required to save England).

Warne carried on at the Pavilion End after tea, using the slope to help his leg-break. He had a huge shout for lbw at the end of his first over after the interval, but Aleem Dar was unmoved yet again. A slow-motion replay showed that there was a little bit of bat involved in the overall mix of pad, ball and dust, so the decision was a good one. Strauss breathed again. He was not playing Warne with any real confidence, padding up to another one in the next over, and probably only being saved by the fact that his foot was a long way down the wicket. He was managing to put away the occasional bad ball, but he did not look like the Strauss of his great season in 2004. Against Bangladesh he had failed to cash in as the other batsmen had done and for the greater part of the season, he had not looked to have any rhythm. This was a worry for England at the top of the order.

When Strauss did get out, in Lee's next over, he was undone by a good ball and an even better piece of fielding. Lee banged in a short ball at Strauss, who could only fend it off and it bobbed up to silly mid-off. Lee, seeing that there was nobody there to take the catch, threw himself forward in his follow-through, and like a demented goalkeeper pulled off a superb catch diving full length almost at Strauss' feet. Where England had been putting down all sorts of catches, some of them simple ones, the Australians, as personified by Martyn in the first innings and Lee here, were holding on to stunning catches and creating opportunities for victory out of nowhere. This was Lee's eleventh over, and even with the recent tea break, would have been tired. Strauss might have considered himself unlucky to be out to such a remarkable piece of fielding, but England needed to take on board the lessons of Lee's commitment: never give up and never assume a match-winning position is a match already won.

Still, 80 for one was a great deal better than 79 for six, as England had been first time round. Trescothick was looking secure, and was now joined at the crease by his captain, who hit the second ball he received from Lee for a typical four, deliberately guided past the slip cordon. Trescothick hit two fine fours off Warne's next over, a sweep and a straight drive, and England's batsmen were looking confident. That was the cue for McGrath to re-enter the fray, and he began with a maiden over to Vaughan. At the other end, Warne made the decisive inroad into England's batting by deceiving Trescothick who thick-edged the ball to Hayden at slip, who does not miss those ones. Suddenly, England were 96 for two, with two new batsmen at the crease, against Warne and McGrath, the pair with almost 1,100 Test wickets between them. Ian Bell, the new man in, tried hard to counter Warne by using his feet to get out of his crease and to the pitch of the ball, and he took the total past 100, but Warne's ability to use flight, swerve and that unpredictable dip makes getting to the pitch a hazardous task. It worked for Bell until the drinks interval, which he can hardly have relished coming as it did barely three overs since his arrival in the middle. How much thirst can a man work up making 8 runs in a quarter of an hour? At the other end, Vaughan, who had survived quite some time without adding to the four he took off his second ball, also looked as though he would rather carry on batting than break his concentration with a sip of liquid energy.

The drinks break worked for Australia. Warne deceived Bell with a straight-onner, and the poor lad was pinned against the stumps and would probably have walked even if the umpire's finger had not been raised. 104 for three, and the rot had set in. There were still 334 runs needed to win, a figure that has totemic qualities for Australians, but only spells disaster for Englishmen. Pietersen, the hero of the first innings, joined Vaughan, to a huge cheer, but there was nobody left now who actually thought England could win. Now it was simply a question of the size of the defeat. Pietersen, like Vaughan, was off the mark with a boundary second ball, and we all hoped he would score a little more quickly than his captain after that. Vaughan played out another maiden from Warne, and by the time Lee was brought on to replace McGrath at the Pavilion End, Vaughan had faced 23 balls in the best part of three-quarters of an hour without scoring a run. It was Lee who put him out of his misery. The first ball of his new spell was nudged for a single by Pietersen, but the second was a perfect length ball outside off stump which kept low and jagged back enough to take Vaughan's off stump. The pitch might have had something to do with the height the ball reached, which certainly made a very good delivery virtually unplayable. The worrying fact, from the English point of view, was that

Lee adds to Vaughan's misery, bowled again for 4.

Pietersen displayed admirable circumspection in the first innings, but decided to hit out in the second.

the captain had been clean bowled in both innings of the Test, for a total of 7 runs painstakingly put together over 46 balls. The man was clearly in no sort of form at all.

A quarter of an hour later 112 for four became 119 for five. Flintoff, taking his cue from several other batsmen, scored 3 runs from the first delivery he received and then shut up shop. Lee was certainly very fast in this spell, pumped up and going for the jugular. It was the first real contest between Lee and Flintoff of the series, although Lee seemed more interested in Pietersen, who was hit a couple of times by some very rapid bouncers. He carried on, apparently unperturbed. Flintoff was the fifth victim, well caught by Gilchrist as the batsman attempted to cut Warne's slider, which he read as a leg-break, and just got a thin nick as it thudded into the 'keeper's gloves. The cheer that greeted his entry was in complete contrast to the silence that heralded his return. Flintoff's first Test against the Australians had been a failure – just 3 runs in two innings, and four wickets for 173 runs, and a dropped catch. If Australia could prevent Flintoff imposing himself on the series, the Ashes were safe. They looked safe enough already, but England without Freddie firing on all cylinders should be easy to beat.

The new man, England's last hope, was Geraint Jones. He was completely beaten by Warne's second ball to him, which fortunately did not catch an edge, so Jones survived. Pietersen decided that attack was probably the only option at this stage, and decided to open his shoulders when the opportunity arose. This was not a case of a one-day slog, at which he had already shown himself to be adept, but a controlled innings with power when power was needed. One hit off Lee for six crashed into the upper tier of the Grand Stand, and caused Lee's immediate withdrawal from the attack, but apart from that and a handful of boundaries, there were no significant successes for the English batsmen. However, there were also no more significant successes for the Australian bowlers. By virtue of some intelligent batting against tiring bowlers, Pietersen and Jones added 37 runs before, much to their obvious joy and the Australians' disappointment, the thickening clouds and gathering gloom caused the umpires to offer the light to the batsmen, and their offer was eagerly accepted. At the end of another slightly short but still tense day, albeit one that was not to England supporters' tastes, another 261 runs had been scored and another nine wickets fell. For England, needing a further 264 runs to win, the only hope was thunder, lightning and a plague of frogs for two full days.

Day 3, Close of Play:

Australia 190 and 384.
England 155 and 156 for five wickets (Pietersen 42 not out, GO Jones 6 not out).

The fourth day began with optimism for the England camp, because the rain was falling. It was by no means a deluge, merely a persistent drizzle, and the forecast was for a break in the showers long enough to get some play on both Sunday and, if needed, Monday. So the weather was unlikely to come to England's aid. Throughout the morning, everybody at Lord's sat around, sheltering from the splutters of rain and reading, if they so chose, the lambasting the British press were giving their cricket team, who had only flattered to deceive by winning matches throughout the previous twelve months. The masters of world cricket were still Australia, and the main message of the reports was 'I told you so.' It made depressing reading for most England supporters, the more so because deep in our hearts we agreed with it.

It was not until 3.45, after a few false starts, that play was finally able to get underway. England, in the persons of Pietersen and Jones, needed to bat out the rest of the day – a maximum 42 overs were scheduled – and then hope that Monday's forecast understated the likelihood of rain. Australia, in the persons of McGrath and Warne, needed to take the remaining five England wickets before the rain, to wrap up the victory Australia certainly deserved. It took Australia just fifteen balls to make the breakthrough. Jones, having not added to his overnight score, attempted to hook McGrath, a policy that has been abandoned over the years by many better batsmen, and merely scooped the ball to Gillespie at mid-on. It was 158 for six, and Giles strode to the wicket.

Two balls later he was striding back to the Pavilion, having edged McGrath to Hayden at gully. Whatever his shortcomings as an opening batsman, Hayden's catching is still as safe as ever, his huge hands easily pouching one of the more straightforward offerings of his career – 158 for seven. Now it was Hoggard. But before the Australians could really get stuck into Hoggy, the rain started again, and the players decamped back indoors. Would the rain save England? Ten minutes later, rain relented, and the teams were back out, even though as they re-established themselves in the middle, the rain started again. The players took no notice of it, and the light drizzle soon went away again.

So did Hoggard. After a stay of four overs and a bit, without getting off the mark, Hoggard succumbed, leg before to McGrath to a ball that kept low. He had no chance and was extremely out. That was the final ball of the over. Steve Harmison came out and stood at the bowler's end while Pietersen faced Warne. They took a couple from the first ball, and single from the second ball. To the third, Harmison was another leg before victim, and just like Hoggard he could have had no quarrel with the decision. Warne now had four wickets, and still had the chance to take a fifth, and secure for himself a place on the Lord's honours board, the one accolade he had not yet received in his brilliant career.

The last man Simon Jones joined Kevin Pietersen, with only 253 more needed to win. For the record, this was 123 more than the record last wicket partnership for England against Australia, set by Tip Foster and Wilfred Rhodes in Sydney just over a century before. It was also pointed out that no partnership lower than the fourth wicket had ever put together so many runs for England in Ashes history, so it was a big ask for the two men. The expectation was that defeat would follow shortly.

It did, but not before Pietersen had displayed his defiance by smacking Warne for a huge six over midwicket, and then five balls later, hitting him elegantly over long-off for four more. They proved to be the final runs of the innings, as to the first ball of the next over, from McGrath, Jones was drawn into a shot and edged it to Warne at first slip, who does not drop these, especially when there is a Test to be won. So Warne denied himself the chance of his name on the honours board to go with his portrait in the Long Room, but Australia were the winners, comprehensively, by 239 runs. The final five wickets had fallen for 22 runs in five overs, and nobody except Pietersen had scored a run all day. He was left on 64 not out, a highly praiseworthy innings in his debut Test, even if he has still to learn the art of protecting the tail and shepherding them to greater things.

Glenn McGrath was declared Man of the Match, which was no surprise. His bowling in the first innings, when he reduced England to 21 for five, was the match-winning performance, and established Australia as winners from the end of the first day. McGrath, the 35-year-old, said after the game, 'I've never felt younger than I do now,' but he would say that, wouldn't he. Hoggard, who had suggested that the Australians might be too old to last out a five match series which includes back-to back-Tests, was lampooned for what the *Wisden Cricketer* called 'idiotic pre-match rhetoric' which 'came back to haunt him'. Time would tell, time would tell.

One down and four to play is not the ideal situation when you are up against the Australians. Next stop Edgbaston.

England v. Australia, First Test Match

At Lord's Cricket Ground

21, 22, 23, 24 July 2005

Result: Australia won by 239 runs

Toss: Australia

Australia

JL Langer c Harmison b Flintoff	40	run out (Pietersen)	6
ML Hayden b Hoggard	12	b Flintoff	34
*RT Ponting c Strauss b Harmison	9	c sub (Hildreth) b Hoggard	42
DR Martyn c GO Jones b SP Jones	2	lbw b Harmison	65
MJ Clarke lbw b SP Jones	11	b Hoggard	91
SM Katich c GO Jones b Harmison	27	c SP Jones b Harmison	67
+AC Gilchrist c GO Jones b Flintoff	26	b Flintoff	10
SK Warne b Harmison	28	c Giles b Harmison	2
B Lee c GO Jones b Harmison	3	run out (Giles)	8
JN Gillespie lbw b Harmison	1	b SP Jones	13
GD McGrath not out	10	not out	20
Extras (b 5, lb 4, w 1, nb 11)	21	(b 10, lb 8, nb 8)	26
Total (all out, 40.2 overs)	190	(all out, 100.4 overs)	384

Fall of Wickets First Innings: 1-35 (Hayden), 2-55 (Ponting), 3-66 (Langer), 4-66 (Martyn), 5-87 (Clarke), 6-126 (Gilchrist), 7-175 (Warne), 8-178 (Katich),9-178 (Lee), 10-190 (Gillespie).
Fall of Wickets Second Innings: 1-18 (Langer), 2-54 (Hayden), 3-100 (Ponting), 4-255 (Clarke), 5-255 (Martyn), 6-274 (Gilchrist), 7-279 (Warne), 8-289 (Lee), 9-341 (Gillespie), 10-384 (Katich).

Bowling First Innings: Harmison 11.2–0–43–5; Hoggard 8–0–40–1; Flintoff 11–2–50–2; SP Jones 10–0–48–2
Bowling Second Innings: Harmison 27.4–6–54–3, Hoggard 16–1–56–2; Flintoff 27–4–123–2; SP Jones 18–1–69–1; Giles 11–1–56–0; Bell 1–0–8–0

England

ME Trescothick	c Langer b McGrath	4	c Hayden b Warne	44
AJ Strauss	c Warne b McGrath	2	c & b Lee	37
*MP Vaughan	b McGrath	3	b Lee	4
IR Bell	b McGrath	6	lbw b Warne	8
KP Pietersen	c Martyn b Warne	57	not out	64
A Flintoff	b McGrath	0	c Gilchrist b Warne	3
+GO Jones	c Gilchrist b Lee	30	c Gillespie b McGrath	6
AF Giles	c Gilchrist b Lee	11	c Hayden b McGrath	0
MJ Hoggard	c Hayden b Warne	0	lbw b McGrath	0
SJ Harmison	c Martyn b Lee	11	lbw b Warne	0
SP Jones	not out	20	c Warne b McGrath	0
Extras	(b 1, lb 5, nb 5)	11	(b 6, lb 5, nb 3)	14
Total	(all out, 48.1 overs)	155	(all out, 58.1 overs)	180

Fall of Wickets First Innings: 1-10 (Trescothick), 2-11 (Strauss), 3-18 (Vaughan), 4-19 (Bell), 5-21 (Flintoff), 6-79 (GO Jones), 7-92 (Giles), 8-101 (Hoggard), 9-122 (Pietersen), 10-155 (Harmison).

Fall of Wickets Second Innings: 1-80 (Strauss), 2-96 (Trescothick), 3-104 (Bell), 4-112 (Vaughan), 5-119 (Flintoff), 6-158 (GO Jones), 7-158 (Giles), 8-164 (Hoggard), 9-167 (Harmison), 10-180 (SP Jones).

Bowling First Innings: McGrath 18–5–53–5; Lee 15.1–5–47–3; Gillespie 8–1–30–0; Warne 7–2–19–2
Bowling Second Innings: McGrath 17.1–2–29–4; Lee 15–3–58–2; Gillespie 6–0–1–0 Warne 20–2–64–4

Umpires: Aleem Dar (Pakistan) and RE Koertzen (South Africa)

Man of the Match: GD McGrath

4

Not Fade Away

The Second Test Match, Edgbaston

In between the excitement of the Lord's Test, which despite its ultimate one-sidedness was a thrilling and highly emotional match, and the Second Test at Edgbaston there were ten days for the two teams to regroup and plan their paths through the rest of the series. It had never been much of a punt to begin with, but now the two-horse race looked even more like a walkover. There were few takers for an England series victory.

I took some time out by going down to Cornwall for a few days' break. It's not a county immediately associated with top-class cricket, with only two men from the county – the two Jacks, Crapp and Richards – who have earned full England caps. But it still has many deep cricketing connections. At Mawgan Church, on the Lizard peninsula, I came across a tablet to the Rev. Horatio Mann, of Linton Park in Kent, who had been the rector there for 36 years in the first part of the nineteenth century. This Horatio, or Horace, must have been a relative (perhaps a nephew) of the cricket promoter and gambler Sir Horace Mann, also of Linton Park in Kent, a key figure in the early development of cricket as a national game, whose bankruptcy just before the turn of the century may have been one of the reasons why his namesake was an impoverished clergyman in Cornwall rather than a wealthy landowner in Kent.

At Lord's I had bumped into Chris Old, the former Yorkshire and England fast bowler who in 1974 had finished off a Lord's Test against India before lunch on the fourth day. He and Geoff Arnold dismissed the hapless Indians for 42, and gave England a victory by an innings and 285 runs. I had planned a very pleasant day at headquarters watching some close-fought cricket, and I have always blamed Messrs Old (five for 21) and Arnold (four for 19) for the fact that I failed to get full value for my ticket that day. Old now runs a fish restaurant on Praa Sands near Penzance, as good a place for an idle Saturday lunch as you can find. We chatted about the England team, and Old, like everybody else in England, was not optimistic.

We discussed potential changes in the side for Edgbaston, but there seemed to be few options. Thorpe had announced his retirement, and by picking Bell against Bangladesh, that seemed to rule out Rob Key of Kent. Anyway, how could you drop Bell after one match? So the batting line-up had to remain as it was. Flintoff had had a poor match at Lord's, but he is a proven match-winner, so his place was secure too. For the same reason that Bell was safe, so was Geraint Jones. The selectors had made their move for batsman over 'keeper, Jones for Read, and there was nothing to be gained by switching back now.

Now there was only the bowling to consider. Ashley Giles may not be in the class of Rhodes, Verity, Lock, or even Tufnell, but he is the best England have got, and on his day he can bat a bit. What's more, Edgbaston is his home ground. The four quick bowlers seem to be the front runners at present, and Harmison and Simon Jones certainly did little wrong at Lord's. If there was a doubt, it was with Hoggard, the blond smiler from Leeds, whose personality was, in many people's view, enough to keep him in the side even when he is not bowling at his best. And who would replace him? The bowling stocks were remarkably low, especially as Gough and Caddick were on the shelf, Anderson was not back to anything like his best form, and all the others who occasionally got a mention were not seen to be of Test class. 'Fast bowling at the moment is not good,' said Old. 'There's nobody coming through.'

Another option that was being discussed in the columns of the broadsheets (and of the tabloid ex-broadsheets) was to bring in Paul Collingwood at the expense of a bowler, perhaps Ashley Giles. That would mean using the part-time bowlers a bit more than at Lord's – Vaughan, Collingwood, even Bell and Pietersen – but it would strengthen England's batting, and equally importantly our fielding, which is what had let us down at Lord's.

'Collingwood I coached as a lad', Old told me. 'He was just a tiny boy but he had more talent than the others I saw at the time.' But as a grown man, Collingwood seems to have been stuck with the title of one-day cricketer. His two Test caps have brought him just 89 runs at 22.25, and no wickets. He has taken six Test catches, though, a tribute to his superb fielding skills.

The problem with England's batting did not seem to be the basic quality of the players themselves, but simply that they were hopelessly out of form. Strauss looked as though he could not hit a croquet ball, let alone a fast reverse-swinging yorker, and Michael Vaughan was also clearly struggling. 'Cricket's a matter of rhythm,' says Old. 'Whether batting or bowling, it's all about rhythm. And you don't get your rhythm back in the nets. Michael Vaughan is out of form and there's no point in having more nets – he needs time in the middle.' The Team England policy of not allowing its centrally contracted players to play much cricket outside the international calendar was not helping the England players work themselves back into rhythm and form.

A few days later, Vaughan was released to play for Yorkshire in a totesport League fixture against Kent at Headingley. Vaughan scored 116 not out, though Yorkshire still lost the match. But at least it was a few more runs under his belt. On 30 July both Marcus Trescothick and Andrew Flintoff were released to play for their counties in the Twenty20 Cup Finals, and they duly met in the final. Trescothick's Somerset were the winners, but the games did little for either man's Test form. We already knew they were good at Twenty20. What we needed to know was whether they were in form for the very much longer version of the game.

At any rate, the selectors could not come up with any options that the mass of amateur selectors up and down the country had not considered, with the result that the squad for the Second Test was unchanged, as follows:

M.P. Vaughan (Yorkshire, captain), M.E. Trescothick (Somerset), A.J. Strauss (Middlesex), I.R. Bell (Warwickshire), K.P. Pietersen (Hampshire), A. Flintoff (Lancashire), G.O. Jones (Kent, wicketkeeper), A.F. Giles (Warwickshire), M.J. Hoggard (Yorkshire), S.J. Harmison (Durham), S.P. Jones (Glamorgan), and C.T. Tremlett (Hampshire).

Tremlett obviously has little idea how to ingratiate himself with the captain. Bowling to him in the nets, he caught Vaughan a nasty crack on the elbow, and as Vaughan has shown a remarkable ability to pick up odd injuries at the last minute, there was a hurried call to bring another batsman into the squad. It was not Robert Key who got the nod this time, but Paul Collingwood, and the Durham man came rushing down to Birmingham in case the elbow did not heal. Fortunately for England – and by that I mean no disparagement to Collingwood who was about to begin a succession of innings that would prove him to be in the form of his life – Vaughan's elbow proved sturdier than his back, his knee and other parts that have troubled him at the wrong moment in the past. Vaughan played, Collingwood went north to Chester-le-Street and as at Lord's, Tremlett was the man left out of the twelve on the morning of the match.

The Australians seemed to have no such troubles. They pottered down to Worcester for a three-day fixture against the county, which was reduced by rain to two days and an over, and rattled up 406 for nine in 98 overs. A pernickety critic might have pointed out that the top scorer was reserve 'keeper Brad Haddin, with 94, and that Gillespie made more runs than Ponting, Clarke and Katich combined, but Kasprowicz took five wickets as Worcestershire crumbled for just 187. In their brief second innings, Clarke and Ponting hit fifties, but the game proved very little. Not that the Australians were worried.

They moved the short distance from Worcester to Birmingham and prepared for what should be a second victory, putting dreams of England's Ashes on ice for another few years. Their team selection was straightforward, the same eleven as at Lord's. But in the warm-up session on the morning of the Test, something happened which could well have changed the entire Ashes summer. Glenn McGrath, Man of the Match at Lord's and the only Australian pace bowler that the English batsmen really feared, trod on a ball and tore ligaments in his right ankle, and was unfit to play. His place was hurriedly taken by Mike Kasprowicz.

The team that came on to the field was: R.T. Ponting (Tasmania, captain), M.L. Hayden (Queensland), J.L. Langer (Western Australia), D.R. Martyn (Western Australia), M.J. Clarke (New South Wales), S.M. Katich (New South Wales), A.C. Gilchrist (Western Australia, wicket keeper), S.K. Warne (Victoria), B. Lee (New South Wales), J.N. Gillespie (South Australia) and M.S. Kasprowicz (Queensland).

McGrath's injury was hugely significant. It upset the balance of the Australian attack, and it meant that Warne would have to bowl as both an attacking bowler, his strength, and as a containing bowler, which is not what a wrist-spinner usually does. If Brett Lee was to be given

free rein to blast out England, then Kasprowicz and Gillespie, as experienced a pair of back-up bowlers as Australia had fielded in some time, would have to apply the brakes. The news of McGrath's injury spread like wildfire through the England camp and out into the crowd, and the overall view was that this was England's chance, and a chance that just had to be seized. However great it is to see a world-class fast bowler in action, we had seen that at Lord's, which was quite enough, and would be happy to see less of it at Edgbaston, at least less of it in Australian colours. Nobody would wish an injury on anybody, but perhaps this was the sort of thing that happens to 35-year-old ankles which might not happen to 25-year-old ankles. As McGrath hobbled around the ground over the next few days on crutches, the word was that he would be bound to miss the next Test at Old Trafford, played back-to-back with the Edgbaston Test, and may well be out for the whole tour. Nobody was counting chickens, but a number of top-order England batsmen were breathing a little easier.

As if the injury to McGrath was not enough of a bombshell, Ricky Ponting compounded the bizarre news of the day by winning the toss and putting England in. Could the Australians really be afraid of their opponent's attack, as Nasser Hussain clearly was, despite denials, at Brisbane on the last tour? Why on earth would you put the opposition in on a flat pitch without your leading strike bowler? At a stroke the advantage was handed to England, who knew now that not only would they not have to face McGrath at all, but also they would not have to face Warne in the fourth innings on a wearing pitch. It was an odd decision.

Ponting justified it by turning to history. Apparently only one of the last thirteen Tests at Edgbaston had been won by the side batting first. Having noted that much, he should perhaps have gone on to consider that in 2004 England won the toss against West Indies here, batted first, scored 566 for nine (Flintoff 167, Trescothick 105) and went on to win by 256 runs. In 2003, the match was drawn, but South Africa, batting first, made 594 for five, with Smith (277) and Gibbs (179) putting on 338 for the first wicket. In 2002, England did indeed wipe out Sri Lanka by batting second, and four years earlier, at Edgbaston, Steve Waugh had won the toss and fielded, to romp home by an innings and 118 runs. But in each case, the winning side had its full force of bowlers. Without a reliable bowling attack, Edgbaston can be a runmaker's paradise.

Whether this particular wicket would ooze runs was a much more difficult question to answer. The English summer weather has always been uncertain, but nobody could have imagined that a tornado would hit Birmingham, no more than a quarter of a mile from the ground, just a few days before the Test was due to start. The result of this freak storm was that an inch of rain fell on the pitch area in about a minute, a massive and torrential, if very brief, soaking. To say that this made it difficult for the ground staff to prepare the strip would be stating the obvious, but that is what Steve Rouse and his team had to cope with. He was quoted as saying it was the worst possible preparation leading up to a Test match, and even he had no real idea exactly how it would turn out. Everybody assumed there would be moisture under the surface,

Opposite: Jones poised to take the catch that sealed England's victory.

and a rather crusty top to the pitch. A very fast wicket was out of the question: a slow seaming wicket of the typically English county variety was the most likely outcome. It is probable that this doubt regarding the pitch was also a factor in Ponting's decision to field first.

What Ponting did not know – apart from how the pitch would play – was that the England team had been having some fierce tactical discussions after the debacle at Lord's, and had decided that the only way to play these Australians was to attack them. If the Ashes were to come back home, then they would not be won by faint-hearted and defensive tactics: the England team had to go for broke. The strategy that had begun with the selection of Pietersen over Thorpe was to continue with aggressive field placings, precise bowling to an attacking plan and, first of all, by playing the Australians at their own batting game and scoring at a rapid rate to give the bowlers plenty of time to take the 20 wickets required for victory.

Brett Lee and Jason Gillespie opened the bowling for Australia in the absence of McGrath and became unwilling participants in a day's cricket that transformed the summer. Trescothick played the first over carefully, even though Lee's first ball of the match was a wide, and Strauss sized up the bowling for the first three balls of Gillespie's over. They seemed to agree – nothing much in it for the bowlers, with the ball bouncing rather low and often not getting through to Gilchrist on the full. Flat, no pace, not much bounce, all in all a strip made for batting.

Trescothick's favoured sweep shot.

Warne dismissed Strauss twice at Edgbaston with extravagant turn.

Strauss, having had as little to do as possible with the first half of Gillespie's over, leant into the fourth and gently guided it between the slips and gully down to the third-man boundary for four. Raw power is not needed when there is timing to get the ball to the fence. On the other hand, raw power is fun to watch and fun to wield. Trescothick had had enough of this pussyfooting about, and hit the first ball of Lee's second over to the cover boundary, probably the shortest boundary when the bowling is from the City End, but even so, the fielder would never have beaten the ball to the fence even if there had been another twenty yards to play with. Trescothick decided he liked the feel of ball on bat, and the fifth and sixth balls of Lee's over were treated with similar disdain. Both went to the cover boundary, but the sixth ball in particular was hit with huge force. Any fielder who tried to get in the way of that would have been rubbing his fingers for hours to come.

The gauntlet had been thrown down, and England set about the Australian bowling in a way that was thrilling to watch, all the more so for being totally unexpected. In Gillespie's next over, Strauss nicked one very low down to Warne at slip, but he did not get down quickly enough, and the chance was missed. But apart from that little error, there seemed to be no alarms for England as the openers began to build a solid partnership. The Australians played their part by keeping up the attacking fields – when Lee bowled to Strauss he had four slips and a gully – and this may have accelerated the run scoring. After only eight overs, the score was 36 for no wicket, most of the runs having come in boundaries. After ten overs, England were at 44 for no wicket, including nine fours. Lee was taken out of the attack and went off to lick his wounds, having been hit for 24 in his first five overs. He did not help himself by bowling a few no-balls, but his main problem was Trescothick. The Somerset man had scented blood and was on the rampage. The score rattled along at just over four an over, with Trescothick playing very much the leading role. But he was not slogging wildly, or playing one of his one-day innings when the feet do not move at all and the runs come from his uncanny hand–eye coordination and his ability to judge the line so well. This was a disciplined innings as well as being an aggressive one. He was enjoying himself.

So were the crowd. The Australians may have been wondering why their captain did not take first go on this belter of a batting wicket, but there was not too much sympathy for them around the ground. On a day of only mediocre weather, often in not very good light, the performance of the entire England side was a revelation, and the crowd loved it. It was not long before that mixed blessing, the Barmy Army, dusted off their collective tonsils and began singing. The festival atmosphere seemed complete, despite the cloudy skies. When Strauss jumped out and hit Warne back over his head for four to bring the score to 60 for no wicket, the umpires decided that it was time for drinks. The fact that it was the middle of Warne's over did not seem to matter. The ball had, it seemed, been hit out of shape by the combined bats of Strauss and Trescothick, and it needed a little attention. We were only in the fourteenth over of the innings.

And so it went on. Strauss threatened to catch up with Trescothick when they were both in the low thirties, but Trescothick settled that particular contest with a huge six back over Warne's head. Even Warne was being made to look ordinary by the invigorating hitting of the England opening pair. Two more fours from Trescothick in Kasprowicz's next over confirmed the suspicion that the batsmen were enjoying themselves. When was the last time that England had made 86 for no wicket in the opening 20 overs of a Test, let alone an Ashes Test, and let alone in a series in which they were already one down? Trescothick's fifty came up in the 22nd over, when he had faced just 74 balls, and England's hundred came up in the 23rd over, when Strauss cover-drove Kasprowicz for yet another four. This was the new England, and we liked it.

After 25 overs, England had reached 111, and Warne bowled to Trescothick. His powerful square drive brought out the best in Michael Clarke the fielder, but they still managed an easy single. Then it was Warne to Strauss. The thing about Shane Warne, and the reason why he has 600 Test wickets, is that at any time he can produce the unplayable ball. No batsman can ever feel at ease against him. Despite the fact that he had gone for 37 in his first six overs, at a rate of more than a run a ball, the English batsmen knew they could not take liberties. Strauss tried to, by aiming to cut a ball that was pitched wide outside his off stump. It turned almost square and Strauss was clean bowled. I am not sure he could quite believe it, any more than Mike Gatting could believe it all those summers ago when he was the victim to Warne's 'ball of the century', but it is in the scorecard now, so it must be true. Strauss had made 48 out of the opening partnership of 112, in only 25 overs. For the first time this summer, Strauss was looking as though he had recovered some of his fluency, what Chris Old would call his rhythm.

The new man in was Michael Vaughan, with hardly more than an over to go before the lunch break was due. He got off the mark with a single, but it was the next over that really got the crowd going. Lee bowled the final over of the morning to Trescothick, and conventional wisdom would have it that the Somerset man should play a careful maiden and go into lunch a happy and secure man. Trescothick is a man who prefers unconventional wisdom. The first ball of the over from Lee, bowling around the wicket, was quick enough but a little short and a little too wide outside off stump. Trescothick simply steered the ball between gully and backward point to the third-man boundary. The next ball was again short and even wider. Trescothick turned himself round and quite deliberately hit the ball for six over third man. The crowd were cheering. Lee's happy smile had gone walkabout. The third ball was played carefully back to the bowler, but the fourth was crashed through cover for another four. The fifth ball was another dot ball, but the sixth was virtually a carbon copy of the fourth – a cover boundary. That was the cue for Trescothick to turn and stride off back to the pavilion for a very enjoyable lunch break, having taken 18 runs off the final over of the session, leaving him on 77 not out, and England very healthily placed at 132 for one. It had been a sensational morning.

Marcus Trescothick is a much better player than the Australians gave him credit for at the start of the summer. They knew him as a man who had averaged only 29 against them in two full series, with a top score of 76. But in the other 51 Tests he had played up to the start of the Ashes series, he had made 4,193 runs at just a heartbeat under 50. I know that included free runs against Bangladesh, but you might just as well exclude Hayden's monumental 380 because it was against Zimbabwe. Anybody with a Test average against allcomers of 45, with twelve centuries, is a very good batsman. By common consent the problem with Trescothick is in the feet. Great batsmen move their feet. 'Get your foot to the pitch of the ball' is virtually the first thing any boy learns in the nets, but it seems that Banger missed lesson one. He makes up for it by having a great eye and, increasingly, the peculiar skill of leaving the ball at the last minute. Where once the fact that his bat was often a long way from his body made him prone to slip catches, he now leaves those he decides not to reach for, which makes him a far more difficult player to get out than he used to be. He still hits the ball very hard, and scores at a rapid rate, but his innings are lasting longer these days. The Australians had not quite appreciated this at the beginning of 2005, and assumed the England vice-captain would continue to be their bunny. They were rapidly proved wrong.

After the lunch break, the combination of Gillespie and Kasprowicz began to show the signs of wear and tear that had been so effectively glossed over in the First Test. Neither Trescothick nor Vaughan, who was helped on his way by four overthrows from an over-eager Michael Clarke, seemed in any trouble, and the pair picked off boundaries almost as they pleased. If that makes the play sound indolent, then it was anything but. There was an energy in the batting of both men, in the way they looked for the attacking option for every ball, and the way they ran each run as though it might be their last, which kept the score racing along. By the end of the 31st over, the score was 162, a rate of well over five an over, respectable enough in limited-overs cricket, and positively blazing by Test standards, even by the standards of the Australians in full swing. The Australians looked deflated, and Ponting was finding it impossible to think of something that might stem the flow of runs. Trescothick surged past his previous highest score against Australia, 76, also made at Edgbaston, and seemed well on course for a superb century when he contrived to get himself out. Allowing himself a momentary lapse in concentration, he played at a respectable but not searching delivery from Kasprowicz, and just touched it through to Gilchrist. The main antagonist was gone. Trescothick's 90 had come in a mere 102 balls, and had included fifteen fours and two sixes. It was the innings that set the tone for England, and established a strong base from which the later batsmen could launch their own ferocious attacks on the increasingly insipid Australian bowling.

Bell, the next man in, played a little gem of a knock. Unfortunately it was such a little gem that it was barely visible. He hit the first ball into the leg side and took 2 runs. He leant back and hit the second ball hard to the third-man boundary, and was out to the third ball, in exactly the same way as Trescothick had been three balls earlier. The spirit was willing in Bell's case, but the flesh, the concentration and the discipline was weak. Three balls for 6 is a quick innings, but a short one.

This let the Australians, for probably the only time in the day, think they might be back in the game. A score of 170 for three is a lot better than 164 for one. As Geoffrey Boycott so sagely says, time and time again, add two wickets to the score and see if it is still a good one. Well, it was still a good one, but not what this belter of a wicket deserved. Pietersen, the English batting hero, if there was one, of the Lord's Test came out to join his captain, and to face the Gillespie–Kasprowicz partnership that was trying to bring some sanity to the proceedings. But Pietersen and Vaughan never allowed the bowlers to settle. Kasprowicz got the no-ball yips, overstepping twice in one over, which was enough for KP to step across his wicket and flick the first, one-day style, to the midwicket boundary. Vaughan was the recipient of the second no-ball, and he played the classic off drive as only he, and perhaps Rahul Dravid, can, for another four. Kasprowicz, once again, was taken out of the firing line.

Warne was brought back in his place, but it was Gillespie who struck next. Vaughan, who had made 24 without ever looking in any sort of trouble, suddenly had a go at a short delivery, and got it too high on the bat. It soared high into the air, but on its downward path found the safe hands of Brett Lee, who had had to run round to fine leg to take the catch. It was a very good catch, but Vaughan really committed suicide: he had no need to play the shot at all.

One hundred and eighty-seven for four (in a breakneck 37 overs) was definitely the sort of score Australia could cope with, especially after the gamble of putting England in. If Flintoff, who had scored 3 runs in his two innings at Lord's, were to fail, then Australia would certainly be in control. What nobody realised was that Trescothick's fine knock, and the other smaller cameos, were just curtain raisers for the top-of-the-bill act, Pietersen and Flintoff, who between them put Australia to the sword. They added 103 in 17 overs, at a rate of a run a ball as near as dammit, giving all the bowlers equal respect – very little. Flintoff plays straighter than most batsmen of his generation, which can be very disheartening for the bowler who thinks he knows a way past most people's bats, while Pietersen has a technique that looks ridiculously unsafe, all wristy right hand and cross-batted pull shots, but which works.

The two men hoisted the fifty partnership in only 50 balls, and the Australian attack began to look very ragged once more. When Flintoff hooked Lee with his eyes shut (Flintoff's eyes, not Lee's, although they might as well have been) over square leg for six, to bring up the 250, you could see the body language of the Australians saying, 'This is not supposed to happen.' But it was. To prove he could make big hits off anybody, in the next over Freddie hit Warne over long-off for another six. It was by no means a violent shot: he just leaned into it and caressed it over the boundary. Flintoff can make very big shots look almost effortless, and he plays them so correctly that the fielding side cannot at first imagine that there could be anything more than a well directed four. To see the ball sailing into the crowd from a shot like that is not good for team morale. And Flintoff did it five times in the course of his innings.

Pietersen was losing much by comparison with Flintoff, who was really steaming. In the same over from Warne, they both hit boundaries, Flintoff's a thumping cover-drive to bring up

Flintoff put a disappointing start to the series behind him at Edgbaston, and never looked back.

A rare success for Gillespie – during the series he took just three wickets at a hundred runs apiece.

his half-century, and Pietersen's another shot through cover, but to combat the flight he changed tack at the last minute and almost seemed to turn himself inside out to play it. It still went for four, the shot of a very high-class batsman. The two batsmen were obviously enjoying themselves, allowing themselves a free rein to attack and giving the Australians new problems to think about. By the time they reached tea, England had scored 289 for four after only 54 overs. This was hectic stuff, and the crowd were loving it.

The tea interval produced the result that Australia wanted. Three balls after the players were back on the field, Gillespie induced an injudicious shot from Flintoff, and he was out, caught by Gilchrist. This was Gillespie's 250th Test wicket, and had he but known it, almost his last. The partnership had put on 103 in 105 balls, including five sixes (all from Flintoff) and twelve fours. The Australians, still assuming they would win because they always did, took great heart from this further breakthrough. When Geraint Jones went, also caught behind but this time off Kasprowicz, just a few overs later, the score was 293 for six, and England would seem to have squandered the unexpected chance of batting first on this strip. 500 was what was needed to be safe, but teams do not score 500 against Australia.

The most encouraging aspect of the England innings, apart from the general attacking intent shown by all, was the way that the tail did not just fold up, as it had in the second, very feeble, innings at Lord's. Pietersen was at the other end again to cluck around his partners like a mother hen (every so often giving the ball a mighty swipe in a manner that was most un-mother-hen-like), but this time, instead of four ducks, we got four double-figure innings, some hefty blows and a sense of purpose and enjoyment that had been missing at Lord's. Giles made 23 before Warne did for him, leg before to a straight one that was pitching on off stump and would have hit it, but not before he had seen Pietersen through to his third fifty in his first three Test innings. They had added 49 for the seventh wicket, but when Pietersen was out in the next over, two balls after hitting Lee for a six to match most of the five that Flintoff had struck, the brakes seemed to be on. Pietersen's highly entertaining innings of 71 in 76 balls ended when he tried another big hit off Lee, but could only scoop it to Katich, who accepted the chance eagerly. It was the worst shot of his innings, and could have cost him his maiden Test century, and England another 50 runs. England were now 348 for eight, in the 67th over, with only Hoggard, Harmison and Jones to hold up the Australians. Langer and Hayden no doubt took advantage of the drinks break to talk about batting on this wicket, and to begin to get their minds into their batting trousers, so to speak.

Unfortunately for them, the tailenders had other ideas. It only took them one more over to bring up Warne's century: after 20 overs, his analysis was two for 100, a statistical indignity that the great man cannot have suffered too often in his career. His fellow leg-spinner on the tour, Stuart MacGill, held the record in this department – four consecutive Test innings, the first and second innings of two consecutive Tests – in which he was hit for at least 100 runs. This is a difficult feat to achieve: how often do teams need to make so many runs in their second innings that one bowler will be hit for 100 runs, let alone in consecutive matches? All the same, against England at Melbourne and Sydney in 2002/03, he took two for 108 and five for 152 at Melbourne, and two for 106 and three for 120 at Sydney. No wonder the Australians used him sparingly on tour, and not at all in the Tests.

Harmison in particular enjoyed himself. Lee lined up his three slips and a gully, and waited for Harmison to get himself out. He dug one in short and Harmy, having learned from Flintoff and Pietersen, got himself underneath it and hooked it high into the stands beyond fine leg for six. There was, it must be admitted, an element of luck in the shot, but there was no luck involved in the next ball, just skill. It was another short ball, but it did not get up, and Harmison pulled it forward of square for four more. That was Lee's hundred up, as well. In the next over, Harmison decided to try dancing down the wicket at Warne. What's good enough for the top-order boys must be good enough for him. Four more over long-on was the inevitable result, but next ball Warne had his equally inevitable revenge. He beat Harmison in the air, and, uncertain whether to go forward, back or sideways, Harmison played all around the ball and was bowled. Still, 17 in twelve balls only added to the impetus, and now it was Simon Jones' turn at the crease.

In one over from Gillespie, Jones hit him massively for six and Hoggard hit him beautifully through the covers for four. The 400 came up, and the pair punched gloves like real batsmen

Harmison regularly roughed-up Australia's top order.   Not for the first time, nor for the last, Langer is the unfortunate target.

do. It could not last much longer, and Warne eventually picked up his fourth wicket of the innings when he had Hoggard leg before, trying to sweep. Last-wicket stands are a real nuisance for the fielding side. This one only added another 32 in ten overs, but it set the seal on England's day. If England had slid from 187 for four to 270 all out, or even from 290 for five to 350 all out, Australia would have been in with a very good chance to win, and with McGrath in their attack, they probably would have done. By totalling 407, and in fewer than 80 overs, England could justifiably claim to have put the Australian attack to the sword. It is true that they were all out, but the speed with which the runs were scored, and the confidence with which they played the good balls and scored off the bad balls represented a huge turnaround from Lord's. This was the biggest score that England had made on the first day of any Test match since the Second World War. That's how good it was.

The rest of the day was a let-down. Just as the players came out to start the Australian innings, the light faded and then the rain came down. The players scampered off again before a ball could be bowled.

Day 1, Close of Play:
England 407 all out.

The newspapers the next morning could hardly believe it all. 'Whirlwind England Rekindle The Ashes' was a typical, if unimaginative, headline. The question for the full house pouring into Edgbaston was, 'Could England follow up their brilliant batting with an equally impressive bowling performance?' or in more colloquial language, 'Go get 'em, Harmy.'

It was Hoggy who went and got 'em first. After a maiden over from Harmison to Langer, which included a ball that hit the unfortunate batsman on the head, Hoggard bowled to Hayden. He and Vaughan had set that peculiar 'Hayden position', a kind of straight short cover, or deep silly mid-off, who stands practically on the non-striker's toes. Strauss was the man posted there, eager to get in on the action. He did not necessarily expect anything quite so soon, but to the very first ball of the over, Hayden played his trademark straightish clip, straight into the hands of Strauss – 0 for one. There is nothing so satisfactory for the fielding side as a well thought-out plan that pays off, and with the dangerous Hayden back in the pavilion already, the England team's high fives were even higher than usual. Ponting, on the other hand, is a batsman in quite a different category, with a wide variety of shots at his disposal, and no real propensity for get-ting out to one rather than another. Strauss ambled off to field elsewhere, his job done.

Ponting and Langer set about building an innings and Ponting especially tried to play the kind of aggressive cricket that served England so well the day before. Hoggard's second over, with two no-balls and two boundaries for Ponting, allowed Australia to gain some sort of perspective on the day, and England realised they were in for a tough fight to get this fine batting side out. But they had done it twice at Lord's, and there was no reason why they could not do it again.

Langer was continuing to receive the close attention of Steve Harmison. Having hit his helmet in the first over, Langer was soon bent double again as a short ball smacked into his midriff. In the Bodyline series of 1932/33, this sort of an attack would not have been considered fair, ('There's two teams out there, Mr Warner, and only one of them is playing cricket'), but in 2005, the only thoughts from the commentary boxes were, 'Well bowled'. The England supporters relished seeing an Australian opener jumping about like a prawn on a hotplate, but all the same, Langer survived. Harmison's opening spell was very fast and very hostile, but not in the end lethal for either batsman, and he probably bowled one or two overs too many. He came off after seven overs during which neither batsman had had a chance to settle, but which both had survived. Hoggard, after his first success, looked less effective, and Vaughan turned to Flintoff and Simon Jones to try and establish England's superiority once and for all. Australia's fifty came up in nine overs, at least as fast as England's frenetic rate the day before.

Jones began with consecutive maidens, and at the drinks interval, after thirteen overs, Australia were 61 for one, with Ponting on 39 and Langer on 16. Ponting had already hit seven fours, and hardly needed to step up a gear, but whatever was in those drinks gave his batting a further kick. One thing that seems to keep happening in this series is that every time there is a break, for lunch, tea or drinks (and there are too many breaks, it has to be said), the next over seems to provide a surprise of some kind. The break seems every time to snap the concentration of either the batsmen or the bowling side, to give the other team a brief advantage. In this case, it was Simon Jones who came back unrefreshed. His third ball was dismissed by Ponting with disdain to the long-off boundary; the next ball, a half-volley, was played slightly across the line to the long-on boundary for another four; and the fifth, a rather poor full toss, gave Ponting the chance to thump it through midwicket for a third consecutive four, and his fifty, in only 51 balls. The total was only 74, and this was becoming a contribution to rival Trescothick's at the start of the England innings. That was enough to induce Vaughan to take Jones out of the firing line and bring Giles on instead.

Ashley Giles, the 'Wheelie Bin', the King of Spain, in England's side only for lack of a rival for the slot, has been for a long time a bit of a joke among international cricketers. The accepted line seems to be that everybody knows he is not really good enough for Test cricket, but somehow he retains his place in the England side and, when the opposing batsmen are feeling generous, takes a wicket or two. Not even Ashley Giles' biggest fans would suggest that he is one of the all-time great left-arm slow bowlers, but in an era when over-protected wickets have made life very hard for finger spinners, Giles has been among the best of his breed. It may be considered negative to bowl over the wicket into the rough, but his control of line and length in recent years have made him very hard to get away, and he manages to gain some sort of control over the batsmen even though he will rarely run through a side. He has only taken five wickets in a Test innings five times, and has never taken six. But he is now an essential cog in England's bowling machine, a fact that was not fully realised until 2005, despite successes against Brian Lara and others in previous summers. He took 24 wickets in first-class cricket in April 2005, the sort of start to a summer that any bowler would hope for, and with the consistent and firm support of Duncan Fletcher and all his England team-mates, he has gained the confidence to regard himself a member of the team on merit, whatever his critics in the media may say. We like our heroes to be human, like Giles and Hoggard, for example, rather than invincible, like Steve Waugh used to be.

It did not take long for Giles to get into the scorebook. In only his third over, he tossed one up and tempted Ponting into a sweep shot. He only managed a top edge which dollied up for Vaughan at short fine leg to catch – 88 for two, and Ponting gone for 61 in 76 balls. The ovation for Giles at the end of the over as he took up his fielding position was a sign not only of how popular the home town man is in Birmingham, but also of how dangerous Ricky Ponting was proving to be. Langer, 21 not out at this time, was pottering on, playing Test cricket as we have always imagined it ought to be played, a dour, orthodox but highly valuable innings for his side. From here on, it was a matter of England working their way through Australia's middle order, hoping that Langer would go away eventually.

Martyn set off at full speed, as though the Australians were still trying to emphasise that they were the team who hit big runs fast, not England. He had almost caught up Langer when the fable of the tortoise and the hare was proved right yet again. In the final over before lunch, Martyn, the hare, decided to try to steal a single off Flintoff, and played the ball towards Michael Vaughan at mid-on. He must have thought there was an easy single because he dawdled, tortoise-like for a moment almost as though deciding whether to run. Langer, the batting tortoise but the running hare, set off at once. Vaughan, in one brilliant movement, picked up the ball, turned round and threw at the stumps at the bowler's end. A direct hit and Martyn was gone, and a direct hit it was. Lunch was taken with Australia on 118 for three, in one ball short of 25 overs. It was still a hectic scoring rate, but whereas England were only one down at lunch the day before (and with a few more runs in the bank) Australia had already lost three. England's morning.

The rebuilding after lunch was done by Langer and Clarke, the top scorer at Lord's. Clarke was something of an unknown quantity before he came to England. He had a season with Hampshire in 2004, but failed to excite much interest or score many runs, and since most county games go by without anybody actually being there to watch them, there were few who had seen much of him before this tour. But his talent is undeniable. He came into the Australian side a year earlier, and hit a century in both his first Test at home and away. With a Test average of almost 42 (compared with 35 for Hampshire) and a wonderful innings at Lord's behind him, he was already established as a batsman that England had to think hard about. Naturally aggressive and exciting to watch, he fitted into the Australian batting mould easily. As one of only three right-handers in Australia's top seven, he was to find that England's emphasis on getting rid of the left-handers gave him and the other right-handers, Ponting and Martyn, a slight advantage as England's bowlers tried to adjust their line and rethink their strategies. The right-handers scored more than their share of runs in a low-scoring series by Australian standards. It might have been because the English bowlers were thinking more about the left-handers, or it might just have been that the right-handers were better batsmen.

Clarke announced his arrival after lunch with two fours in the first over he faced, from

Jones, and from then on he and Langer set out their stalls for a long stay. They were together for the best part of the afternoon session, 20 overs, and added 76 before Clarke, who had made 40 in 68 deliveries, was deceived by Giles' flatter and quicker delivery and could only thin edge it through to Geraint Jones, who took a smart catch. Langer soldiered on. Simon Katich lasted only long enough to hit one four off Giles, and then he had a stab at a ball from Flintoff that was moving away from him. Caught behind, 208 for five. Gilchrist came in to be Langer's sixth partner of the innings, and the third with whom he built a fifty partnership. None of them went on to be century partnerships, and nobody scored a century for Australia. I suppose that is being a bit churlish when nobody scored a century for England either, but at least England did develop two century partnerships. The truth is, surprisingly, that the England bowling, of which Giles was the central cog, was just too good to take lightly. Every time they went on the attack, they seemed to lose a wicket.

Langer eventually succumbed to Simon Jones, who got a little reverse swing and trapped him lbw for 82. It had taken him four and a half hours, and he had been at the wicket for 61 overs. He had hit only seven fours, the same number as Clarke who had scored just less than half Langer's total, but it was the rock around which his fellow Australians built their response to England's cavalier 407. There had been no real alarms, apart from one stumping chance when he was on 78, which went to the third umpire, but the verdict was in the batsman's favour. Gilchrist had by this time made only 25 off 44 balls, a most un-Gilchrist-like innings. For a change, it was Gilchrist picking up the tempo from his partner rather than the other way around. In truth, Gilchrist had hardly looked at ease in any of his innings in 2005, and was underperforming significantly. This, his biggest Test innings before the Oval, was a patient knock in which he relied on basic batting skills rather than his unique ability to hit almost anybody out of the ground. It was a valuable innings, but it also demonstrated that even Gilchrist was vulnerable.

Once Langer had gone, the innings subsided quite quickly. Warne hit two thumping fours, one off Giles and one off Jones, both to the cover boundary, but then jumped out to hit Giles into the campus of the University of Birmingham, missed it and was bowled. Embarrassment for Warne but delight for Giles. The next man in, Lee, lasted until yet another drinks break on this cool summer day. On resumption he immediately edged Simon Jones to Flintoff at slip, and the big man with the huge hands made no mistake. I assume that Flintoff's and Hayden's hands are the biggest in the two teams, but there is no record of which man has the biggest of all. Anyway, if you are going to snick, avoid Flintoff and Hayden.

That was 282 for eight. Gillespie helped Gilchrist add 26 in 51 balls, of which Gillespie faced 37. This is hardly shepherding the tail to a big score, and when Flintoff trapped Gillespie leg before, with a ball that might well have been going down leg side, the score was 308 for nine, and Gilchrist was on 49. Flintoff's next ball, to Kasprowicz, was not going down leg. It was a fast inswinging yorker, the type of ball that every fast bowler longs to bowl at every tailender, and it was far too good for Kasprowicz. Two lbws in successive balls, and Australia were all out for 308. England's lead was 99.

England had about 35 minutes to survive that evening, although survival was not the thought uppermost in the openers' minds. Adding to the lead was the point of this little session, as amply proven by Trescothick's response to Lee's first ball, a beautiful cover drive for four. Australia were missing McGrath.

Warne was given the seventh over of the innings, when the score was already 25 for no wicket. As was becoming usual in this series, Warne set about changing the game immediately. His first ball turned a mile, but it was always going wide. The second ball also turned a mile. Strauss tried to get a bat or a pad or anything in the way, but it cut inside his defences and bowled him. It was a quite brilliant delivery, totally unexpected from the state of the pitch, but never unexpected when a player of Warne's supreme class has the ball in his hand. Strauss, bowled for 6, learned an important lesson that evening.

Day 2, Close of Play:

England 407 and 25 for one wicket in 7 overs (Trescothick 19 not out, Hoggard 0 not out). Australia 308.

The third day's play, in retrospect, decided the match. If the first day had provided spectacular batting from an England team not thought capable of defying the Australian attack, and the second day had given us the sight of an Australian top seven underachieving against a disciplined and united England attack, then it was the third day, on which seventeen wickets fell, that turned the losers at Lord's into winners at Edgbaston. The fourth day was just there to give all England supporters the screaming habdabs. Not that England's progress on this third day was particularly straightforward: the Australians never let go of the idea that they ought to be the winners, and one or two played as though they deserved to be the winners.

Trescothick and nightwatchman Hoggard came out once again to bat. The wicket still looked good, and the day was set fair. Lee began the task, from the Pavilion End, of getting rid of the English batsmen. He warmed up with a maiden to Trescothick, and then, inevitably, Shane Warne came on at the City End, carrying on his spell from the evening before, when he had shown how easy it is to rip the heart out of the English batsmen. All you have to be is a bowling genius. All the same, it was not Warne who was the first to strike. Brett Lee, bowling very quickly, struck in the fifth over of the morning, when he induced one of those flat-footed wafts from Trescothick that we were hoping he had dropped from his repertoire, and Gilchrist took the catch. England were now at 27 for two, with both the openers out and looking rather more hesitant than they should be with a lead of 126. Three balls later, they looked even more hesitant.

Michael Vaughan is a man whose Test statistics point to an extreme shakiness at the start of his innings. Work on him at the very beginning of his innings, and he is as nervous as a kitten up a tree, as Johnny Mathis used to sing. Let him get accustomed to the wicket, the light and the bowling, and he will make you pay. He is good at making very big scores, but he also has a weakness for very low scores. This morning, Lee bowled him one on his pads, which the England captain had no bother with, playing it down to fine leg for an easy single. To the next ball, Hoggard finally got off the mark with another straightforward single into the leg side. It was the nineteenth delivery he had faced; once again he was proving his worth as a nightwatchman.

Unfortunately it was the specialist batsmen who were not doing their job. Vaughan's second ball from Lee was a ripper, but the England captain turned it into a better delivery than it actually was. He remained anchored in his crease and attempted to play back to a full-pitched ball. The way he played it made it look as though it might have kept low, but in truth it did not misbehave, except from an England point of view, when it knocked Vaughan's stumps over. For a very fine Test batsman, Vaughan was getting bowled far too often. He needed time in the middle to get over his uncertainties, and the Australians were making sure he did not have it.

Twenty-nine for three became 31 for four in Lee's next over, when Hoggard's resistance was ended. Just as he was becoming a nuisance to the Australians, 27 balls faced for 1 run, Lee persuaded him to cut at a slightly wider delivery, and steer the ball simply enough into the massive hands of Hayden at gully. The two men now holding the fort were Pietersen and Bell, the two most inexperienced men in England's side, and Lee was on the rampage. Pietersen, true to character, did not merely try to watch or defend Lee first ball to him, but rather tried a flick at a leg-side delivery and there was a strong hint of glove as the ball sped safely into Gilchrist's gloves. The appeal, a very determined one from everybody around the bat and some in the outfield, not to mention every Aussie in the crowd, was turned down. Pietersen was lucky.

By the end of the over, Lee had figures of three for 18 in seven overs, while at the other end, Warne had one for 1 in four overs. Australia were in the ascendancy, and it would take something spectacular from England to wrest back the initiative, and build on the big first-innings lead that they had worked for and deserved.

Pietersen and Bell began the process. The obvious thing would be to batten down the hatches and build for the long term. After all, there was still plenty of time. Twenty-three wickets had fallen and we had still not reached lunch on the third day. The game had all the makings of being over in four days, so time was not a factor. Take as much as you like, boys, Vaughan would have said. Just give us as lead we can work with.

Pietersen took his time. He allowed himself one ball to take a look at the bowling of Warne, his Hampshire team-mate, and then walloped the second ball of the over, slog-sweeping it from outside the off stump into the stands at midwicket. The startled look on the Australian fielders' faces told the story. Only Shane Warne himself seemed to be happy – give them enough rope and they will hang themselves has been his philosophy for many a season.

Perhaps he began to wonder whether he was giving Pietersen too much rope when the batsman hit the fifth ball into the stands once again, this time beyond long-on. The crowd, having endured the fall of three England wickets in barely half an hour, were loving it. But even after that assault, Australia still held the whip hand – England 44 for four. Warne and Lee kept making Bell and Pietersen work for their runs, but it was becoming increasingly clear that, without McGrath, there was no reliable back-up for the two strike bowlers. Lee was certainly not inexpensive, and bowled rather more no-balls than he should have done, but at least his burst of three wickets was keeping the England batsmen honest. Australia would have to rely almost exclusively on Warne to restrict England's lead.

Drinks breaks in Test cricket are now established in the playing conditions set down by the ICC. They are scheduled every hour, theoretically in mid-session. But on a quiet and compara-tively cool Birmingham morning, the break is more to do with television companies and adver-tisers than with the well-being of the players. They have energy drinks available on the boundary. There is a need for the ICC to ensure a continuous flow of play in Test cricket: The matches are not limited-overs games, except that there is a requirement that at least 90 overs must be bowled in a day. The problem is that there is no effective sanction to prevent teams from slowing down play when it suits them. The ICC has added to the problem by permitting players to leave the field of play and to return at their whim. The endless delays in play have resulted in extended final sessions each day to ensure the mandatory 90 overs are bowled, which is in nobody's interest. On occasions the ICC has also seen fit to fine fielding captains for slowing the over-rate, even when the game has been a thriller brought to a positive conclusion well within the allotted time, and even when it is often the batting side as much as the fielders who slow the play down by such devices as taking guard incessantly, prodding the pitch, calling for new gloves, new bats, new helmets, new ideas. The situation has become so confused that steps must be taken to sort it out. It is wishful thinking that it can be sorted out taking only the interests of players and paying spectators into account, but it should be. The requirements of television broadcasters, their advertisers and journalists are well enough catered for as it is.

Still, this particular drinks break served only to allow the Australians to swap Lee for Gillespie at the Pavilion End. Lee had conceded three runs an over despite his three wickets and any con-tainment was being left to Warne. The run-rate from his bowling was two an over, despite Pietersen's big hitting. And it was of course the blond genius who made the breakthrough, with a great deal of help from Adam Gilchrist behind the stumps. Warne bowled to Pietersen, who tried to sweep but only got glove or perhaps a little bat on to the ball. Maybe he missed it alto-gether, but anyway it looped up, and Gilchrist, diving full stretch, took a truly great catch one-handed down the leg side to get rid of Pietersen. This was the first time that Pietersen had been out for less than fifty, but his score of 20 maintained his Test average above 70. A score of 72 for five was better than 31 for four, but the lead was still not 200, and now the smart money was moving back to Australia, the pre-series favourites. Flintoff came in, hoping to prove that his first-innings 68 was more typical of the man than his 3 runs in two innings at Lord's.

The innings proved to be Flintoff's apotheosis, the moment when the Australians knew they had an opponent they needed to respect and to savour, if not to fear. But before he could really get going, he lost his first partner, the last proper batsman in the side. Bell was undone by Warne, as many greater batsmen than he have been undone before, by choosing to play at a ball that pitched outside leg stump. It is easy to say from the distance of the boundary's edge

and beyond that all he had to do was pad it away, but the variations of flight and line and length are not a series of independent questions being asked: they are an examination and the answer to the ball before affects the response to the next ball. Warne can get wickets from his lesser balls because the batsmen do not know they are lesser balls. This was Bell's fate. A thin tickle through to Gilchrist and the long walk home had begun for Bell. England were now 75 for six, with 'last man 21' writ large on the scoreboard.

Geraint Jones came out to join Flintoff, and with time on their side, but no Australians, they had no need to go for the big hits. Another Flintoff knock like his first innings was unlikely, unnecessary and perhaps even foolish, we all thought. Just build solidly on the 99-run lead of the first innings, and put victory out of sight for the Australians. Do nothing foolish because there is no further room for mistakes. But what did we know?

The partnership started very shakily. Flintoff had only made 7, including a four off Jason Gillespie, and Jones 2, when Flintoff played a punched back-foot shot off a quicker, flatter ball from Warne. There was no run, but Flintoff immediately reacted as if in great pain. The England physio, Kirk Russell, immediately came out on to the field to take a look at what the trouble might be: it appeared as though Freddie had damaged his left shoulder. After some time for treatment, Flintoff decided to bat on, but that harmless little dab to a comparatively innocuous Warne delivery could have been the end of any hope for England. For some balls, some overs indeed, Flintoff seemed very cramped and impeded by his shoulder, and we were all wondering not so much about his batting, which is perhaps his second string at present, as his bowling. If Flintoff could not bowl any more in the game, or even in other games of the series, then this could be as big a blow to England as McGrath's absence from this game would prove to be for Australia.

It was not until Warne uncharacteristically bowled a leg-side full toss to Flintoff, which the big man gratefully hit for four, that Freddie looked back on his game. That was in the over before lunch, however, which was taken at 95 for six, and during the interval Flintoff was given painkillers and came back out looking rather more relaxed. Clearly the diagnosis of whatever the trouble was had shown that the injury was not likely to be a long-term problem. However, if that was the good news for England immediately after lunch, the bad news came in Lee's first over. Having hit him for a good boundary to bring up the 100, Jones got a real snorter of a ball that lifted on him from a length. He could do no more than edge it to Ponting, and the score reached the depths of 101 for seven. Was the pitch going to play an even bigger role as it became more unreliable to bat on? Now Flintoff was surrounded by the tail, and his side were at least 80 short of a safe target to set Australia, and at least 50 shy of a sporting target. If the last three wickets crumbled for 20, Australia would surely canter home.

Flintoff had other ideas. The assault began with two fours off Lee's next over but even then, it seemed that he was content to take the 1s and 2s where they were available, and to let Giles fend for himself as any good number eight ought to. He and Giles put on 30 runs together, in

Opposite: Warne's appeals never lack conviction.

eleven overs, many of which were patient encounters with Warne who was wheeling away at one end without hope or expectation of relief. Then Warne managed finally to winkle Giles out, forcing him to make involuntary contact with a sharp turning leg-break, which flew low to Hayden at slip. The catch was a good one, but Hayden rarely misses chances. 131 for eight, which became 131 for nine next ball, when Harmison, who took a huge stride in the direction of Warne's well-flighted delivery, just allowed his bat to tickle the ball on to his pad, and thence to Ponting at silly mid-off. The England innings was now in a shambles: with nobody of the calibre of Warne in their side, a lead of 230 was not enough.

Simon Jones announced his presence by letting the hat-trick ball go harmlessly by and hitting the second ball he received for four. It was the next over, bowled by Kasprowicz, that gave England's supporters a little more hope. To the first ball, full and quick, Flintoff took a huge swing and a miss. The second ball was a no-ball, fairly full and swinging in to Flintoff. He hit it easily over midwicket for six. The next ball was hit hard, but straight to mid-off, so there was no run. As Kasprowicz delivered the third ball, Flintoff took a step to the off, swung his bat and hit the ball way back into the stands at midwicket, a huge blow that had the crowd in ecstasies. Never mind the match situation, hitting like this is worth a cheer at any time. The match situation, incidentally, was that England brought up the 150 with that second six. The next ball was another no-ball, off which Flintoff took an easy single, but if Kasprowicz thought that bowling to Simon Jones would be any less painful, he should have known better. Jones slashed the next ball past the slips to the third-man boundary for four. One more no-ball followed before the over was finished, meaning that a total of 20 runs came off the over, and Kasprowicz had figures of 3-0-29-0. Ponting switched to Plan B.

Warne still turned arm and wrist at the other end, but Lee came back on in place of Kasprowicz at the Pavilion End. The first three balls of his second over were hit by Flintoff for six, four and six, the first of which was reckoned by many the biggest hit they had ever seen. When Brett Lee got to Nottingham, he would himself produce some monstrous blows, but certainly the Edgbaston crowd were revelling in the sheer strength of the man with the wrenched shoulder. Lee went for only 18 in all in that over, and had an lbw appeal against Jones turned down by umpire Billy Bowden that certainly seemed a pretty good shout. Still, it made no real difference (or so we thought at the time) as Warne ended Flintoff's innings with only 1 more run added to the total, bowling him as he came down the wicket for another expansive heave. Warne had taken his sixth wicket of the innings for just 46 runs in 23.1 overs, England were all out for 182, Flintoff was out for 73, and Australia were set 282 to win. Flintoff's innings brought his total of sixes in the match to nine – a record by an English batsman in an Ashes Test – but the value of his innings was more than the size of the hits. It was a counter-attacking innings that gave heart back to England, and to their supporters, at a time when there was a very real danger of England slipping to an ignominious and heavy defeat. The match was not yet won, not by a long chalk, but it was not lost, either.

Australia's mighty batting line-up was still expected to win from here. A score of 282 is a big fourth-innings target, but it has been achieved often enough before. World champions against the underdogs – should be a doddle. They set off steadily enough. Harmison and Hoggard worried Hayden and Langer a couple of times, but once Hayden was off his king pair with a four, they set about the task of scoring 282 for victory. At this stage, although the winning target was a formidable challenge, most of the received opinion was that Australia would get there. As Hayden and Langer approached the fifty partnership without any real alarms, there was no reason to start hedging bets. Ashley Giles was brought into the attack in only the eighth over, another example of Vaughan's inventive captaincy, but this particular invention did not work: Hayden hit the last ball of his first over for a one-bounce four over Giles' head. It was after twelve overs, with the score at 47, that Flintoff first came into the attack, taking over at the City End from Harmison, whose six overs had cost only 13 runs. Flintoff was on a hat-trick, having finished the first innings with two lbws to remove Gillespie and Kasprowicz, but the field placing did not reflect that. Flintoff began bowling round the wicket, the line that England believed tended to limit all the Australian left-handers, a belief that was beginning to have some substance. His first ball, for the hat-trick, was driven by Langer to cover for no run, but the next had Langer playing away from his body. The ball deviated just enough to take an inside edge and cannon on to the stumps. Langer, bowled Flintoff 28. The first breakthrough had been made, and Flintoff had three wickets in four balls.

The rest of the over will remain in Ricky Ponting's nightmares for some time to come. It was an over that compared to the famous one Michael Holding bowled to Geoffrey Boycott at Bridgetown, Barbados in 1981. In that over, Holding dismissed Boycott for a duck with the final ball of the over, having beaten him with all five previous deliveries. It was an over that prompted the remark that with any other batsman at the wicket, England would have been 0 for six rather than just 0 for one, but it confirmed the brilliance of Holding, and the domination of the West Indian fast bowlers over England for a generation or more. We cannot say now that this over of Flintoff's will have repercussions in Ashes Tests until 2020, but Ponting will not want to face another like it, and by the end of it, was able to wander back to the pavilion to contemplate in the shower how good a bowler Flintoff had become. The first ball he faced, the third of Flintoff's over, jagged back from outside the off stump, and Ponting was hit on the pad, evoking a huge appeal from Flintoff. Too high, says umpire Billy Bowden. The next ball, just short of a length and on that tight line outside off stump, this time did not jag back, and Ponting played it edgily and uneasily to slip. This was followed by another outside off, which came back in to Ponting enough for there to be another lbw appeal, but once again Bowden was unmoved. The next ball was a no-ball, but Ponting could not make the most of it. This time at least he managed to get his bat out of the way, and it went through to the 'keeper. The final ball of the over, and of Ponting's innings, was a little fuller and it lured Ponting into the drive. It had just enough on it to move away as it brushed the edge of Ponting's bat, and Geraint Jones took a straightforward catch. It was a great over: two wickets and the complete, and far from temporary, unsettling of the Australian captain.

The Australian middle order had not yet proved themselves under Test conditions in England, although one had to assume they soon would. At Lord's Michael Clarke, thanks to a let-off early in his innings, Damien Martyn and Simon Katich had all made an impression on the game, but despite Clarke's useful 40 here at Edgbaston first time around, nobody had imposed themselves forcefully on any game. They did not do so this time either. Hayden, who looked more and more out of touch as his innings wore on, survived until the score had reached 74, when Simon Jones was brought into the attack. It was an eventful over, and spectators soon grew to expect someting special at the start of Simon Jones' spells. Hayden hit the first and fourth balls for four, one to the leg side and one a straight drive, before nicking the fifth ball to Trescothick, or at least within range of Trescothick, at slip. The catch was in the end a very good one. That made it 82 for three, but still the pundits were taking Australia to win. Martyn and the new batsman, Michael Clarke, took 13 runs off Harmison's next over, so it seemed as though normal service was being resumed, until Giles and Hoggard came back into the attack. Vaughan was mixing up his bowlers as much as he could, and this seemed to be unsettling the Australians. This can only be done if there is no weak link in a bowling attack, but England's five-man barrage was working pretty well at Edgbaston. Whoever was bowling, there was no rest for the batsman, no opportunity to milk the bowling at one end at least, while saving all the powers of concentration for the other end.

Hoggard took a wicket with his first ball back in the attack, when Martyn clipped the ball lazily to Bell at midwicket. Bell may not yet be making the runs expected of him, but his fielding has been superb and his catching faultless. The Edgbaston crowd for the first time began to sense that something wonderful just might be possible. Katich took two fours off the next five balls bowled by Hoggard, but his innings was destined to become another middle-order cameo that was the curse of Australia's batsmen all summer. Ashley Giles brought about Katich's undoing, inducing an outside edge which flew quickly to Trescothick at slip who took his second good catch of the innings. Australia were now 134 for five, and the balance had suddenly swung back firmly to England. The fate of the next man in, Adam Gilchrist, could decide the direction of the match. But within the space of four balls, Australia slumped from an even money bet to a 500/1 against no-hoper. Giles did the first piece of damage, persuading the ever attacking Gilchrist to flick the wrong ball to mid-on, where Flintoff (who else?) had a very easy job to complete the catch. To the second ball of Flintoff's next over, the new batsman, Gillespie, was thoroughly yorked by Flintoff for a duck. At 137 for seven, they were dead in the water. The crowd were going wild as only cricket crowds can: the beer was no doubt beginning to take its toll this late in the evening, but the wit and the singing remained. There were even hints of congas starting in the cheap seats.

Michael Clarke had been reduced to a virtual spectator at the non-striler's end as the Australian innings crumbled. Now he was joined by the one man you could be sure would do his best to stop the rot, the man whose efforts had kept Australia in the match, if indeed they were still in the match. Enter Shane Warne. Warne played aggressively but bravely and

Harmison produces a beauty of a slower ball to deceive Clarke.

England, watching the way he walked across his stumps to batter the ball to the leg side, claimed the extra half hour. They had an extra eight overs to take the final three wickets. Warne's response was to hit Giles, the man who had ripped out the two wickets that brought England so close to the winning line, for two sixes over square leg. Clarke and Warne stayed together right through the extra half hour, dashing England's hopes of an extra day off between the back-to-back Tests, until the fourth ball of the final over of the day. Harmison was given the last over, and made the most of it, giving Clarke a thorough working over. The fourth ball, after several thunderbolts, was a much slower ball which Clarke did not pick at all, and he was clean bowled. It was a wonderful delivery from a bowler who had not bowled his best in this Test match, and it turned the tide psychologically if not physically towards England for what seemed to be the final time. It meant that although England had not won the match in three days, they had reduced Australia to 175 for eight, still needing 107 more to win, with only Warne, Lee and Kasprowicz to carry them there. It looked all too easy for England to bring the series back to one-all, and confirm the suspicion that this England team is not such a bad one after all.

Day 3, Close of Play:

England 407 and 182.

Australia 308 and 175 for eight wickets in 43.4 overs (Warne 20 not out).

The fourth and presumed final day might only have lasted two balls, but the ground was full. The prospect of an England victory over the all-conquering Australians was just too much of an occasion to miss. And anyway, the tickets were paid for, so why waste them. If there was anybody who decided to give the Test a miss because it would only last a few minutes, or even worse to give their tickets away to somebody else, then they will neither own up to their folly nor forgive themselves for missing out on a chance to witness sporting history. This was the day that made cricket in England popular and newsworthy once again.

The Australians had all the time in the world, two days, to score 107 runs or lose two wickets, so they could have set their stall out to get 'em in singles. But that is not the way the Australians play, especially Warne and Lee when in batting mode, and we all expected a short but entertaining morning session, or half a session at most. Entertaining it was, if your idea of entertainment is having your heart pulled out and run through the mincer while your nerves are being stretched on a rack, but it was certainly not short. For most people watching, it lasted several years even if in reality it was only about 22 overs, bowled during an hour and three-quarters of play.

There is a skill in bowling out tailenders, a skill which is very useful to have. Some bowlers almost seem to pride themselves on the fact that they take top-order wickets, but the bowlers a sensible captain also treasures are the ones who can mop up the tail. In essence there is little difference, except that you do not have to be so subtle with a tailender. You do not have to tempt them into making mistakes because they will anyway. They will not distrust loose balls because they see them as the only scoring chances they are likely to get. And they will not read one ball in the context of the next, largely because there may well not be a next. Vaughan was unlucky that morning that he did not have anybody on the field who really knew how to get rid of a tail. Harmison tried bouncing them out, but they just ducked or mishit for four, or swatted the less well directed attempts. Hoggard was not getting much swing, but what he was getting was too good for numbers nine, ten and eleven. Giles is steady, but even tailenders can hit slow loose balls for four without worrying too much about the risks. And Flintoff, Vaughan's trump card, was not quite getting it right.

Warne and Lee, both of them good enough batsmen to play at least one place higher in any other batting order, milked the opportunities and rode their luck. They also capitalised on England's frustration, knowing that as time passed and the score mounted, the tension would rise faster in English breasts than in Australian ones. Mind you, it rose even faster in the breasts of those watching and unable to take part in the action. The 200 came up, and the fifty partnership was looming as England searched in vain for the breakthrough. Vaughan's tactic of switching the bowling regularly, which had seemed so clever the day before, now seemed to

Trescothick, standing deep at slip, stops an edge off Katich.

smack of desperation. Warne and Lee were both hitting boundaries, sometimes with unorthodox shots, but sometimes with classical purity, and nothing could stop the inexorable march to victory. Surely England could not slip up now? The whole of Test match history was in their favour, as was the whole of the country. Even at eleven o'clock on a Sunday morning, the television audience was larger than Channel Four had attracted for cricket for some time. Public interest had been caught, and the public was mesmerised and terrified by turns.

Then suddenly a piece of pure theatre, a wicket from a source as unexpected as it is rare. Shane Warne trod on his wicket. In trying to give himself enough room to play Flintoff out into the off side, Warne lost his bearings and trod on his stumps. Hit wicket bowled Flintoff 42, a gutsy knock which, if only it could have been duplicated by almost anybody else, would have won the game. But the score was now 220 for nine, there were 62 more runs needed to win, and only Michael Kasprowicz to help Brett Lee get there.

They tried. They really tried. Kasprowicz survived an lbw appeal and a fast inswinging yorker from Flintoff before turning his attention to Giles and hitting him for consecutive fours and suddenly the target for Australia was under 40 runs. Still, we had to believe England would win, but who exactly was going to take the final wicket? Both batsmen looked quite solid and quite unconcerned. Smiles and punched gloves greeted every minor triumph, while the English body language tried its best not to show disheartenment. When the drinks break arrived, 30 more were needed. The pause in play merely built the tension.

The moment when the English supporters finally thought the game had gone was probably when, with 14 more runs to win, Flintoff bowled a no-ball to Lee which went leg side, flicked his pad and went too wide for the diving Jones to reach. Four leg-byes on top of the no-ball, and suddenly it was 9 to win. The tension was unbearable. Inside the ground everybody had gone quiet, concentrating wholly on the game. Nobody was strolling round the ground, looking for beers or the gents. Nobody was singing. Outside the ground, in millions of homes, in cars, in shops, buses and cafes, the English public was tuned in, or trying to tune in, to watch or listen to the final overs. Many televisions and radios were switched off again because the tension got to great, but for those who stayed with it, the only thing that made the excitement bearable was that, one way or another, the end was nigh.

That Flintoff over produced 9 runs, and at the end of it, Australia needed only 6 to win. Harmison, at the other end, had to make the breakthrough. Lee squeezed a single off the first ball, and Harmison almost yorked Kasprowicz with his third ball, but the pair survived. Five to win now, and Flintoff took the ball again. This time there were no no-balls, just six fine deliveries which tested Lee. Despite a couple of wafts at balls outside the off stump, there was no sign of a wicket, and on the last ball, Lee stole a single to keep the strike, dropping his bat in his nervousness as he did so. He did not stop to pick up the bat – he just kept running, and got safely home.

Now it was Harmison again, with just 4 more runs required. The big man came thundering in to Lee, but his attempted yorker was a full toss, which Lee hit well to the off side. Vaughan had posted his sweeper there, however, so only 1 run was scored, and Kasprowicz had to face five balls of the over, with 3 more needed to win. He had made 20 by this time, though, and was playing as sensibly as a man could do in these extreme circumstances. He played the first of the five carefully back to the bowler. Harmison then decided to bang one in short, and Kasprowicz, in taking evasive action, just gloved the ball through to Geraint Jones, who took the catch. The moment between the ball landing in the 'keeper's gloves and the umpire's finger being raised seemed like an eternity, but when Kasprowicz was given out, the entire ground went wild. England had won by 2 runs. The release of all that tension in 20,000 chests was transformed into the sound of cheering, shouting and singing. It would be a churlish man indeed, or an Australian, who would point out that slow-motion replays showed that when the ball hit Kasper's glove, his hand was not on the bat, so technically he was not out. At the time, at full speed, nobody saw it, nobody suggested that the appeal was spurious or that Kasprowicz and Lee did not accept their fate immediately. Nobody cried foul, as no foul had been committed. Only the unforgiving eye of the slow-motion television camera spotted the error, but to the credit of the Australians, none of the team ever complained about that particular umpiring decision, even though it could be argued it cost them the match.

It had been the most astonishing Test that most of us had ever seen. The close finish contributed to that, of course, but the individual performances and duels throughout, the fluctuating fortunes and the fact that England had been virtually written off before the match began, all made the game one of the truly great contests. We all knew it, and the players knew it too. As Brett Lee sat on the ground, desolate after the close defeat, Flintoff went up to him and placed a consoling arm on his shoulder. It was a moment when two men who had given their all in a great contest acknowledged each other's contribution, and it underlined the atmosphere in which the series was played. For many it was the image of the summer – great cricket played by great players in the right way.

On to Old Trafford. It cannot get any better than this.

England v. Australia, Second Test Match

At Edgbaston, Birmingham

4, 5, 6, 7 August 2005

Result: England won by 2 runs

Toss: Australia

England

ME Trescothick c Gilchrist b Kasprowicz	90	c Gilchrist b Lee	21
AJ Strauss b Warne	48	b Warne	6
*MP Vaughan c Lee b Gillespie	24	(4) b Lee	1
IR Bell c Gilchrist b Kasprowicz	6	(5) c Gilchrist b Warne	21
KP Pietersen c Katich b Lee	71	(6) c Gilchrist b Warne	20
A Flintoff c Gilchrist b Gillespie	68	(7) b Warne	73
+GO Jones c Gilchrist b Kasprowicz	1	(8) c Ponting b Lee	9
AF Giles lbw b Warne	23	(9) c Hayden b Warne	8
MJ Hoggard lbw b Warne	16	(3) c Hayden b Lee	1
SJ Harmison b Warne	17	c Ponting b Warne	0
SP Jones not out	19	not out	12
Extras (lb 9, w 1, nb 14)	24	(lb 1, nb 9)	10
Total (all out, 79.2 overs)	407	(all out, 52.1 overs)	182

Fall of Wickets First Innings: 1-112 (Strauss), 2-164 (Trescothick), 3-170 (Bell), 4-187 (Vaughan), 5-290 (Flintoff), 6-293 (GO Jones), 7-342 (Giles), 8-348 (Pietersen), 9-375 (Harmison), 10-407 (Hoggard).

Fall of Wickets Second Innings: 1-25 (Strauss), 2-27 (Trescothick), 3-29 (Vaughan), 4-31 (Hoggard), 5-72 (Pietersen), 6-75 (Bell), 7-101 (GO Jones), 8-131 (Giles), 9-131 (Harmison), 10-182 (Flintoff).

Bowling First Innings: Lee 17–1–111–1; Gillespie 22–3–91–2; Kasprowicz 15–3–80–3; Warne 25.2–4–116–4

Bowling Second Innings: Lee 18–1–82–4; Gillespie 8–0–24–0; Kasprowicz 3–0–29–0; Warne 23.1–7–46–6

Australia

JL Langer lbw b SP Jones	82	b Flintoff	28
ML Hayden c Strauss b Hoggard	0	c Trescothick b SP Jones	31
*RT Ponting c Vaughan b Giles	61	c GO Jones b Flintoff	0
DR Martyn run out (Vaughan)	20	c Bell b Hoggard	28
MJ Clarke c GO Jones b Giles	40	b Harmison	30
SM Katich c GO Jones b Flintoff	4	c Trescothick b Giles	16
+AC Gilchrist not out	49	c Flintoff b Giles	1
SK Warne b Giles	8	(9) hit wicket b Flintoff	42
B Lee c Flintoff b SP Jones	6	(10) not out	43
JN Gillespie lbw b Flintoff	7	(8) lbw b Flintoff	0
MS Kasprowicz lbw b Flintoff	0	c GO Jones b Harmison	20
Extras (b 13, lb 7, w 1, nb 10)	31	(b 13, lb 8, w 1, nb 18)	40
Total (all out, 76 overs)	308	(all out, 64.3 overs)	279

Fall of Wickets First Innings: 1-0 (Hayden), 2-88 (Ponting), 3-118 (Martyn), 4-194 (Clarke), 5-208 (Katich), 6-262 (Langer), 7-273 (Warne), 8-282 (Lee), 9-308 (Gillespie), 10-308 (Kasprowicz).
Fall of Wickets Second Innings: 1-47 (Langer), 2-48 (Ponting), 3-82 (Hayden), 4-107 (Martyn), 5-134 (Katich), 6-136 (Gilchrist), 7-137 (Gillespie), 8-175 (Clarke), 9-220 (Warne), 10-279 (Kasprowicz).

Bowling First Innings: Harmison 11–1–48–0; Hoggard 8–0–41–1; SP Jones 16–2–69–2; Flintoff 15–1–52–3; Giles 26–2–78–3
Bowling Second Innings: Harmison 17.3–3–62–2; Hoggard 5–0–26–1; Giles 15–3–68–2; Flintoff 22–3–79–4; SP Jones 5–1–23–1

Umpires: BF Bowden (New Zealand) and RE Koertzen (South Africa)

Man of the Match: A Flintoff

5

Out of Time

The Third Test Match, Old Trafford

An email to me from an Australian living in London:

'I am thinking of writing a personal letter to Ponting to tell him that he has ruined my summer. I am tired of having my English colleagues turning up at my office door on Monday mornings hopping around from foot to foot like dancing bears, and going on about how my lot are on the edge of losing the Ashes. To be fair, England have played better than I expected and my lot have been rubbish, except for the Pigeon, the pie thrower and Sparkles.'

And this was after only two Tests. For the record, 'Sparkles' is Brett Lee (also known as 'Bing').

At this stage, even though the whole of England had been enervated by the closeness of the Edgbaston Test, and then boosted by the final result, everybody outside of the England dressing-room still expected Australia to dominate the series. England had almost thrown away a victory that should have been comfortable and even Michael Vaughan admitted that coming back from 2-0 down would have been difficult.

It would have been unfair, too, as England outplayed Australia, crucially minus McGrath, in the Second Test. But now, immediately, we all decamped up to Manchester to watch some more cricket with just three days to get our breath back. There were also just three days for the teams to overcome any injuries and get themselves to the start line for what promised to be a very close struggle. Before the Edgbaston game, nobody really expected England to make much of a fist of it, given the beating they had taken at Lord's, but now the caravan had arrived at Old Trafford with the series tied at one apiece, expectations were higher. And with McGrath still sidelined, as he surely must be with that ligament injury, England may very well start as favourites.

England certainly had no real problems in selecting their side. There were no injuries and so the twelve picked themselves:

M.P. Vaughan (Yorkshire, captain), M.E. Trescothick (Somerset), A.J. Strauss (Middlesex), I.R. Bell (Warwickshire), K.P. Pietersen (Hampshire), A. Flintoff (Lancashire), G.O. Jones (Kent, wicketkeeper), A.F. Giles (Warwickshire), M.J. Hoggard (Yorkshire), S.J. Harmison (Durham), S.P. Jones (Glamorgan), and C.T. Tremlett (Hampshire).

Australia, on the other hand, had several problems to deal with. Apart from the lack of form shown by several of their players in both Tests, which was a concern, there was the injury to Glenn McGrath and the sudden hospitalisation of Brett Lee, who spent two nights after the Second Test in hospital with an infected left knee, caused by a graze picked up while diving in the field at Edgbaston. The Australian physio, Errol Alcott, rated both players no more than 50:50 to play, and the 29-year-old pace bowler Stuart Clark was summoned from Middlesex to bolster the squad. The English players were no doubt rubbing their hands in glee at the prospect of a pace attack consisting of any combination of Gillespie, Kasprowicz, Tait and Clark, a far cry from the lethal Australian opening attacks of a few seasons back.

To take their minds off their troubles, the Australians travelled to watch Altrincham F.C. take on Bangor City in a pre-season friendly, a fixture pretty well at the opposite end of the professional sporting scale to Test cricket. Their long-standing coach driver, Geoff Goodwin, was chairman of Altrincham, and the Aussies hoped to take some sort of inspiration from the result of the game: Altrincham 5, Bangor City 0. It must be quite a posh bus to have a football club chairman driving it.

Whatever inspiration they needed, it seemed to work, for on the morning of the Test, the Australians were able to announce that both of their fast bowlers had been passed fit, and would play. There was still a doubt about McGrath in particular. He had not looked match fit in his brief workout in the nets the day before, and the England camp suspected that a bit of gamesmanship was involved in the selection. Remembering Steve Waugh's astonishing come-back from injury at the Oval four years earlier, when he had put together a brilliant century on one leg, the Australians were probably gambling on the mere fact of McGrath's presence in the side being enough to dumbfound the English batsmen and offer them up like lambs to the McGrath slaughterhouse.

So the Australian side, in the end, was:

R.T. Ponting (Tasmania, captain), M.L. Hayden (Queensland), J.L. Langer (Western Australia), D.R. Martyn (Western Australia), M.J. Clarke (New South Wales), S.M. Katich (New South Wales), A.C. Gilchrist (Western Australia, wicketkeeper), S.K. Warne (Victoria), B. Lee (New South Wales), J.N. Gillespie (South Australia) and G.D. McGrath (New South Wales).

McGrath for Kasprowicz was the only change, and the Australians were back to full strength, on paper at least. England left out Chris Tremlett on the morning of the game, despite some journalists suggesting he be given a first Test cap in place of Matthew Hoggard, who had not done very much in the first two Tests. But England stuck to the same eleven for the third Test in a row, the first time this had happened for some while.

Michael Vaughan then did the decent thing, and won the toss, or to be more accurate, Ricky

Previous pages: Bell scored two half-centuries at Old Trafford. This appeal, however, was answered in the affirmative.

Ponting lost it. Although the day was hardly a scorcher, it was obviously a batting wicket, and Vaughan had no difficulty in deciding to do just that. Trescothick and Strauss came out to face the recuperating McGrath, coming in from the Stretford End, and the equally crocked Lee, from the Brian Statham End (a.k.a. Warwick Road). Trescothick, following on from his match-defining 90 at Edgbaston, tried to go on the attack at once, but apart from edging the second ball he received from McGrath through the slips for four, he was at first kept in check by some fine bowling. At the other end, Lee, as if to prove he was never sick, was reaching speeds of 90 miles per hour in his first over, but the most significant event of that first Lee over was when Strauss played the ball quite safely and gently to Clarke at gully. Clarke bent down to pick the ball up and something went in his back. So the youngest man in the Australian side, and one of their best fielders, had to go off for treatment, and would not be seen again for the best part of two days. Brad Hodge, another fine fielder, came on as substitute for the rest of England's innings.

Trescothick had only made 13 when he was dropped, in only the fifth over of the morning, by Gilchrist off McGrath. It was a straightforward edge by Trescothick, the Man Whose Feet Never Move, to first slip, but Gilchrist, diving across, dropped the catch. It was to prove costly on a day of dropped catches and missed chances for the Australians. Gilchrist's season, which had begun only averagely, would not get any better. By the end of the summer, his statistics did not compare favourably with England's much maligned Geraint Jones, and his lack of performance was a symptom if not a cause of Australia's poor showing. Finishing up with a batting average 30 runs below your lifetime Test average is a serious underperformance, and although he took, as ever, some wonderful catches, he also grassed a few and was no longer the reliable Gilchrist, the hub of the fielding effort, that he used to be.

In Lee's fourth over, Strauss was hit on the helmet as he mistimed a hook, and the grille clattered into his ear. There is no doubt that the blow hurt him, and he was still probably befuddled when in Lee's next over, he completely misjudged a slower ball, played all over it and was bowled. Strauss was still struggling for runs, and although we can excuse that dismissal as being caused more by the crack on the head than the delivery itself, Strauss, bowled by Lee for 6, was now in need of a major innings.

So was Vaughan, the next man in. He was helped in his mission for big runs by the temporary withdrawal of Lee from the attack, after five overs for 6 runs and the wicket of Strauss, who was replaced by Gillespie, the whipping boy of the Australian attack. However hard the Australians tried to disguise it, however loyally they supported him, and however often Ponting brought him into the attack, the facts remained the same: Gillespie, once a very fine Test bowler who commanded respect from all the world's batsmen, had lost his zip. This was one tour too many and even a fully fit Gillespie was no match for a half-fit McGrath or Lee. Vaughan greeted him with two fours and a 2, 10 runs off his first over, all taken with gentle dabs towards third man and beyond. McGrath soldiered on for eight overs before Lee had to be brought back into the attack. It was noticeable that although McGrath was giving it his all when he bowled, he was moving very gingerly in the field. He clearly was not fully fit, and the

England batsmen had seen it. Ponting's resources were scant, and this was barely past drinks on the first morning.

And so it continued. Vaughan, who took most of the strike from Gillespie, overtook Trescothick when they were both in the thirties, and by lunch, taken after the 25th over, England were coasting along at 93 for one wicket, with Vaughan looking almost at his best on 41, and Trescothick happily poaching runs wherever he could find them, on 35. After lunch, even with McGrath back in the attack, Trescothick took every ball of the first two overs, and used them to sneak past his captain to his fifty, a mixed bag but full of his specialities – the stand-up-tall-and-whack-it off-side shots and the clips off his toes. The fifty came up with a straight driven four off Gillespie, a lovely shot that had the crowd on its feet and cheering. England were now 110 for one after 28 overs. All looked serene.

If there was one moment in this game when the initiative passed firmly to England and was never really lost, it was in McGrath's next over. The second ball was short and a little wider outside off stump, and Vaughan decided to cut it. He was beaten by the height and could only edge it to first slip where Warne was waiting. Gilchrist saw it too and threw himself in front of Warne, but could only get a little bit of glove on it, and deflected the ball to third man for four. What was a straightforward catch for Warne had been turned into four more for the England captain by yet another mistake from Gilchrist. And the next ball was even more cataclysmic. McGrath bowled a beauty that beat Vaughan completely and knocked the off stump out of the ground. Then we noticed umpire Steve Bucknor's arm outstretched. It was a no-ball! Vaughan and Trescothick ran 2 runs and McGrath, instead of having two wickets under his belt, stomped off to third man at the end of the over with an analysis of none for 50 in ten overs. Gilchrist's dropping of Trescothick cost 50 runs, but his drop of Vaughan, and McGrath's no-ball, were to cost Australia over 100 runs. You can not give away 150 runs through fielding mistakes and expect to win the game. England learned that lesson at Lord's.

The next over brought Vaughan his fifty, and he and Trescothick sailed serenely on. It was not until the 34th over that Shane Warne, on 599 Test wickets, was brought on to bowl, even though there had been rumours of the Old Trafford pitch turning square from the first day. Clearly Ricky Ponting did not believe these rumours, and he was right not to, but Shane Warne can extract turn and bounce from a blancmange, and it was surprising that his main strike bowler did not have a bowl until well into the afternoon session. Warne had said before the match began, 'If Strauss is still in after five or six overs, I might be thrown the ball earlier than usual,' so we have to assume that with the departure of Strauss, he was thrown the ball later than usual.

His appearance did not immediately slow down England's progress. Vaughan handled him carefully at first, but also hit two fours off McGrath's next over, provoking Ponting into bringing Lee back into the attack once more. Even so, England passed the 150 before drinks were taken, in 38 overs. However, the end of this big partnership was nigh. With the score on 162, Trescothick attempted a sweep against Warne, but could only make contact with a bit of bat, a

An untidy dismissal, but a hugely significant one. Gilchrist catches Trescothick and Warne becomes the first player in Test history to take 600 wickets.

bit of pad, a bit of glove, and probably a few strands of shirt and a slice of arm guard. The ball spooned into the air, and Gilchrist, never one to do things the easy way, let the ball hit him on the thigh and bounce up for him to take the catch. Trescothick was gone for 63, and Warne thereby took his 600th Test wicket, the first man to reach this improbable target. It was by no means the best of his wickets, but it was the one that counted, and Old Trafford rose to him as surely as if he had been an Englishman bowling the ball that won the Test. Trescothick, who had also been McGrath's 500th victim at Lord's, had another memory to pass on to his grandchildren.

Ian Bell in the first two Tests had been something of a walking wicket, so the Australians were no doubt queuing up to bowl at him in Manchester. He started slowly, but at least he did start, and once he got going, he looked as secure as anybody. For the first time in this series, it became clear why the selectors had such faith in him. Bell had been very lucky to edge out Rob Key for the final batting place against Bangladesh, and having scored so heavily against them, he was very difficult to drop. Certainly there was no case for picking Key ahead of him, even though Key scored very heavily for Kent all through the summer, but the Pietersen/Bell/Thorpe debate at the beginning of the Ashes series had developed quickly into a

Pietersen v. Thorpe debate, and Bell was assumed to be a part of the starting line-up. He is a great fielder, he can bowl a bit, he is young, but it is his batting he is picked for, and after two Tests, there was a groundswell of opinion that felt there must be something better out there somewhere. So it was the right time to make a fifty.

Australia brought Katich and his left-arm wrist-spin into the attack, presumably to give the front-line bowlers a bit of a rest, but it only served to give Bell the chance he needed to get a handful of runs under his belt, and the confidence that goes with them. When he had made 10, he almost gave a caught and bowled chance to Katich, but even diving at full stretch, Katich could get no more than his fingertips to it. From then on it was plain sailing. At tea, England had reached 195 for two wickets, with Vaughan on 93 and closing inexorably on his fifteenth Test century, and his sixth as captain.

The century came up just after tea, when Vaughan drove a fullish delivery from McGrath through midwicket for 3 runs, the cue for the crowd to go wild – a bigger cheer than any heard so far that day. The 200 was past and all looked fine for England. When McGrath dropped Bell, who had then made 18, off a comparatively simple caught and bowled chance, then the day was destined to belong to England. Bell was stuck on 18 for 38 balls, clearly leaving the expansive shots to Vaughan, and the captain obliged. As soon as Gillespie came back into the attack, he was deposited into the midwicket crowd for six, and then steered past third man for four

Vaughan made Australia pay for dropped catches and no-balls with 166 – the highest score of the series.

with consecutive balls. It was sad to watch in many ways, because we knew we were witnessing the end of a very good bowler's Test career. By the time the afternoon drinks came round, Gillespie's fourteen overs had gone for 75 runs, and neither Vaughan nor Bell seemed to be in any difficulty against him. Indeed, it was only when Warne was bowling that they seemed to have anything to think about. It was an afternoon when England dominated in a way they had not against Australia for the best part of twenty years.

The drinks break should have taken another wicket, but Warne was out of luck. Vaughan hit his first ball, not a good one, for four and then tried to cut the second. He only got an edge and the ball flew to Hayden at slip, who put it down. Vaughan was on 141 at the time. Australia were so reckless with their generosity to England that even the England of old would have been hard pressed not to hold the upper hand at this stage. The England of 2005 just ground the Australians a little further down with each mistake.

Vaughan's 150 came up in the course of three thrilling shots to consecutive balls from poor old Dizzy Gillespie. The first, a classic Vaughan cover-drive, gave the fielder no chance and thrilled the crowd. It is the very best shot in word cricket today, and English fans would love to see it even more often than we do. The second, an on-drive, was the one that brought up his 150 (to more tumultuous applause) and the third was a pull through midwicket from a ball that was hardly more than a medium-paced long-hop. But his end was not long coming.

Simon Katich, middle-order left-hand bat and part-time wrist-spin bowler of the Michael Bevan variety, came back into the attack, and you could almost see Vaughan's eyes light up. The 200, which he had missed on two previous occasions by under 10 runs, was there to be taken. But whether it was overconfidence, tiredness or carelessness, or a mixture of them all, he put a Katich full toss straight down the throat of Glenn McGrath at long-on. England were 290 for three, Vaughan was out for 166, a really soft dismissal to end one his most authoritative Test innings since the 2002/03 tour of Australia, and Katich had a lucky wicket. Nevertheless, Vaughan had now spent the time in the middle that Chris Old had advocated earlier in the season, and all his rhythm was back.

Pietersen was the next man in, and with the new ball almost due, we were expecting to see Lee and McGrath against the English middle order. But Ponting kept Warne going, brought Lee back for an over or two and then turned again to Katich, and did not take the new ball finally until the 87th over, by which time England had reached 331 for three, and Bell had his fifty, brought up by a clip to square leg off Katich. Pietersen had made a quick 19 when he faced the first over with the new ball, bowled by Lee. He hit the first ball for 2 runs, but the second ball did the trick. Lee banged the ball in short, and Pietersen fell for the sucker punch. He hit the ball fairly well, but too high up the bat, and it flew directly and safely into the hands of Brad Hodge, fielding as substitute for Clarke on the midwicket boundary. Pietersen was beginning to gain a reputation as being more mouth than trousers, and another cameo was not going to help his cause. The blue streak down his hair, which followed the red streak and preceded the white streak on show at the Oval, was fine by Duncan Fletcher, the England coach, but only if it did not get in the way of the wonderful team spirit that he and Michael Vaughan had engendered over the past two years. As far as team spirit was concerned, Pietersen certainly talked the talk, but he needed to do a little more than score bright twenties if the wrath of the media was not to descend upon him. In this he was quite different from the almost invisible Ian Bell, who had not made the runs Pietersen had, not by a long chalk, but who by nature kept out of the limelight and tried to get on with his job. The press were not likely to be hounding him for some time yet.

The score was now 333 for four, and England sent in Matthew Hoggard as nightwatchman. The averages show that Hoggard only scored 45 runs, at an average of 6.42, all series, but he stuck around for 229 balls in the process, an average of pretty well 29 balls per dismissal. At Lord's, he stuck around for 31 balls yet still bagged a pair. He makes the perfect nightwatchman because he knows how to defend and he can keep the best bowlers at bay for a few overs, which is all that is needed at the end of a day. If he does not stick around in the morning, so be it. Let the proper batsmen get on with the job. This time, he came out to join Bell with no more than three overs to go, one of which was fast and furious, from Lee to Hoggard. The final ball, coming at the unfortunate Hoggy at well over 90 miles per hour, was far too good for him, and his off stump cartwheeled out of the ground. So England went in at the end of the day on 341 for five, with Bell on 59 and Flintoff to bat first thing in the morning. The day belonged to England, but Australia were not entirely out of it, especially if they could take England's remaining wickets for no more than fifty runs. It was still a good batting track.

Day 1, Close of Play:

England 341 for five wickets after 89 overs (Bell 59 not out).

At this stage I want to write a little about the transportation arrangements to get to and from Old Trafford. There is no easy way to organise the trip, wherever you come from, unless you have a helicopter and a parachute at your disposal. We decided this time to take the tram from Manchester Piccadilly, along with half the population of Lancashire. The transport authorities of Manchester seemed to have failed to grasp the fact that there was a Test match on that week, and there were no extra trams, nor extra coaches on the existing trams. So jump on and breathe in. The tram stops conveniently at Trafford Park, next to the ground, and from there it is a quick walk to the ground, except on Test match days, when it is a very slow shuffle under a tunnel and towards the gates, in the company of several hundred other cricket-goers. Given the huge public interest that had suddenly built up for the Tests, and given the proximity of Manchester United's Old Trafford stadium, it was surprising that the public transport system was not more efficient, and on the return journey the chaos was even greater. We wanted to travel via Altrincham, home of the Australian bus driver's football team, but so did 10,000 other people. Whichever way you try to get in and out of Old Trafford, it is a problem. On the final morning, even the cricketers were in danger of being late.

Still, enough of our grumbles about transport. Let's move on to grumbles about the ground. It is an astonishing fact that in Manchester, where the average rainfall really is greater than in most other cities in Britain, there is a Test cricket ground with far fewer covered seats than anywhere else in the country. With the exception of the pavilion (the only square-on pavilion among Test grounds in England) and part of the Washbrook Stand, all the seats are uncovered. And above the covered seats in the Washbrook Stand, there is a leak in the roof, so if you are sitting in the wrong seats down below, it can be as wet as, or even wetter than, being in the open. Still, we had umbrellas and the forecast was not bad, and it is a friendly ground, if ripe for redevelopment.

The second day began very well: Andrew Flintoff, local hero, strode to the wicket with the not-out batsman, Ian Bell. Huge cheers greeted him: throughout the summer the volume of noise that England's supporters gave their team was greater than I can ever remember, and that is not merely because of the presence of the Barmy Army, who were led at Old Trafford not only by their trumpeter but also by a W.G. Grace lookalike, 100 years out of time. The support that the England team were given at every ground must have boosted them, and on occasion must have disheartened the Australians. When England were not playing very well in the 1990s, the support was still good in numbers, but not very vocal. Home advantage was thrown away by crowds not getting behind the team. Now, with a winning side, the vocal support is ear-splitting. I know cricket should be played and watched for cricket's sake, but to watch a winning side is a whole lot more fun.

Flintoff did not disappoint. He lost Bell early on, attempting to pull Lee but just getting a thin edge through to Gilchrist. He had not added to his overnight score, and England were 346 for six. This brought Geraint Jones to the wicket, and optimistic memories came back of previous Flintoff–Jones partnerships. They set about the Australian attack carefully at first, although they did not let the loose balls pass harmlessly by. They added 28 runs against Lee and McGrath, and the only alarm was when a half-hearted streaker ran on to the pitch, but then pulled his trousers back up before everybody could say how shocking it all was. His day of watching cricket was therefore complete before Shane Warne was brought back into the attack, at about the same time that the drizzle began. We had all been warned that rain was likely, so we all had our defences planned. Within a very short time, about fifteen thousand umbrellas were up, and at 375 for six, halfway through a Brett Lee over, the players ran back in to the pavilion.

The break lasted no more than twenty minutes, and Flintoff and Jones came back to resume their stand, at an accelerated pace. The pair added 50 in the next seven overs, as Lee, Warne and Gillespie were treated with little respect. Jones danced down the wicket to hit Warne for four, and Flintoff went down on one knee to sweep him backward of square. Gillespie tried bowling short, and the result was predictable – four through midwicket every time. When Jones guided a wide ball from Gillespie down to third man, Justin Langer ran to cut off the boundary, slipped and watched helplessly as the ball crossed the ropes. The big TV screen immediately announced Gillespie's century – 0 for 100 in 16.2 overs. That did no good for rela-tions between Gillespie and Langer, but the opener was not at fault when Flintoff smashed the final ball of Gillespie's over back past the bowler for another boundary. We were watching the twilight of a fine Test career, and it was sad to see, but it seemed Gillespie could do nothing to stop the flow of runs.

However, within a couple of overs, both Langer and Gillespie were redeemed, in part at least. First, Warne tossed one up to Flintoff, who could not resist the bait and, just failing to get to the pitch of the ball, lofted a difficult catch to long-on, and Langer made no mistake. Flintoff was gone for 46, and the partnership of 87 was broken. Then in the next over, on the stroke of lunch, Jones got an inside edge to a straight ball from Gillespie, and played on. So England went in to lunch at 434 for eight wickets, with Jones out for 42 off only 51 balls, an innings that did not suffer in comparison with Flintoff's. When Jones bats like this, he looks like a man who should be averaging 40 for England, not 30. Given the chance, one day I expect he will.

After lunch (and in particular I thought the rice salad with prawns went down well. Oh, and the duck wraps. It is amazing what picnics at cricket grounds are like these days) it did not take Australia long to finish off the England innings. Harmison rubbed salt into Gillespie's wounds by cover-driving him beautifully for 3 runs, but it took Warne no time to find the edge of Giles's bat and give Hayden yet another slip catch. 438 for nine became 444 all out when Simon Jones, having survived a huge lbw appeal from Warne in the previous over, took a wild swing at a leg-break (an off-break to the left-hander) and was bowled. Warne finished with four for 99 and Lee four for 100. McGrath, clearly not fully fit, took no wicket for 86 runs, the worst innings analysis of his entire Test career. How different it all was from Lord's.

Four hundred and forty-four was a good score, but for England to press home the advan-tage, the view was that a couple of quick wickets would be needed. The opening partnership of Hayden and Langer had not yet given Australia the start they are used to, and if England could keep them on a leash, the prospects were good, especially as Michael Clarke had not fielded since the second over of the previous day, and was still back at the team's hotel, no doubt flat on his back. But the Australians had other ideas. With Langer taking the lead, as was to become the habit throughout the series, the openers started to build something approaching a solid start. By this time the sun was out, the weather was set fair, and batting conditions were good. Langer took two consecutive fours from Hoggard's second over from the Brian Statham End, the second the shot of the day: a superb cover-drive. Harmison was bowling too short, and did not look his usual devastating self. After six overs, with the score already on 30, Flintoff replaced Harmison and quickly showed how to bowl at left-handers. His short balls were quick and well directed, but his length was mainly fuller than Harmison's, and his round-the-wicket angle made the ball harder to get away. All the same, by the time drinks came, after eleven overs, the score was 41 for no wicket. Shortly afterwards, Simon Jones was given one over

Opposite: Though a slow bowler, there is no lack of effort in Warne's delivery.

from the Brian Statham End, which was a good maiden, but then Vaughan decided to give the ball to Giles to see what he could do with all the rough outside the left-handers' off stump. It was an inspired move. In his first over, he had Langer playing and missing (well, he might not have missed: there was a huge appeal for a catch behind the wicket, but umpire Bowden said no) and then next ball, he made the breakthrough. The ball was not as good as the previous delivery, and Langer got the meat of his bat to it and aimed to clip it through midwicket. Bell, at short leg, stuck out a hand and took a very fine reflex catch. Australia were 58 for one.

Billy Bowden, who is getting a reputation as a very good umpire despite his histrionics, seems to be a 'not outer' in the way that Dickie Bird used to be, or in the way that Aleem Dar is not. That is fine if everybody knows it and expects it, and he keeps a consistency of decision throughout a match and a series. But he certainly does need a lot of persuading. Although he made some very good decisions indeed, Hawkeye showed that some of his not out lbw decisions should have been given out, although virtually none of the ones he actually gave during the summer were unkind to the batsman. In the case of the caught-behind the ball before Langer actually departed, the Snickometer supported Bowden's view that there was no contact.

Langer's departure was the key moment of the day. Vaughan persisted with Giles (who might originally have been given the over merely in order that Jones could change ends), and the spinner bowled for the rest of the day, 21 overs on the trot. His bowling took the headlines in the papers the next day, ample revenge for the insults, real or perceived, heaped on his head after the Lord's Test. At tea, Australia had moved to 73 for one wicket, with Ponting on 7 and Hayden on 33, still nowhere near his belligerent and fluent best.

Simon Jones' first ball after tea did for Ponting. It was a short ball, and Ponting misjudged either the length or the pace. He tried to fend it off but could only lob the ball to gully where Bell took another catch, at the other end of the scale of difficulty from his earlier effort. At 73 for two, with the captain gone, it could have been the start of a crisis. But Simon Jones was having difficulty with his direction, giving away 8 byes in an over, with a wide ball to leg followed by a beamer, both at Hayden and both giving Geraint Jones no chance at all. The confusion caused by this rather wild bowling was added to when umpire Bucknor, who signalled no-ball for the beamer, forgot to signal four byes when the ball sped to the boundary. The correction was not made until the next morning, when Australia suddenly found they had 4 more runs than they thought. The ball after the beamer produced a huge appeal for leg before (but then all appeals are huge, if you want to convince the umpire it is out: Bucknor said no), and the strong suspicion that Jones was getting reverse swing on the ball, only 22 overs old.

In the next over, Billy Bowden, the not outer, raised his crooked finger to remove Hayden, who looked absolutely plumb, playing back to a Giles spinner that turned sharply out of the rough. 86 for three (or 82 for three as we thought at the time) was not good for Australia. Katich, who came in to join Martyn, was almost leg before to the next ball, but Bowden returned to his not out ways. The pair put that initial alarm behind them and settled down to build a revival of Australia's hopes. Giles wheeled away, looking dangerous when the ball pitched in the rough and demanding respect from the batsmen. At the other end, Simon Jones was beginning to find the control to make his reverse swing more effective, and there were no easy runs to be taken. It was a long session, with 36 overs eventually bowled in it, and both teams were determined to win the session. When drinks arrived twelve overs after tea (emphasising the slowness of the over-rate), the score was 115 for three.

Yet again, the drinks break brought a wicket. Flintoff bowled to Katich, who left it, only to see his off stump ripped out of the ground. It was put down to an error of judgement, which it obviously was, but there were mitigating circumstances. By that stage in the day, the sunlight was beginning to reflect off the hover dryer stored at the Stretford End of the ground. The plastic cover gave off quite a glare, and it was distracting even from where we were positioned, at third man at the Brian Statham End. For the batsman it must have been even more difficult. Eventually, but not for a few more overs, a non-reflective cover was put over the plastic one, and the batsman and fielders could concentrate again. I suppose that sunshine at Manchester is such a rare thing that nobody had noticed the glare from the cover before. The new man was Adam Gilchrist, the next in line of Australian under-achievers, and it confirmed the fact that Michael Clarke was still not fit to bat. Word had by this time gone from Old Trafford to the hotel to tell Clarke to get to the ground as quickly as he could hobble, but it was assumed he would not be next man in if a wicket fell soon.

Gilchrist showed all the signs of playing a typical innings. He stepped down the wicket to each of the first two deliveries he received from Giles (net profit: 1 run) and took two fours off Flintoff in three balls, but his progress was slowed when Martyn was out. This was probably the best ball that Giles bowled all day. Although Giles contains the left-handers well, it seems to me that he bowls better to the right-handers, and it was Martyn's fate to be the right-hander facing this wonderful delivery that pitched outside leg stump and hit the top of the off stump. Martyn had batted well and had not looked in any trouble, but there was no shame in being bowled by that ball from Giles. He had made 20, and the score was 129 for five. At this point, the Aussies were clearly in deep trouble, 315 behind England, with five wickets down and one man on his sick bed, and three and a half days to go. The crowd were getting very noisy, and W.G. Grace and the trumpeter were leading the celebrations.

They would have been even noisier if England had held on to either of the two chances that came their way in the next over, both from Gilchrist off Flintoff. The first one was no more than a quarter chance, as Gilchrist looped the ball into the air and the diving Bell could only just get a fingertip to it, but the second chance was through the diving Pietersen at short cover when it should really have stuck. So should the chance in the next over. The shot was by Warne off Giles, the fielder was Pietersen again and the result was the same. When Pietersen finally holds a catch in Test cricket, and by the law of averages that must happen some day, there will be a huge if somewhat ironic cheer, not least from his England team-mates.

While Giles held down one end, Vaughan juggled his quick bowlers at the Stretford End. Flintoff was the most threatening, Harmison the most unpredictable and Jones the most likely to take a wicket. Hoggard did not get a bowl at all. More drinks were wheeled out after 44 overs, but this time on resumption they did not take a wicket immediately. It was Simon Jones, with the first ball of his third spell, who made the breakthrough, with the help of Jones the Gloves. Gilchrist just waved at a fairly standard loosener, and took an edge through to the 'keeper. Australia were 186 for six (or 182 for six according to the scoreboard at the time) and Michael Clarke came in, walking in a spritely enough manner to the wicket, accompanied by his runner, Matthew Hayden.

Watching people bat with a runner is usually the moment when high farce invades the cricket pitch, but for an Australian side facing a tragedy of King Lear proportions if they were to go one down with two to play, this was not the time for levity. It was, however, as far as Clarke was concerned, a time for brevity. He clearly had little freedom of movement, and his usual flowing style of batting was hardly seen. One glorious cover-drive reminded us of what a good batsman he is, but otherwise crabbed movements, the occasional squeezed single and therapeutic exercises at square leg were the order of his 20-minute stay. He met his downfall by attempting an ambitious drive off a slower ball from Jones, which only got as far as Flintoff at mid-off. That made it 201 for seven – although we all still thought the 200 was 3 runs away – and Clarke and Hayden trudged back to the pavilion.

Warne brought up what he thought, and we thought, was the 200 with a huge six off Giles. By this time Warne, who had been punishing every loose ball and defending carefully when he needed to, had taken his score into the 40s, and was the one Australian batsman who looked as though he was in control of the situation. Warne's batting was even more influential than his bowling in this match, a statement that cannot often be made. So was Gillespie's, but as his bowling was only influential insofar as it helped England to that big first-innings score, that is not much of a tribute to his batting, which was courageous and good in the first innings. He and Warne saw out the remains of the day, with Australia finishing on 210 for seven, to be advanced to 214 for seven overnight when umpire Bucknor's oversight was corrected.

Day 2, Close of Play:

England 444.

Australia 214 for seven wickets after 56 overs (Warne 45 not out, Gillespie 4 not out).

When was the last time that Shane Warne or Jason Gillespie batted through a complete day's play in a Test? Well, rewrite the record books, because on Saturday, 13 August, the two Australian bowlers, each with a Test batting average of just over 16, somehow kept the England bowlers at bay during the very limited play that was possible between showers. Fourteen overs of cricket were played and Dizzy and the Fat Boy survived them all. As it had only taken fifteen overs earlier in the innings to dispose of Ponting, Hayden, Katich and Martyn, this was no mean achievement.

It was just past 3.00 p.m. when the teams were able to take the field for the first time, and the umpires decreed that 38 overs of play were still possible. They were clearly more optimistic than the soggy spectators in the stands, who clearly felt that more rain was on the way. Even so, there was no noticeable thinning of the crowd. They could see that a big upset was on the cards, and even though it could not be completed on Saturday, they wanted to be able to say they had seen part, at least, of Australia's downfall. It was a very small part. Giles, as ever, wheeled away from the Brian Statham End, while Simon Jones had first crack at the batsmen from the other end. Progress was slow. Warne eventually struck the first four of the day, off Jones, and a couple of balls later hit Giles safely out to long-on to bring up his fifty, a very valuable contribution to the Australian cause. Even by this stage, pretty well exactly halfway through the series, Warne was standing out as the one match-winner that Australia still possesses, and the sad thing for Australia was that this impression did not change during the second half of the series. He gave one chance, when he was on 55, when he danced down the pitch to wallop Giles back over his head, missed, and should have been stumped. All the newspapers, and most of the radio and television commentators and the spectators in the ground felt that it was an easy chance, which could cost England the chance of enforcing the follow-on, and with it the match, but although it was a missed chance, and it should have been taken, it was no sure thing. It turned a long way and bounced more than usual, despite Giles giving no extra spin on the ball. All the same, it proved that the England 'keeper had a long way to go before he would be England's clear first choice behind the stumps.

The follow-on soon became academic. Australia were 211 runs behind when Warne took matters into his own hands by hitting Giles for 12 runs in an over, averting the follow-on with the final ball thumped over mid-off for four. With that the rain came down again, and play was delayed until ten past six, when it was clear enough to risk six more overs. That was just enough time for Jones to miss another chance, this time a regulation nick from Warne off Flintoff, that there was little excuse for dropping, apart from the setting sun and those hover covers. The debate about who was England's best wicketkeeper was dead (the answer was Chris Read as always) but the debate about who was England's best wicketkeeper–batsman was hotting up.

A brief word about npower's contribution to the television displays of the summer, which were fairly irritating everywhere, but which reached a peak of incompetence at Old Trafford. All through the Test series, npower persisted in giving us 'Red Hot Facts' on the big screen, most of which were neither Red Hot nor Facts. Consider, 'England's win ratio at Old Trafford is 50 percent'. Quite apart from the fact that ratios and percentages are different things (as confirmed by my actuarial mate sitting next to me), does that mean we have won half the Tests played at Old Trafford against Australia? Well, no it does not. Before this Test England had actually won seven and lost seven, but had also drawn thirteen, making the win ratio and/or percentage something quite different. Then consider the statement about Steve Bucknor, who 'now stands in 102 Tests'. What? All at once? Who teaches English grammar at npower's advertising school? Or what about the fact that Australia's top score at Old Trafford was a 'red hot 656 for eight declared' in 1964. Anybody who remembers that series and that match will immediately acknowledge that the 656 for 8 was anything but red hot. Bobby Simpson ground out 311, and Ken Barrington hit 256 for England in reply, to bring the match to a stone-cold boring draw. Why do sponsors and advertisers fill the screen with useless information like this? Is it just to show off their ignorance of maths, English and cricket history all at once? The cricket is thrilling enough as it is, without these incompetent attempts to ratchet up the excitement to red hot levels.

After several attempts to find the best way to get away from Old Trafford, we took the pretty route via Jodrell Bank this time. No better than before. How do you get into and away from Old Trafford when there is a crowd of more than fifty or so?

Day 3, Close of Play:

England 444.

Australia 264 for seven wickets after 70 overs (Warne 78 not out, Gillespie 7 not out).

The weather improved on the Sunday, and although the sky was overcast, a full day's play was expected. In an attempt to catch up on time lost from the day before 98 overs were scheduled. The ground was filled to capacity as Flintoff began the day with a no-ball to Gillespie, but from then on the day moved England's way. Harmison took over from Giles, who had bowled 28 consecutive overs from the Brian Statham End since Friday, but it was when Simon Jones replaced Flintoff that the eighth wicket fell. Warne, who had battled for three hours at the crease to get to 90, finally ran out of patience and tried to hook a short ball for six. Giles on the boundary made sure it did not carry. It was a fine innings by Warne, and easily his highest Test score against England. By taking the score along to 287, and scoring 90 of the 158 runs added while he was at the crease, he gave the Australian total some substance and avoided the unheard of ignominy of the follow-on.

Brett Lee found Simon Jones and his reverse swing too much to cope with, but lasted a quarter of an hour for a single, before edging one to slip, where Trescothick made a good diving catch. Jones had his five wickets and it was 293 for nine. At this point England took the new ball; Gillespie of all people hit it for six over midwicket with what was to be the final scoring stroke of the innings, and then he fell, leg before to Simon Jones. Australia were all out for 302, and Simon Jones had career-best figures of six for 53 in 17.5 overs of wonderfully controlled, fast swing bowling.

England batted again with a lead of 142 on first innings. The aim was to make up for lost time, put sufficient runs on the board quickly enough to permit a declaration and leave time to bowl Australia out again. Simple enough. Just do it.

Trescothick and Strauss planned the work and worked the plan, as 1970s business gurus used to say. Lee, bowling in excess of 90 miles per hour, hit Strauss on the helmet grille for the second time in the game, and this time drew blood. Strauss spent the rest of the match with a large white plaster on his left ear, a badge that he wore with some pride. He also wore a new helmet grille. Trescothick avoided injury, and when he hit Lee very powerfully for four through cover point to bring his score to 5, he racked up 5,000 runs in Tests. Among the sixteen Englishmen to have achieved this, only Hobbs, Hutton, Hammond and Barrington got there in fewer matches. Exalted company indeed. All of those men had been on Ashes-winning teams, though, and Trescothick did not wish to remain the odd one out.

At lunch, England had reached 26 without loss, although Strauss did edge a four between Warne and Ponting in the slips, and neither man went for the catch. After lunch Trescothick took on Lee again, and won the battle. The fifty came up in thirteen overs, with England jogging along at four an over and building a big lead quickly. But when Trescothick had made 41, he defended a ball against McGrath, but did not realise the ball was rolling back on to his stumps. The bail was dislodged and Trescothick had to go. Vaughan never really got going, and was caught on the fine-leg boundary by Brad Hodge, fielding substitute for Michael Clarke again. He made 14, but by this time England were on 97 and on top. Ian Bell, half-century maker in the first innings, came in to join Strauss. He started very slowly, but Strauss made up for that. A six off Brett Lee, to show he had got over the dreadful whack on the helmet in the first over, and two fours off Shane Warne in the final over, the first of which brought up his personal fifty, showed that the Middlesex man was feeling good. At tea the score was 128 for two after 35 overs, and Gillespie had not yet had a bowl.

He got his chance immediately after tea, but failed to take it. His fourth over was a nine-ball mess of no-balls which went for 14 runs, and England's lead was almost 300. Bell, who had been very careful at the start of his innings, now hit Warne for two fours, to bring his score to 24 from 55 balls, but from then on he started to bat more freely. He needed to; with Pietersen and Flintoff next men in, the best thing Bell could do if he was not going to score fast would be to get out and let them have a go. Strauss at the other end passed his previous highest score of the season (69 against Bangladesh) and forged on towards his hundred. At the drinks break, England were on 187 for two, and Bell hit the second ball after the break, from McGrath, over the bowler's head for six. McGrath, despite having taken Trescothick's wicket, was clearly not fit and England were able to treat him as just another bowler. It was by hitting a short delivery from the once feared McGrath for four through midwicket that Strauss brought up his century, his sixth in Tests and his first against Australia. It was a very good innings, just what England needed, and it blew away the last of the cobwebs from a slow start to the season. Australia had Warne, Warne and Warne to keep the game within reach, and it was Warne who congratulated Strauss at the end of the over.

Just before Bell reached his fifty, McGrath struck twice. His first wicket was the big one, that of Strauss, who was caught off a nothing ball on the square-leg boundary by Martyn, and the second was Pietersen, first ball lbw, a yorker and McGrath's best ball of the match. England

were now 225 for four, but look on the bright side – Flintoff was the next man in. He did not last long either, bowled by McGrath, playing a wild slog across the line. Then McGrath completed the most outrageous five-wicket haul of his career when Bell was caught by Katich for 65 – on the long-on boundary! He is going down fighting, at least. His final analysis was five for 115 in 20.5 overs, almost a run a ball conceded.

His fighting spirit was sorely tested by Geraint Jones, who played an innings few others could play: 2 . 2 2 . 4 off McGrath, then a single off three balls from Warne, and finally 6 4 . 6 off McGrath, giving him 27 off fourteen balls, one of which was a no-ball. At this point Vaughan declared. England had made 280 in 62 overs, and left Australia 423 to win in a little over a day. Had it not been for the rain, England might have left them over 500 to get in a day and a half or so. But in Manchester it rains, so you adapt your game accordingly.

Vaughan's declaration was a big psychological blow. It showed who was emerging as the power in the series, how rapidly the young England side was overtaking the ageing Australians, and how unconcerned Vaughan's men were about setting a target which, although difficult, would not have seemed beyond the powers of this Australian side last time they met in 2002/03. England were top dogs already, even if Ricky Ponting was not ready to believe it.

By the end of the day, Australia had made 24 without loss, but, as Andrew Strauss told the press, 'We're not going to blow them away, but there are definitely ten wickets out there tomorrow.'

Day 4, Close of Play:

England 444 and 280 for six wickets declared.
Australia 302 and 24 for no wicket after 10 overs (Langer 14 not out, Hayden 5 not out).

The final day of the Old Trafford Test was one of the most remarkable in post-War Test history. The day dawned clear. There was no prospect of rain. At least 50,000 people had the same idea – let's go to the Test match. Fifth day tickets were only on sale that morning, for £10 per adult and £5 for a child, and with such a close finish expected, it was a great day to throw a sickie and head for the Test match. The ticketed capacity of Old Trafford is around 21,000, and the queues began to form at midnight. By 6.00 in the morning, the queues were six deep around the ground. By 8.40 a.m. the ground was full, with up to 20,000 more outside trying to find a way in. Police in the centre of Manchester were advising about 10,000 more milling about near Piccadilly station not to bother going to the ground. The appeal of Test cricket was firmly re-established, and the success of this summer's series was assured. All England had to do to cap it all was win this game and one more to take the Ashes.

When the England team came out to begin the day, the atmosphere was compelling. We noted

Opposite: Strauss returned to form with a typically workmanlike century.

Ponting's was a true captain's innings, and Australia's batting highlight of the series.

it at Lord's, and at Edgbaston, and it would be there at Trent Bridge and the Oval too, but it was at Old Trafford where the feeling was deepest. Here was a huge body of ordinary Englishmen and women willing eleven blokes to win a game for them. All around the country, televisions and radios were tuned in, and millions more were adding their hopes and prayers, and groans and cheers, to the twenty thousand lucky souls who were there to witness it at first hand.

From the beginning it seemed the prayers would work. Hoggard took the second over of the day, and with his first ball, a beauty that swung across Langer, he induced a little edge and Jones the Gloves did the rest. Australia were one wicket down and the day had hardly begun.

This brought in Ricky Ponting, a captain under siege. His leadership was for the first time being seriously questioned, firstly because he won the toss and fielded at Edgbaston, a decision that probably cost the Test match; and secondly because his world-beating colleagues were not delivering the goods when he asked them, Shane Warne always honourably excluded. If ever he needed to show the world that these Australians still had the talent and the fighting spirit that made them great, the time was now. The situation was a new one for Ponting. Since his Test debut at the end of 1995, he had been part of a victorious Australian side, a side that bullied its opponents into submission, and trampled them into the ground. Ponting himself had gone some way to get rid of the unfriendly image that had begun under Allan Border and reached its apogee under Steve Waugh, so trampling opponents into the ground was not part of the Australian game plan, but they still relied on their sheer power to make their opponents quake in their boots. England had deliberately targeted Australia in the first day of each game, the first session and the first hour, to make sure that they made an impact on the game early. These Australians had not encountered this before, and they found it difficult to cope with. The Old Trafford Test was in many ways the most successful display of this English tactic. They had hardly conceded a single session, and now Ponting had to come in to face a rampant England who had done what they wanted to do already by making an impression on the first hour of the day. A captain's knock was required.

A captain's knock was delivered. Until Kevin Pietersen's innings at the Oval, this was undoubtedly the best innings of the series. It also established Ponting as unquestionably the best batsman in the Australian side and a captain who may not be the greatest tactician ever to don the baggy green, but who can certainly lead by example. From the depths of 25 for one, with 398 runs still required to win, and almost one hundred more overs to survive, he engineered one of the great escapes of Test cricket. He had little help. Only three other members of his team made more than 30, and Ponting's final score of 156 was exactly four times more than the next highest scorer managed. He added 71 with Hayden, having survived a stumping

Giles was the target of sniping criticism from the press all summer. This ball to Martyn was excellent riposte.

appeal when he had made only 7. He hit a Flintoff no-ball for a flat six over square leg, and survived a silly run attempt when he set off for a quick single and Hayden turned him back. It was a busy start to his innings, and when Hayden went, bowled round his legs by a great ball from Flintoff for 36, there was still a possibility that Australia could get the runs. At lunch, taken with seventy more overs remaining, Australia were 121 for two, and the match, though still England's for the taking, was a little less obviously wearing the blue cap with the crown and the lions.

Help was at hand, in the form of umpire Steve Bucknor, who shortly after lunch gave Martyn out lbw to Harmison, despite a thick inside edge noticed by almost everybody on the ground. It was a terrible decision. Martyn, whose batting needed all the help it could get, was getting none, and was gone for 19, shaking his head all the way back to the dressing- room. By this time, Australia seemed to have given up thoughts of victory, for they were not pressing hard and now needed about 4.5 runs an over to win. They were also up against an England attack bowling really well, with no obvious weak link. Simon Jones and Andrew Flintoff were getting reverse swing, and the Australians were finding it tough going, even on a wicket that was still good for batting. The crowd, of course, loved it. Every English advance was greeted with huge cheers, every sharp piece of fielding, every bowling change, even every drinks break was a cause for more celebration. The afternoon session was a raucous one, based on the assumption that by the end of the day, England would be within sight of the Ashes.

The new man, Katich, stayed with Ponting as the captain reached his fifty with a cut down to third man off Simon Jones, but did not manage to stick around for long. He had made 12 in 23 balls when he chased an outswinger from Flintoff, who was in the middle of a devastating spell, and could only edge it to third slip, where Giles took a good catch. The score was now 164 for four, Ponting had made 69 and there were 58 more overs in which to make 258 more runs to win, or for England to take six wickets, one of which was the crippled Michael Clarke. The game was boiling up, without it ever looking as though Australia could get away with it.

Gilchrist came in next, ahead of Clarke again, and his disappointing series continued. He took as many as five balls to get off the mark, and even played a complete maiden over from Flintoff (when did Gilchrist last play a maiden over in a Test?), but the new supercautious Gilchrist was even less prolific than the earlier crash bang version. After facing 30 balls in over half an hour at the crease, he fell in exactly the same way as Katich had, caught chasing an outswinger from Flintoff. This time it was Bell who took the catch in the gully. At 182 for five, and fifty overs to go, Australia looked dead in the water.

Clarke hobbled in, without a runner this time, and played with much greater freedom than in the first innings. Vaughan brought himself into the attack for three overs, and Clarke and Ponting helped themselves to a couple of easy boundaries apiece, and at tea the score was 216 for five, with the captain on 91 not out. After tea, Clarke and Ponting continued to build their partnership into the biggest of the innings, and a small element of doubt began to creep into England's collective mindset. Ponting brought up his century with a beautiful cover-drive off

Steven Harmison's slower ball, and both he and Clarke were hard on Giles. In the event this pitch, that some people had said would turn square after the first day, did not yield a wicket for either Warne or Giles in the third and fourth innings. It was a true batting wicket, and only the quicker bowlers could get much from it.

Clarke's effort was finally ended by Simon Jones. Jones bowled an inswinger, Clarke did not pick it, and just raised his bat high in the air to let the ball pass by. It did, but took the off stump out on its way. We thought at the time that that would be the mistake that put England back on course for victory. Australia still needed 160 runs to win in 33 overs, and England only needed four more wickets. We all knew that Australia were just hoping for a draw when the next man appeared. It was not Warne but the arch-defender Jason Gillespie. Australia had clearly ruled out all hope of winning, and now merely wanted to stave off defeat.

The tactic did not work. Gillespie lasted just five balls before being trapped leg before by Hoggard's big inswinger. Now Australia were 264 for seven with 31 overs still left to bowl. A wicket every ten overs against the tail should be no problem. But of course, two of the wickets to fall were held by the captain, Ponting, now on 112, and the one man who would never give his wicket away, Shane Warne. They dug in and battled away. After more than fifteen overs of defiance, Warne hit one off his pads to his Hampshire team-mate Pietersen. It was not an easy chance, but they have to stick if Tests are to be won, and this did not stick. Warne, on 30 at the time, lived on. At the end of the next over, the umpires signalled the start of the final fifteen overs of the Test, and drinks were rolled on for a final time. The tension was mounting, and all around the country, television sets were being switched on to watch the final overs. By the end of the broadcast, Channel Four's audience had reached 7.7 million, a figure even greater than for the Edgbaston Test (which ended on a Sunday morning, of course) and larger even than their flagship programme *Big Brother*. For once real life sporting drama was proving more popular than reality television, and far more compelling.

The end of Warne was almost another tale of missed chances. Ponting had just reached his 150, an epic effort lasting 247 balls, when next over, Warne edged a ball from Flintoff hard to Strauss at second slip. Strauss could not hold it, but managed to palm the ball towards the 'keeper, past Trescothick at first slip. Jones, seeing what was happening, changed direction and threw himself to his right to take the rebound almost at Trescothick's feet just before it hit the ground. It was a stunning catch – a piece of pure reflex athleticism which, we all thought, would at last seal the match for England. Warne was gone for 34, and Australia were 340 for eight with just under ten overs to go.

Brett Lee, another fighter with bat in hand, came out to join Ponting. There was no fat lady singing, only the fat men of the Barmy Army, so the game was not over yet. Vaughan continued to shuffle his bowling attack, seeking the last two breakthroughs, but now suddenly it looked as though time would run out on England. Well, we said that at Edgbaston too, and look what happened. But then Jones pulled up lame just as he was about to start his 18th over of the innings, and he had to go off. It was, we found out later, only cramp, but it deprived

England of one more option in these final tense overs. Harmison took over at the Stretford End, and it was Harmison who brought England even closer to victory. It did not happen at once, but with the last ball of the 104th over of the innings, with just four to go after it, he enticed Ponting into playing at a quick leg-side delivery. Ponting could only get a glove on it, and it went through to Jones who took the catch. Ponting's truly wonderful innings of 156 had brought Australia to the very brink of safety, but as he walked disconsolately back to the pavilion, to a generous standing ovation from the crowd who were certainly getting their money's worth, he must have thought the game was gone. How could McGrath and Lee survive four overs from Flintoff and Harmison?

To be honest, I do not quite know how, but they did survive. Flintoff bowled the first of the four overs to Lee, who tried for a single on the last ball to keep the strike. He hit it too hard and England let it go for four so that Harmison, who had taken the final wicket at Edgbaston, could be unleashed on McGrath. He bowled fast and well, and McGrath had to work hard to dig out a yorker second ball, but he survived. What's more, he hit a streaky four to fine leg to boost his series average. Now it was Flintoff to Lee for a last time. Once again, Lee was able to play the over safely, although this time there was a furious if rather half-hearted lbw appeal when the ball hit him on the foot. He was rightly given not out. It would have been a travesty if England had won on a doubtful leg before decision. But like the previous over, Lee tried to take a single off the final ball, but England let it roll for four. The final over was to be Harmison to McGrath once again..

There were now 23,000 people in the ground hyperventilating, not to mention the 7.7 million watching television and probably an equal number listening to the radio or following over the Internet. For the second time this summer, the result of a Test match, and quite probably the destination of the Ashes, had come down to a final over, bowled once again by Harmison. We could not watch, millions could not listen. How could Harmison hold the ball to bowl, or McGrath his 'X-Factor 61' bat? Stuart MacGill suddenly came rushing out on to the pitch with advice for McGrath, but what possible advice could the Aussie twelfth man give? Don't get out? Play for the draw? Get a single and let Lee do the batting? I suspect that all these ideas had occurred to McGrath already. Maybe MacGill was just taking the order for drinks at close of play.

When finally the over began, Harmison gave it everything. His third ball, though, was not quite on line, and McGrath took that single he and his fellow Australians so desperately wanted. Lee had to face the last three balls. He staved off the fourth and fifth, and the final ball, which Harmison tried so hard to turn into a leg stump yorker, was turned down to fine leg for four. Australia had done it! They had saved the match against all odds. The relief on the faces of the Australian batsmen told the story. They had got away with it and knew they were lucky to have done so. The Australian balcony emptied and the players all came out on to the field to celebrate with their rearguard heroes. For the Australians, the draw was a victory. Who would have guessed three weeks earlier that the mighty Australians would have been so relieved not to be beaten by England? It was a match that England should have won, and if there had been no rain it was a match they would have won, but there were no complaints.

For England, the draw could have been taken as a defeat, but it was not. They huddled on the pitch after the final delivery and Vaughan used the moment to point out how happy the Australians were not to be beaten, because they knew they deserved to be. England had not gained an absolute advantage in the series by going 2-1 up, but they certainly had the psychological edge. Glenn McGrath's view that 'They must be wondering what they have to do to beat these guys' was sounding as hollow as his 5-0 forecast at the start of the series. England were on the road to glory, the weather and fitness permitting.

It cannot get any better than this. On to Trent Bridge.

England v. Australia, Third Test Match

At Old Trafford, Manchester
11, 12, 13, 14, 15 August 2005

Result: Match Drawn
Toss: England

England

ME Trescothick c Gilchrist b Warne	63	b McGrath		41
AJ Strauss b Lee	6	c Martyn b McGrath		106
*MP Vaughan c McGrath b Katich	166	c sub (Hodge) b Lee		14
IR Bell c Gilchrist b Lee	59	c Katich b McGrath		65
KP Pietersen c sub (Hodge) b Lee	21	lbw b McGrath		0
MJ Hoggard b Lee	4			
A Flintoff c Langer b Warne	46	b McGrath		4
+GO Jones b Gillespie	42	not out		27
AF Giles c Hayden b Warne	0	not out		0
SJ Harmison not out	10			
SP Jones b Warne	0			
Extras (b 4, lb 5, w 3, nb 15)	27	(b 5, lb 3, w 1, nb 14)		23
Total (all out, 113.2 overs)	444	(for 6 wickets declared, 61.5 overs)		280

Fall of Wickets First Innings: 1-26 (Strauss), 2-163 (Trescothick), 3-290 (Vaughan), 4-333 (Pietersen), 5-341 (Hoggard), 6-346 (Bell), 7-433 (Flintoff), 8-434 (GO Jones), 9-438 (Giles), 10-444 (SP Jones).
Fall of Wickets Second Innings: 1-64 (Trescothick), 2-97 (Vaughan), 3-224 (Strauss), 4-225 (Pietersen), 5-248 (Flintoff), 6-264 (Bell).

Bowling First Innings: McGrath 25–6–86–0; Lee 27–6–100–4; Gillespie 19–2–114–1; Warne 33.2–5–99–4; Katich 9–1–6–1
Bowling Second Innings: McGrath 20.5–1–115–5; Lee 12–0–60–1; Warne 25–3–74–0; Gillespie 4–0–23–0

Australia

JL Langer c Bell b Giles	31	c GO Jones b Hoggard		14
ML Hayden lbw b Giles	34	b Flintoff		36
*RT Ponting c Bell b SP Jones	7	c GO Jones b Harmison		156
DR Martyn b Giles	20	lbw b Harmison		19
SM Katich b Flintoff	17	c Giles b Flintoff		12
+AC Gilchrist c GO Jones b SP Jones	30	c Bell b Flintoff		4
SK Warne c Giles b SP Jones	90	(9) c GO Jones b Flintoff		34
MJ Clarke c Flintoff b SP Jones	7	(7) b SP Jones		39
JN Gillespie lbw b SP Jones	26	(8) lbw b Hoggard		0
B Lee c Trescothick b SP Jones	1	not out		18
GD McGrath not out	1	not out		5
Extras (b 8, lb 7, w 8, nb 15)	38	(b 5, lb 8, w 1, nb 20)		34
Total (all out, 84.5 overs)	302	(9 wickets, 108 overs)		371

Fall of Wickets First Innings: 1-58 (Langer), 2-73 (Ponting), 3-86 (Hayden), 4-119 (Katich), 5-133 (Martyn), 6-186 (Gilchrist), 7-201 (Clarke), 8-287 (Warne), 9-293 (Lee), 10-302 (Gillespie).
Fall of Wickets Second Innings: 1-25 (Langer), 2-96 (Hayden), 3-129 (Martyn), 4-165 (Katich), 5-182 (Gilchrist), 6-263 (Clarke), 7-264 (Gillespie), 8-340 (Warne), 9-354 (Ponting).

Bowling First Innings: Harmison 10–0–47–0; Hoggard 6–2–22–0; Flintoff 20–1–65–1; SP Jones 17.5–6–53–6; Giles 31–4–100–3
Bowling Second Innings: Harmison 22–4–67–2; Hoggard 13–0–49–2; Giles 26–4–93–0; Vaughan 5–0–21–0; Flintoff 25–6–71–4; SP Jones 17–3–57–1

Umpires: BF Bowden (New Zealand) and SA Bucknor (West Indies)

Man of the Match: RT Ponting

No one who has witnessed the last fortnight's cricket will allow the game to be declared boring ever again. With that in mind, it is somewhat apt that this match provided a hinterland for the uninitiated as well. Shane Warne's 600th Test wicket was not a collector's item, but his presence – and the supremacy of his performances in these two matches – are a reminder to the thousands who have been turned away over the past decade of what they have been missing.

They are a reminder, as well, of why it is that England has been deep in Australia's shadow for so long. The Ashes are ablaze and the world is watching – and that in itself is a reason to rejoice in today's epic finish.

6

Nineteenth Nervous Breakdown

The Fourth Test Match, Trent Bridge

After the breathless excitement of the back-to-back Tests at Edgbaston and Old Trafford, the two teams, and the English sporting public, could sit back for ten days and consider in the cold light of day exactly what had happened since the one-sided contest at Lord's. What had happened was, probably, the swing of the pendulum of power away from Australia and towards England. The previous two Tests were not just battles that had been fought, both narrowly to England's advantage, but were key contests in a sporting war that was 125 years old. The Ashes were certainly not in England's hands yet, but if it was not the beginning of the end for Australian domination, it was certainly the end of the beginning.

The newspapers were pretty sure that England were on the upswing and Australia were falling apart. Whereas the difference in the Lord's match had been McGrath, at Old Trafford, even with the clockwork destroyer back in their ranks, they came off worst in a tense draw. Now the difference was Flintoff, or Simon Jones, or Michael Vaughan's captaincy or Michael Vaughan's batting, or Andrew Strauss or any combination of England cricketers you care to mention. Australia were shot: Gillespie's Test career was obviously over, McGrath had not recovered from treading on the ball at Edgbaston and was only half the bowler he once was, Gilchrist was having a nightmare comparable with that of Geraint Jones behind the stumps, and faring even worse in front of them, Hayden could not buy a run at a boot fair and really they were a two man team – Warne and Ponting. Where was the pride, the never-say-die spirit of the Australian sporting heroes of the past? Who were these wimps, these apologies for Australian cricketers? Oh my Bradman and my Lillee long ago!

The manic media bore down on the Australian camp, which suddenly was looking beleaguered and very unhappy. Not that the players were unhappy with each other – the Australian team spirit was something that was never diluted throughout the summer – but unhappy with their lot, unhappy with the way they were being treated by the press both in Britain and back home, and unhappy about the standard of cricket they had been producing in the first three Tests. The truth was that doubts expressed (by Matthew Hoggard among others) about whether the comparatively elderly Aussies could stand up to back-to-back Tests were proving most pertinent. The most obvious injury victim was Glenn McGrath, whose misfortune in stepping on a ball just before the start of the Second Test was rather compounded by his decision to play in the Third Test. This was a psychological blow aimed at England, but it did not come off. Apart from his batting, which at the end denied England a victory, Glenn McGrath was a shadow of his best self at Old Trafford. In the first innings his figures of no wickets for 86 runs were the worst of his entire Test career, and the five he picked up in the second innings were taken as England pressed on for victory. How many times before Old Trafford 2005 has McGrath been reduced to having catchers at long-on to get his wickets?

Then there were the players out of form. Watching the one-day internationals, it had occurred to me (and to a lot of others) that the mighty Australian batting machine was spluttering along, with several of its stoutest components looking dented and out of sorts. Matthew Hayden, who just under two years earlier had made the world's highest-ever Test score of 380, was scratching around like a rooster by the roadside, living dangerously and seldom scoring. Justin Langer was in better touch, and generally stayed longer at the crease than his opening partner, but their partnerships, usually so prolific and so fast, had been reduced to 35 and 18 at Lord's, 0 and 47 at Edgbaston, and 58 and 25 at Old Trafford – an average of 30.5 in the three Tests. Compare that with 67 and 30, 101, 31, 195 and 67, and 36 and 5 by the same pair in the 2002/03 series. Then they averaged 59, so in 2005 they were only half as good as they had been last time. The lack of a century opening partnership so far was a particular surprise. Everybody assumed that they would build a big score at least once in the series, but there was no sign of it so far.

Ricky Ponting had played one of the great captain's innings to save the Third Test, but that was the first time he had really looked in good form. Martyn, Clarke and Katich had all had their moments, Clarke with a flashing blade and brilliant timing, but always a look of insecurity about his play. Katich had played the anchor role, settling in for the long term each time he came to the crease, the only one of the Australian side prepared to play like Ken Barrington used to do, with the national flag stitched to his backside. He was not quite as successful as Barrington used to be, probably because he is not as good a player as Barrington used to be, but the principle is what counts. Of all the Australians apart from Ricky Ponting, Katich most gave the impression that the Englishmen would have to prise him from the wicket with a crowbar if they wanted him back in the pavilion. Damien Martyn, a right-hander like Ponting and Clarke, had not made a big impression, his 65 at Lord's in the second innings being his only contribution of note, and the general view was that he would need a big score at Trent Bridge if his place was to be secure beyond 2005. The Australians had only brought with them one batting reserve, Brad Hodge, so as more than one batsman continued to play well below form, the selectors had a major headache. Names like Mike Hussey, who had played well in the ODIs and who was having another successful county season, was a name being bandied about as a possible replacement, but the expectation was that Australia would stick to the line-up they had used in the first three Tests, on the basis that somebody has to come good some day soon.

In a nutshell, their problem was that the top six batsmen had so far failed to score heavily and, as important, their number seven, Adam Gilchrist, was having a poor series by his standards.

Since Gilchrist came into the Test side in November 1999, he has transformed the Australian performance, and Test match cricket around the world, with his wonderful ability to score heavily and very fast. It seemed not to matter whether he came in at 100 for five, or 370 for five, he still blazed away and, as often as not, took the game away from the opposition. To boast a batting average of 53.78, as Gilchrist did coming into the Trent Bridge match, batting at number seven, is a truly remarkable feat. Fifteen centuries, twenty 50s and a strike-rate that would be highly respectable in limited-overs cricket have made him the most dangerous batsman in world cricket, the one that bowlers least want to bowl at. Yet this summer so far, his contributions, though quick, have been very disappointing – 26 and 10 at Lord's, 49 not out and 1 at Edgbaston, and 30 and 4 at Old Trafford. 120 runs at 24 per innings is way below his usual standards. In the same Tests, Geraint Jones scored 30 and 6, 1 and 9, 42 and 27 not out; 115 runs at 23 per innings. So the much maligned Jones was, as a batsman, on a par with Gilchrist in the series so far.

All of this meant that some responsibility for making runs passed lower down the order, to Shane Warne and Brett Lee. They took on the responsibility well, but the more time a bowler spends batting, the greater the chances that tiredness will affect his bowling performance. Flintoff was already putting the lie to this theory, as many players have in the past, but a team's main strike bowlers should not be expected always to have to make up for the deficiencies of the top-order batsmen, if the team is to be working smoothly.

While the England bowling quintet of Harmison, Hoggard, Flintoff, Simon Jones and Giles were wheeling away contentedly, healthily and successfully, the Australian bowlers were in all sorts of trouble. Nobody had expected that by the mid-point of the series, it would be the Australians who were looking ragged in the field, but that was how it was turning out. In Glenn McGrath and Shane Warne, the two oldest members of the touring party, they still had two of the greatest bowlers ever to put on the baggy green, but McGrath's fitness was proving fitful, and without him, the balance between the two sides was changed. Brett Lee, playing his first series under the captaincy of Ricky Ponting, was a revelation. His bowling remained fast, accurate and frightening throughout the tour, and his batting and fielding were a huge bonus. His attitude, too, as exemplified in the way he fought for victory at Edgbaston but then accepted Andrew Flintoff's commiserations in the spirit they were given, was exactly right, and his facial expressions, which varied from grimace to smile and back again, depending on whether he was running in to bowl, appealing or walking back to his mark, endeared him to the huge number of television viewers who had become engrossed in this Ashes series.

Those were the plus points. The minus points were in the performance of the two back-up bowlers, Jason Gillespie and Michael Kasprowicz. The two stalwarts of Australian Test sides in recent years were both suddenly and unexpectedly showing their age. The Australian selectors, who had been so good at discarding players the moment they reached the end of their useful life, and not a Test later, seemed to have got it wrong. Darren Lehmann, Matthew Elliott, Mark Waugh and Michael Slater are amongst those who have found their Test careers terminated hastily by the Australian selectors. Not for them the round of final series and retirements when-I-feel-like-it that seems to be the norm for England players, as demonstrated in 2005 by Graham Thorpe and in previous summers by the likes of Nasser Hussain and Michael Atherton. The Australian selectors have traditionally taken the knife to underperforming players even before anybody had noticed they were underperforming. But not so with Dizzy and Kasper. They have been allowed to go on past that bridge too far.

For Gillespie, though, the bridge too far was Trent Bridge. After a toothless bowling performance in each of the first three Tests, finishing with three wickets for 300 runs, Jason Gillespie knew his time had come, and bowed gracefully to the inevitable. The Australian selectors made it clear that Gillespie would not play in the Fourth Test (even if they did not announce it officially), and the interest switched to the county game at Northampton, where the bowling attack was McGrath, Lee, Kasprowicz and the new boy Shaun Tait. It was assumed these four were playing for three places. As McGrath and Lee seemed like sure starters, it was a race between Kasprowicz and Tait for the final place.

In the Second Test, in the absence of McGrath, the obvious choice was Kasprowicz. His figures of two for 109 in the match were hardly encouraging, but he had the experience of 34 Tests behind him now, which was probably what was needed in such a close series and in such a crunch match. At Northampton, the Australians took rather more time over their batting problems than their bowling. Against the usual threadbare attack which counties like to put out against the tourists, Hayden and Clarke scored good centuries (which at least cleared up the issue of Clarke's back) and Langer and Katich hit fifties. It was all very gentle and simple until Northamptonshire began batting. McGrath and Lee took the new ball, McGrath immediately accounting for future England prospect Bilal Shafayat. Lee took a quick wicket, and then Shaun Tait was given the ball. Almost immediately, bowling pretty well as fast as Brett Lee, Tait got rid of Usman Afzaal (remember him?) and yorked David Sales, and then rattled the helmet of Northants opener Tim Roberts, forcing him to retire hurt. He needed five stitches in a cut above his eye, and with that one spell, Tait probably booked himself a place in the Test side.

England had no such problems. Having been brushed aside at Lord's, the strength of the performances at Edgbaston and Old Trafford, along with a refreshing lack of injuries, meant that England could name the same twelve for the fourth Test in a row, a fact that had the statisticians reaching for their record books. Despite all the carping about Geraint Jones (some of it unnecessarily vicious towards a gentle man and a good cricketer), he retained his place as the circus moved to the home of his arch rival, Chris Read. There was really no other issue to think about. Chris Tremlett was included in the twelve once again, but there seemed little likelihood of his playing. Matthew Hoggard had been having a comparatively quiet series, but Trent Bridge, with its new stands, had a reputation for suiting his brand of swing. Hoggard was in.

Australia eventually made it clear that Tait would be the man who came in for Gillespie, and Gillespie was quoted as making all the well-meaning remarks a sportsman has to make when Father Time catches up with him and he sees his career trampled on by a younger man.

Gillespie has always been a hugely popular member of the Australian side, and nothing became his time in the Australian side as much as the manner of his leaving it. But then, as if this summer's series needed another sensation, McGrath, whose right elbow had been troubling him for a day or two, failed a fitness Test on the morning of the match, and could not play. At Old Trafford, it was assumed he would not play and he did. At Trent Bridge, it was assumed he would play, and he did not. For those England fans who had banged on about McGrath being the difference between winning and losing, this was good news. So the final Australian team sheet included both Kasprowicz and Tait, but no Gillespie, and it left a huge amount of responsibility on the shoulders of Lee and Warne. England were elated, even if they trotted out the usual remarks about playing the men on the park, and not worrying about who was in the opposition side, just focusing on the match.

So the teams were:

England: M.P. Vaughan (Yorkshire, captain), M.E. Trescothick (Somerset), A.J. Strauss (Middlesex), I.R. Bell (Warwickshire), K.P. Pietersen (Hampshire), A. Flintoff (Lancashire), G.O. Jones (Kent, wicketkeeper), A.F. Giles (Warwickshire), M.J. Hoggard (Yorkshire), S.J. Harmison (Durham) and S.P. Jones (Glamorgan). C.T. Tremlett (Hampshire) was the man left out of the twelve.

Australia: R.T. Ponting (Tasmania, captain), M.L. Hayden (Queensland), J.L. Langer (Western Australia), D.R. Martyn (Western Australia), M.J. Clarke (New South Wales), S.M. Katich (New South Wales), A.C. Gilchrist (Western Australia, wicketkeeper), S.K. Warne (Victoria), B. Lee (New South Wales), M.S. Kasprowicz (Queensland) and S.W. Tait (South Australia).

England took one look at the sky, one look at the pitch, which Geoffrey Boycott described as 'a beautiful batting track', and one look at the way the coin had landed – in Michael Vaughan's favour – and elected to bat first.

The morning was fresh (the Australians called it cold, but it is never cold in August in Nottingham), but the skies were pretty clear and the forecast was not too bad. A chance of showers was the official verdict. Shaun Tait became the 392nd player to represent Australia in Tests, and in the way the Australians do these things, there was a little ceremony at which Tait was presented with his cap by a former Test player, in this case Michael Slater, who was in England doing duty for Channel Four's television coverage.

The game was started by the two men in white coats striding out to the middle, shortly followed by the Australian team and then Marcus Trescothick and Andrew Strauss. But suddenly there was drama: the two men in white coats were not Messrs Bucknor and Dar, but two impostors who had shuffled out on to the wicket from beside the pavilion. They had not hurried, and the hoax seemed to be working quite well until it was realised they had neither bails nor the ball, nor indeed looked much like the two officially appointed umpires. It was all just

a joke, but in a summer of heightened tension, it said little for Trent Bridge's security that the two men were able to walk up and down the pitch with impunity.

It turned out to be limited impunity, as punity in the shape of several bouncers and policemen quickly escorted the two men away, and that was the last they saw of the Test that day. What a waste of two tickets to one of the most exciting sporting events of the past ten years! But with their disappearance, the match got under way. For the first time since Australia played South Africa in Adelaide in January 1998, they were going into a Test match without either McGrath or Gillespie in their side. Ponting, Warne, MacGill and Kasprowicz, of that 1998 side, were on the 2005 tour, which shows the age of the squad. Brett Lee assumed the mantle of senior strike bowler.

The morning went very badly for Australia. By lunch England had made 129 runs for the loss of one wicket, that of Andrew Strauss. The England openers, no doubt rejoicing in the freedom that the Australian pace attack gave them, got off to a rapid start, Trescothick continuing the blitzkrieg he had begun at Edgbaston and with Strauss in good support. In their attack, they were helped immensely by the number of no-balls the Australians bowled. If anything can be seen to exemplify the loss of discipline on the cricket field, it is in the number of no-balls bowled. It was not just one man with an overstepping problem either. By lunch, sixteen no-balls had been bowled in 27 overs, shared around by Kasprowicz (the main offender), Lee and Tait. By the end of the day, the total had gone up to 22, almost four free overs for the England batsmen. There seemed to be no reason for this sudden explosion of no-balls: Trent Bridge is not a ground with a huge slope, and although the wicket was full of runs for the batsmen, it is not a difficult place to bowl from a technical point of view, as many would say Lord's is, or Canterbury.

Shaun Tait was brought into the attack after ten overs. He bowls quickly, being described on the ground's television monitor as 'right arm fast', unlike poor Freddie Flintoff who, after three Tests of whacking it in at a consistent ninety miles per hour, is still described as 'right arm fast medium'. Tait's action resembles nobody's. It is certainly not out of the coaching manuals. There is a slinging finish to it, a little like Jeff Thomson, but unlike Thomson, a smaller man than the gangling six foot four Tait, his action is not upright. Where Thomson lifted his left arm high and raised himself up on his right toe as he completed his very sideways action, Tait bends his legs and almost stoops to release the ball. This makes his action very skiddy and possibly more difficult to pick up, but it is the direction of his run-up and follow through that give the biggest shock the first time you see it. He runs in at an angle from mid-off to the stumps, and then, in his delivery stride, moves away again back to the off. Contortionists would be proud of his action, but how he can consistently control his direction with an action like that will remain a mystery. At Trent Bridge he did not always control his direction. His opening spell of five overs for 26 runs was good for England, but also good for him as he would have overcome the nervousness most bowlers experience on their Test match debut.

Previous pages: Giles celebrates as England stumble over the winning line.

Shane Warne was brought into the attack in the eighteenth over, with the score at 74 for no wicket. He, like Marcus Trescothick and Kevin Pietersen, was wearing a black armband in memory of Stuart Dove, a young boy who had met the teams at the Rose Bowl on the day of the Twenty20 in June, but who had since died of cancer. Warne was also sporting a goatee on several of his chins, a fashion statement which fortunately nobody else decided to emulate (apart from the now discarded Gillespie, of course). Trescothick was not impressed. It was not long before he smacked Warne back over his head for a big six, to the huge amusement of four Richie Benauds in the crowd. Trescothick reached his fifty when the score was 96 for no wicket, and he would have been hoping to go on to his first Test century against Australia. Strauss was playing second fiddle to Banger's big hitting, but still taking toll of the loose balls as they came along. There was no doubt that batting is a whole lot easier in McGrath's absence. It would be wrong to compare Australia at Edgbaston and Trent Bridge with the New Zealand attack in Richard Hadlee's era, but Graham Gooch described playing New Zealand then as like facing the World XI at one end, and Hampstead Seconds at the other. Nobody would call an attack that can have Warne at one end and Lee at the other as Hampstead Seconds, but when one of them was resting, the support was not there. Trescothick hit the first two balls he received from Tait for four.

It was Warne who made the first breakthrough. At 105, as the openers were both beginning to focus on the lunch break, Strauss tried to sweep and hit the ball down on to his foot, from where it looped gently to Hayden at slip. The Australians all appealed, and the umpires consulted. Did it hit the ground or Strauss's foot? The third umpire showed clearly that it was the foot and not the ground, so the catch was fair, and Strauss was out. The question does arise as to how Strauss could not have known he had whacked it into his foot, and why he did not just walk, or limp, back to the safety of the England dressing- room. But this is Ashes cricket and many cricketers play it as hard as they can.

Michael Vaughan then strode to the wicket, and hit the first ball he received square of the wicket for four. The form he had found at Old Trafford was still with him. At 111 for one wicket, as we were all thinking of former umpire David Shepherd and his hopping routine, Trescothick played on to Lee. Major celebrations all round, and Trescothick set off to the pavilion, only to stop when everybody realised the umpire had called no-ball. This was the third time in the series that Australia had taken a wicket with a no-ball, and they were no doubt hoping that the error would not prove as costly as at Old Trafford, when Vaughan added 121 more runs to his total after being bowled by a no-ball. Trescothick would also have had memories of Trent Bridge four years earlier, when he was given out caught by Gilchrist off Warne after the third umpire had been consulted over the fairness of the catch. The catch was fair, but the ball was a no-ball, which the umpire had failed to call. Trescothick had to go that time. Four years later, fortune was on his side. As if to prove the point, he hit the very next ball – another no-ball – for four behind square, the eighteenth four of the morning, to go with the one six. As Lee bowled the next ball, the entire crowd shouted, 'No ball!' but astonishingly it was a fair delivery.

Lunch was taken with England at 129 for one wicket, clearly with the upper hand. The ball had shown no sign of swinging, which must have concerned Hoggard, but the rest of the England team would have tucked into lunch (if they tuck in to anything more exciting than sports drinks and bananas) with easy minds. Then the script changed: against the run of the weather forecast, it began to rain. On came the covers and up went the umbrellas, and play was postponed. The afternoon proved to be a bit of a stop–start affair: they came back on after lunch for a few balls, adding 5 runs, but then disappeared again. When they re-emerged at 134 for one, it was not long before Tait made the breakthrough that Australia needed, but did not seem to expect. He bowled Trescothick for 65, knocking back the off stump, a significant first Test scalp. By the time he was out, Trescothick had overtaken Jacques Kallis as the leading Test run scorer of 2005, and also, more obscurely, had overtaken Trevor Bailey as the Englishman who has scored more runs against Australia without ever scoring a century. Trescothick's highest score in almost three full series against Australia remains his 90 at Edgbaston two games before, but he had now made 910 runs at an average of 33.70, with seven fifties but no centuries. Trescothick is a far better batsman than he was four years ago, and it remains a mystery why he has just one ODI century against Australia to show for his efforts.

There followed yet another rain break, which ran into tea at 146 for two. Only three overs and a ball were bowled between lunch and tea. During the tea break, 'Land of Hope and Glory' was sung by a tenor with the largest lungs north of Watford, drowning out all attempts at conversation, and probably giving the entire England team a splitting headache. When the teams came back out after the break, Bell was almost immediately caught behind off Tait. It was a good catch off a good-length ball. Bell had made only 3, and there were those around the ground who were wondering whether he quite had the game for Test cricket: what a pity that Graham Thorpe had packed up his cricket bag and gone home! Bell is without doubt a very talented batsman, but he has yet to learn the art of playing no shot at some deliveries. He very rarely plays and misses, and even more rarely decides not to play the ball that ought to be left alone outside the off stump. If he could perfect the leave, as lesser batsmen such as the third umpire in this match, Mark Benson, used to do for Kent, then he would make a great many more runs. His departure was the cue for the entry of Pietersen, back on the ground where he began his career in England, but where it would be fair to say he is not universally loved.

By the evening, the outfield was wet, and the Australians were keeping themselves in the game with some lucky breaks and energetic if somewhat inefficient fielding. Kasprowicz and Hayden were the main culprits of the inefficiency: Kasper missed a caught-and-bowled from Vaughan, and Hayden missed a sharp chance at backward point, also being for the benefit of Mr Vaughan. Pietersen really ought to have been run out by Hayden after a misunderstanding with Vaughan when the score was 197, and Kasprowicz might have caught the rainbow-haired man when he was on 14. Kasper was also the fielder who lost his footing on the wet outfield as Vaughan clipped the ball for what was eventually a four to bring up the 200. The boundary was getting more slippery and more dangerous to patrol. A few balls later and a clip off his toes off Lee brought Vaughan another fifty, and such was the state of Australia's bowling resources that Ricky Ponting decided it was time to bowl himself. Now this is a man with four wickets in 91 previous Tests, at a cost of 215 runs. A little better than Jason Gillespie in this series, but hardly enough to make hardened Test batsmen quake in their boots. He bowls medium-pace dobbers, hoping for a bit of in-swing, which on the basis of his early overs would have helped bring back his deliveries from very wide to merely wide. He even tried a bouncer, recorded at 77.5 miles per hour, against Vaughan, but the England captain was not to be tempted.

It was noticed that Shane Warne had not bowled since lunch, there seemed to be nothing sinister in this. The pudgy genius was fielding at slip as usual, but there was no sign that he was looking to turn his arm over. Tait and Ponting were the bowling attack, and Vaughan hit Tait towards the boundary, where Brett Lee slipped in making the stop and turned his tumble into an elegant long barrier from a sitting position. The boundary was saved. The score was now 213 for three. Then, incredible as it may seem, in the next over Vaughan played at a slightly less wide ball from Ponting, got a thin edge and feathered it to Gilchrist, who took a regulation catch. Vaughan, having made 58 of the most untroubled runs he will ever compile against Australia, was out. He could hardly believe his idiocy, and Ponting could hardly believe his brilliance. At 213 for four in the 56th over, honours were pretty well even, which should not have been the case after England won the toss.

Flintoff joined Pietersen to a huge cheer from the Trent Bridge crowd. This was the moment when, for me, it became absolutely obvious that Freddie Flintoff had become a genuine English sporting hero, rather than just a good cricketer with the right attitude. He has transcended partisan rivalry and although it would be stretching things to say that the Australians relish his cricket as much as the Brits, there is no doubt that even the Australians in the crowd will one day be happy to be able to say to their grandchildren, 'I saw Flintoff play.' By that time the keen memory of defeat may have faded. He is joining the ranks of Botham, Lillee, Compton, Sobers and others in the cricket pantheon, and in popular terms in England, is probably the biggest sporting name of 2005. Football skulks on the inside pages while cricket dominates the back page, a rare event which is largely brought about by the big smiling man from Preston.

By close of play, the two men with the Woodworm bats had brought the score to 229 for four without further alarms. Only 60 overs had been bowled during the day, a loss of one third of a day's play due to rain, and, as the *Daily Telegraph* headlined their report the next morning, England were 'left in limbo'.

Day 1, Close of Play:

England 229 for four wickets in 60 overs (Pietersen 33 not out, Flintoff 8 not out).

On the second day of the Trent Bridge Test, England took the game away from Australia. The weather was cool and cloudy, but there did not seem to be much chance of rain as Pietersen and Flintoff took up the cudgels once more against the Australians. Pietersen was the man wielding his cudgel most effectively for the first few overs, hitting two more fours and dominating the first seventeen minutes of play, making all 12 runs that were added in that time. However, seventeen minutes is hardly long enough when there is a whole day to bat, and when he got a little nick on a full pitched ball from Lee, which cut away and into Gilchrist's gloves, it did not seem to be good news for England. Certainly Australia were glad to see the back of Pietersen for 45, another innings that had promised much more, and then had ended short of expectation. Still, it would be carping to be hypercritical of KP's contribution to the Test series so far, and he must have been as disappointed at the brevity of his innings on Friday morning as any spectator.

Pietersen's departure brought in Geraint Jones, daring to take centre-stage on the ground where Chris Read is considered the only man good enough to keep wicket for England. It proved to be the making of England's victory. As a pair, Flintoff and Jones seem to like batting together. There is little similarity in their cricket or their characters, but they make batting look simple. Flintoff is the big man, usually sporting a couple of days' growth of beard, whose strength is obvious from first glance, and who frightens bowlers by his presence at the crease, and batsmen when he begins that deceptive run-up. Jones is of the Bob Taylor school of wicketkeeping, in his appearance at least. He is neat and compact: all wicketkeepers tend to be compact, but they either seem to be neat (Taylor, Jones, John Murray etc.) or shambolic and eccentric (Jack Russell, Alan Knott). Nobody normal takes up wicketkeeping, but the nearest to normality England have had recently would probably be Geraint Jones. Born of Welsh parentage in Papua New Guinea, the only Test cricketer to date to be born there, he was raised in Queensland and came to Wales a decade or so back to seek his cricketing fortune. He failed to be offered a contract by Glamorgan, but they recommended him to Kent, that home county of great wicketkeepers, and within a season he had usurped Paul Nixon in the county side. Within a further year, he had ousted Chris Read from the England side. It was his batting that earned him his place there, because nobody pretended he was as good a 'keeper as the Nottinghamshire man. A century in only his third Test cemented his place in the side. Critics of his wicketkeeping remained, getting more vociferous with every bye, every missed catch or fluffed stumping. But the baby-faced Jones (29 going on 16) carried on regardless, and at the start of the Ashes series had actually made more dismissals in his first fifteen Tests than either Knott or Taylor.

The Australians, having let it drift a bit on the first day, and sensing an opportunity with the dismissal of Pietersen so early in the morning session, set attacking fields and quickly reintroduced Warne into the attack. Silly point and a slip hovered around the batsmen, but Flintoff showed his intentions by hitting Warne back over his head for four. In truth, it was a mishit, not at all off the meat of the bat, but with Flintoff, half a hit is bigger than most people's full-blooded drives. It was still a good batting wicket, and as the morning session wore on, the sun came out. The Australians were unable to make another breakthrough and slipped ever so quietly back into their shells. Kasprowicz bowled with no slips, and the batsmen found runs to be there for the taking.

The difference between Jones and Read when they bat is that Jones thinks like a batsman, because he is a batsman, whereas Read thinks like a wicketkeeper who may well sometimes stick around for a long while, or bask in a century against a county attack. Read always knows his main value to the side is as a 'keeper, but Jones knows he is valued equally highly for both strings to his bow. He may not always get them both right, but he is a true all-rounder, as Alec Stewart was by the end of his career, and Adam Gilchrist certainly is, but Chris Read is not. Whether Jones is yet a great all-rounder is another debate, but his batting partner Freddie Flintoff was blossoming into one with every ball. The fifty partnership came up in just 42 minutes.

Flintoff was playing very correctly, scoring his runs through his wonderful timing rather than by the use of bat as bludgeon. His shots are beautiful to behold, if less attractive to field against. Many Australians were wringing their hands regularly throughout the big man's innings as they felt the power of his shots. After only 70 minutes of the morning's play, the 300 was up as Jones swept Warne for 2. A strong position was now being established, and the longer they batted the more the game was being taken away from the Australians. Although Geoffrey Boycott in the commentary box was certain that anything fewer than 400 was a poor total on this pitch, Warne was not at this stage bowling particularly well. When this fact was taken together with his absence from the bowling crease for practically all of the after-lunch sessions the day before, the question had to be asked: was Warne fully fit? Were his back and his shoulder playing up? The English partisans could only hope so.

Flintoff pressed the point by sweeping Warne superbly for six to bring up his fifty, and the pair made untroubled progress. Ponting took the new ball at the earliest opportunity, giving it to Shaun Tait, but that hardly stemmed the flow of runs. Jones hit the first delivery through extra cover for four. Lee at the other end looked a little more dangerous, getting a little bit of swing, and moving it off the seam as well. When a bowler can do this consistently at 95 miles per hour, he becomes a difficult proposition. But Flintoff was not to be deterred. One back-foot push-drive straight back past Lee for four was almost the shot of the day – 'almost' only because he hit so many fine shots during his innings that it is hard to say which was the best. Certainly the Australians had no answer. Another over from Tait added 13 to the total, a single from Jones off the first ball followed by three fours by Flintoff – a pull over midwicket, a straight drive just to the off side of the bowler, and another crashing shot through midwicket. Tait was having to learn about Test cricket very quickly. Lee at the other end gave Jones a tough workout, once just failing to trap him leg before by virtue of a faint inside edge on to the pad, and once jagging one back over the top of middle stump, between Jones' body and his bat. At least the Australian plague of no-balls from the day before seemed to have dried up.

The hundred partnership came up in 126 balls, after only 83 minutes, just before a quarter past twelve. This was rollicking stuff and all but the eleven Australians chasing the ball around Trent Bridge seemed to be enjoying it thoroughly. By lunch, after Kasprowicz had been brought

The uncomplicated power of Flintoff's play.

back into the attack following just three overs of Shaun Tait, the score was 344 for five. In 29 overs, England had added 115 runs for the loss of just one wicket. Definitely England's morning.

The very first ball after lunch was a good one from Lee outside Jones' off stump. Jones wafted rather uncertainly and there was a huge and unanimous appeal from the Australians. Not out. And for the next few overs, the batsmen took full toll of the bowling. In the first four overs after the lunch break 38 runs were scored. A quickly run single off Brett Lee gave Jones his fifty. This was Jones' fourth Test fifty, and in many ways his most valuable. Even the reintroduction of Warne did nothing to slow down the run-rate. His first ball was a full toss to Jones, which so surprised him that he failed to take advantage. However, to the next ball he jumped out and hit it straight past the bowler for four. Jones had obviously been studying Flintoff's methods. The 150 partnership came up after only 187 balls, a rate of almost five an over. Australia without McGrath find it very hard to retain control over batsmen who are not afraid to take the attack to them, especially on as good a wicket as this one. The bowling was poor, the outcricket sloppy. This was not a world champion performance, far from it, and England took the fullest advantage.

The 400 came up, with still only five wickets down. Flintoff was nearing his century, his first against Australia, and as if to make it easier for him, Ponting brought back Tait for an over or two. Ponting had not given himself a bowl, despite his success the previous day, nor Simon Katich with his left-arm chinamen, nor Michael Clarke with a Test best analysis of six for 9. The new ball was only twelve overs old, but Tait was bowling with just one slip. That said it all – this fast bowling attack was virtually toothless.

Warne managed to bowl a maiden to Flintoff when he was on 99, and Tait followed up immediately with another to Jones. In the next over from Warne, Flintoff nudged the first ball into the leg side and took the single that brought up his hundred. The crowd stood and cheered, and cheered and cheered. This was a truly great innings, perhaps a match-winning one, and it marked the first time that Flintoff has trusted himself as a batsman to play orthodox shots, albeit very powerful orthodox shots, rather than just hitting through the line and into the stratosphere. His century contained fourteen fours and a six, so it was hardly a Thorpe-like 'nudge and nurdle' display, but a performance of great skill and responsibility. And he smiled all the way through it. He has this perpetual air of somebody who cannot quite believe how good he is, that the things he tries so often bring successes. He is a happy cricketer and it rubs off on to his team-mates and on to the crowds, who simply adore him.

Sadly, the fun did not last much longer. After the pair had added 177 for the sixth wicket, easily the highest partnership of the series for either side so far, Flintoff was deceived by a good ball from Tait, and umpire Steve Bucknor, he of the lingering death, thought about it and then raised his finger. It was, in truth, a good decision, but it ended Flintoff's innings on 102. Another standing ovation accompanied him all the way back to the pavilion. The partnership had done what the Australians, usually with Gilchrist at the forefront, are so good at doing to their opponents. It took the initiative firmly away from the fielding side just when they thought they had a chance of restricting the batting side to a reasonable total. Hopes that had been built up a bit were totally dashed. The Australians were having to learn to take some of their own medicine. As Adam Gilchrist said at the end of the day, 'England are doing to us what we've been doing to other teams for years.' There is no higher praise than that.

It was a little murkier now, and rather more chilly, and not just because Flintoff was back in the pavilion. Geraint Jones carried on with Ashley Giles as his partner, and it looked as though he too would have a hundred to celebrate. However, with the total on 450 and his personal score at 85, Jones misjudged a ball from Kasprowicz and nicked it hard on to his pad as he went forward to play a forcing shot. The impetus of his forward movement helped the ball to loop towards silly mid-on, where Kasprowicz, following through, dived to his right and took a good caught-and-bowled. Giles followed two balls later on the same total, leg before to Shane Warne. Now the England innings was going through the last rites.

Harmison managed to get himself rather comically stumped by Gilchrist off Warne, the big fast bowler falling in an ungainly heap as the bails were whipped off, and it was left to Hoggard and Simon Jones to add another 23 for the last wicket, Jones smiting three fours in his 15. He is a better batsman than Harmison any day. Only seniority allows Harmy the number ten slot rather than number eleven, where he probably belongs. Jones did, however, have one lucky let-off when he was bowled by Lee, off his pads, only to watch as the stumps rattled but the bails did not drop. This was the third or fourth time this had happened in the series: somebody is putting the stumps in too firmly. I suspect the Stumpcam Man. When Hoggard was caught by Gilchrist, also off Warne, 6 runs later, the England innings ended and tea was immediately taken.

A score of 477 all out was a substantial one, even by Geoffrey Boycott's standards, and England should have been reasonably confident as they came out again after tea. Harmison was given first use of the ball and it went as straight as a die, and as fast as a bullet, for the first few overs. Hoggard at the other end was exploring the possibilities of a little swing. The rumours had abounded, possibly based on some circumstantial evidence, that the rebuilding of Trent Bridge, and especially the big new Radcliffe Road Stand and the elegant Fox Road Stand, had created a micro-climate within the ground that encouraged the ball to swing. Well, who knows. All we can say with certainty is that Matthew Hayden struggled gamely for nine overs, making 7 runs before he was completely beaten by a lovely little inswinger from Hoggard to be plumb lbw. Twenty for one wicket was exactly the start England wanted.

Hayden's failure added to the pressure on him: the odds on him continuing his opening partnership with Langer beyond this series were lengthening all the time. Ponting's failure in the very next over was very unfortunate. Given out leg before to Simon Jones for a single, there was television evidence of a thin inside edge which should have saved him. By this time Jones was building up a head of steam and he was a handful: doubtful umpiring decisions were not what the Australians needed on top of the rest of their troubles. It got worse: Damien Martyn, whose series was as unlucky as it was anonymous, got a big inside edge on to his pad in Hoggard's next over, but umpire Aleem Dar, usually a brilliant umpire, raised the finger. At 22 for three, Australia's first innings was broken.

Michael Clarke, bad back apparently completely cured, came in to join Justin Langer, and they tried to patch together some sort of stand that might repair the worst of the damage. His stroke-play was from the outset much more confident and exciting to watch than that of any of his seniors above him in the order. Hoggard was a huge challenge. He did not need the help of the umpires (which he got) to keep the Australian batsmen shuffling about nervously in their crease trying to cope with his swing. For the first time this series, Hoggard was a real handful, and the Trent Bridge crowd were backing him all the way. Hoggard is such an appealing guy – he is as friendly and as open as he looks, which is something that cannot be said about his bowling. When conditions suit him, he is probably the best orthodox swing bowler in the world, and at Trent Bridge the conditions suited him. He was asked later whether he thought the new stands at Trent Bridge had helped his swing. He replied that he did not know, but he hoped they would build new stands at all the grounds he plays at.

After an extended period of defensive field settings when England were batting, it was good to see Vaughan taking every attacking option. They did not always work, but at no stage in the after-tea session did Vaughan allow the batsmen to relax. They had to think their runs as well as hit them. As a unit, his fast bowlers worked together superbly. Hoggard and Jones may have been the main threats with their swing, but Flintoff and Harmison were no easy touches either. Flintoff bowled three more no-balls, a worrying aspect of his bowling that will need to be

Hoggard had a great match at Trent Bridge – Vaughan shares his delight.

addressed sometime after his golden summer is over, but the Aussies never felt comfortable up against him. Who would?

Just as Australia were hoping that the Langer–Clarke partnership would flourish, when it had added 36 in eight overs, Hoggard struck again. In his tenth over of the spell, he swung one just a little more than Langer was expecting, and he nicked a chance to short-leg, where Bell took a good catch. The scoring rate was still pretty fast, as you would expect from these Australians, but the total was not high enough. At 58 for four, the position was looking very bleak. Simon Katich came in and was almost dismissed first ball. He played the ball firmly towards Bell, who instinctively got a hand to it, but it did not stick. It was no more than half a chance. Only a real stickler would classify it as a drop.

Clarke and Katich, the junior members of this batting order, found themselves once again in the position of having to dig their side out of a hole, a job that they have done once very successfully, at Lord's, and on other occasions for less return on their efforts. This was to be a middling effort: on what proved to be the last ball of the day, Clarke misjudged the pace of Harmison and was leg before. England's fourth lbw of the afternoon was a fair decision, but if Australia had any complaints about the umpiring, they ought first to explain to their batsmen that pads in front of stumps are only a good idea if the bat regularly gets in the way between ball and pad: little edges and nicks can easily be missed when the ball is zeroing in on the stumps at 90 miles per hour or more, and umpires are only human.

So the day ended with Australia very much on the back foot at 99 for five. Hoggard had taken three for 32 in eleven overs, and – perhaps the major surprise – nobody found anything to criticise about Geraint Jones' wicketkeeping. England strode off the pitch a happy side.

Day 2, Close of Play:

England 477 all out.

Australia 99 for five wickets in 30.3 overs (Katich 20 not out).

The third day, Saturday, dawned fine. The weather was definitely better than on Friday, but still not without the risk of showers. The crowds flocked to the ground in full costume, as is becoming the norm on the Saturday of a Test match, especially against Australia. A quick glance around the throngs coming through the gates enabled me to spot a gang of Hannibal Lecters, all fully masked up and only now wondering how they were going to get anything to eat and drink all day; a herd of Father Christmasses, minus reindeer and sacks of toys, several Elvisses, and my favourites, a group of Spanish cardinals in full red costumes with birettas and crucifixes, standing around enjoying a pre-match pint. When they got to their seats in the Parr stand, they unfurled a banner, reading, 'Nobody Expects The King Of Spain', a suitable combination of Monty Python and Ashley Giles worship that summed up the mood of the crowd: were we daft to be so optimistic?

It was on the Saturday morning that I attempted to solve one of the great mysteries of the summer, the Nobok Question. Throughout the summer, there had been one advertisement hoarding around the grounds that had been baffling me. There always is: one year it was Durox Supablocks, which turned out to be some kind of building material, and another year it was the big message at Lord's 'Locate In Wales'. That particular advertising campaign never quite got going. In 2005, the simple word 'Nobok' was the message, sometimes accompanied by the extra piece of information, 'Sporting Legends' and a picture of Sir Bobby Robson. I thought of the Edward Lear rhyme about the Akond of Swat. 'Who or why or which or what / is the Akond of Swat?' Who or why or which or what were Nobok? During the first three Tests, several explanations were given. It was a make of sports shoe, like Reebok, only not Reebok. It was an anti-South African organisation, trying to keep the Boks out of Britain. Or it was a misprint for a contraceptive manufacturer, Nobonk. None of these answers seemed very likely. As I was walking behind the Radcliffe Road End with my cousin Bill on our way to our seats in the Larwood and Voce Stand, I noticed an office with the word 'Nobok' on the door, and a helpful looking young lady standing there. Ever one to seize the opportunity, I asked her to explain what Nobok meant.

She did. She gave us five minutes of sales patter about the company she represented, and I did not understand a word. I got the phrase 'mobile phone' in there, and 'sporting legends' which I already knew, but the rest could have been in Swahili for all it meant to me. 'You did very well there,' said Bill. 'At no stage could she tell from your expression that you had no idea what she was talking about. But I'm glad you didn't ask a supplementary question.' Nobok remains a riddle wrapped in a mystery inside an enigma behind the Radcliffe Road End.

Gilchrist came in with Katich at the start of the day's play. There had been some doubt as Brett Lee, the nightwatchman, had stepped on to the field of play the night before when Clarke was out, but it was ruled that the umpires had already lifted the bails for close of play, so Lee had not started his innings after all. Gilchrist, as only he can, set about the bowling with gusto. It is difficult to find different words to describe a Gilchrist innings. They are always rapid and devastating while they last, but England this summer had limited him to brief rations, and the hope was that they could do so again. Gilchrist was not thinking of defence or defeat. He took 22 off a Hoggard over which included two no-balls, three fours and a six: no playing himself in, no adjusting to the light, just pure attack. It is the sort of thing that can put a side off its stride.

But this time his onslaught did not. Vaughan was not intimidated by Gilchrist, and did not remove Hoggard from the attack immediately. He persevered for another over, with Flintoff also taking more stick than usual at the other end, and the runs flowed freely. After half an hour's play, when many of the bewigged spectators were still settling into their seats, the score had moved on to 147 for five, in a mere 6.3 overs. The fifty partnership followed, in 46 balls. Hoggard came out of the attack and Simon Jones took over.

As he tends to do, Jones took a wicket in the first over of his spell. Katich hit the ball to gully, where Strauss took a straightforward catch. That was 157 for six, and the cue for Shane Warne to come in to bat, fresh from his two fine innings at Old Trafford. His first ball was shorter than he expected, he sparred at it, got a leading edge and dollied the ball to Bell at short cover. 157 for seven. Brett Lee, another overachiever with the bat at Old Trafford, was the next man in. He staved off the hat-trick, but for a couple of overs was extremely uncomfortable. Flintoff hit him, as Flintoff has become used to doing, and against Simon Jones poor Lee could not get bat on ball. If only Gilchrist could be winkled out, the innings would surely soon be over.

Gilchrist was winkled out by one of the most astounding catches of even this astounding season. He played hard – as if he wouldn't – at a ball from Flintoff, but did not quite get to it. The ball flew off towards an empty third slip position. Strauss, at second slip, saw the ball out of the corner of his eye and launched himself to his left to take the catch one-handed while flying horizontally through the air. The ball stuck, and Gilchrist was out. With the obvious exception of Pietersen, England's fielders were holding their catches.

At this point, 163 for eight after only 42 overs, the Nottinghamshire management were probably the only unhappy Englishmen in the ground. What if the match did not go into a fourth day? What would that do to club funds? As dark clouds gathered beyond the Radcliffe Road, they seemed to represent the only chance of prolonging the game. The prospect of rain was all that lightened the committee room gloom, a gloom thickened by cigar smoke emanating from Kenneth Clarke MP, the cricket-loving former president of the county club, who was to announce his candidacy for the leadership of the Conservative Party the next day.

When Simon Jones produced one that was far too good for Mike Kasprowicz, and took his off stump, the score was 175 for nine and it was still not midday. 'They're bound to lose,' said Cousin Bill. 'It's just a matter of when.' At this point, with the debutant Tait making his way to the wicket, something obviously clicked in Brett Lee's mind. Almost at once he hit a good-length ball from Steve Harmison way over our heads in the Larwood and Voce Stand, and out into Fox Road and beyond. It was a vast hit, right out of the meat of his bat, one of the biggest sixes I have ever seen. In the next over, he did it again, a hit to the other side of the ground off Simon Jones, and then in the next over, he reproduced his huge hit against poor old Harmy, and the ball sailed once more into the Fox Road. Through it all, Lee was smiling hugely. Harmison was less amused. At least with all the roughing up the ball was getting, it should help Jones' reverse swing. The 200 came up at eleven minutes to midday. In 79 minutes we had seen 101 runs and four wickets go down. By five past twelve we had seen a fifth, as Lee top edged another big hit off Jones down to Ian Bell, who ran along the third-man boundary to take a tidy catch. Lee made 47 in 44 balls, and Australia were all out for 218, 259 behind England. Simon Jones had taken five wickets for 44 runs in 14 overs and one ball. Oh, and Geraint Jones had not conceded a single bye.

There was some debate around the boundary ropes as to whether Vaughan would ask Australia to follow on, what with Warne in the fourth innings and all that, but England had taken the attacking option every time in this series, and they could not start playing safe now. Australia were asked to follow on, the first time this had happened to them for 191 Tests, since the First Test against Pakistan in Karachi in September 1988, Ian Healy's first Test. It was the first time England had enforced the follow-on against Australia since the Bicentennial Test at Sydney in February 1988, and the first time in an Ashes Test since the First Test at Brisbane in November 1986. Mike Gatting, the England captain on those two previous occasions, was there to watch Michael Vaughan join that very exclusive club.

By lunch, Australia had reached 14 for no wicket, with Langer on 9 and Hayden on 5. Simon Jones had opened the bowling with Hoggard, forcing Harmison to bowl first change for once. The ball was swinging, and Vaughan very naturally gave it to the two who could take most advantage of that fact. As a captain, Vaughan was showing a shrewdness that Ponting could not match. Ever since he put England into bat at Edgbaston, Ponting's captaincy was under close scrutiny and even though there were no major errors to point to, there were no clever tactical manoeuvres either, apart from the few overs he gave himself in England's first innings in this Test.

After lunch, Simon Jones did not appear. Instead, Durham's left-handed batsman Gary Pratt acted as twelfth man. This was to have several important implications for the match and the series. The Nottinghamshire Committee were no doubt cheered up by the absence of England's leading bowler in Australia's first innings, as this would certainly stretch the game into a fourth day. Cousin Bill was slightly more worried about whether this would stretch the match into a fifth day: he had a lunchtime barbecue planned. Against a three-man attack of Hoggard,

Flintoff and Harmison, Langer and Hayden battled towards 50, which they reached in the thirteenth over. In the next over, with the score still at fifty, Hayden gave the slips more practice, and Giles held on. Hayden looked out of sorts throughout his innings, not timing anything well, apart from the occasional loose delivery, which he duly punished. His 26 contained four fours. There are those who seek to class Hayden a mere flat-track bully, international successor to Graeme Hick, and their case was bolstered by his performance in the first four Tests. He is a much better player than his recent Test statistics show, but it is a long time – sixteen Tests – since he last scored a century.

Australia then, at last, began to make steady progress in chipping away at this mighty lead of 259. Ricky Ponting came out to join Langer and played another determined second-innings knock. Before this series, Ponting's first-innings average in Ashes Tests was more than double that of his second-innings average. A first-innings average of 52 is fine, but 23.5 in the second innings is less wonderful. In 2005, Ponting began to reverse the statistics, his Old Trafford century being the defining second-innings knock of the series. Now he set about saving the game for Australia, ably assisted by Justin Langer. Slowly, or at least slowly by modern Test standards and at a positive crawl by Australian Test standards, the partnership grew. At 80, Strauss proved he was a mortal by dropping a fairly straightforward chance given by Langer off Flintoff, but otherwise there were no alarms. The 100 was passed, at five to three, and as if on cue, the King Of Spain was brought into the attack for the first time in the match, cheered on by the conclave of cardinals in the Parr stand.

An excellent shot of Langer's second-innings dismissal. Bell took important catches at short-leg throughout the series.

Five minutes later the surrealism of the occasion was hammered home when, with Australia following on and a gangly man from Chertsey known as the King Of Spain bowling left-arm finger-spin into the rough at Justin Langer, Mike Gatting suddenly popped up on the boundary to present a prize for the best fancy dress to three Dame Edna Everages, complete with glasses and gladioli. Is this what the last Ashes-winning captain of England is reduced to? Is there no respect for the greats of our game? And why didn't the cardinals win, anyway? I suspect a few phone calls to Indian bookmakers took place before the result was announced.

That, thankfully, took us to tea, at 115 for one. Langer had just reached his fifty, and Ponting was on 28. England were still very much in the driving seat, but another wicket would be welcome. It came soon after tea, when Langer was caught by Bell, his fourth catch of the match, at short leg off Giles. 129 for two, a useful partnership of 79. Australia had still managed only one century partnership all series, the 155 Clarke and Martyn added at Lord's in the second innings. Langer's departure was a crisis for Australia, but Ponting's was a disaster. Damien Martyn, the new batsman, had helped his captain to add 24 in ten overs – real dour stuff this – when he called for a quick single to the substitute Gary Pratt, fielding at cover. Ponting took off like a startled hare, but still could not beat Pratt's excellent pick up and throw, and he was run out by a yard, and Australia were 155 for three.

As Ponting returned to the pavilion, he aimed a stream of invective at the England team balcony, a précis of which would show that he felt England were not playing fair in their use of substitutes, the assumption being that Jones, if he had still been on the field and not, as was the case, in hospital having a scan on his ankle, would have missed the run-out. Pratt is one of the best fielders on the county circuit. The matter rumbled on and on, resulting in Ponting being fined 75 per cent of his match fee by referee Ranjan Madugalle, and a continued exchange of press releases between the English and Australian camps. Ponting apologised for his outburst, but also said, 'My frustration was compounded by the fact that I was run out by a substitute, an issue we raised before the series began.'

Duncan Fletcher, in an interview, said, 'What were we supposed to do? Jones was off looking after his ankle, and I don't think we could have gone on with ten men. If you want to take a run to the cover fielder and get run out, whose fault is that?' The answer, to most of us round the ground, was Damien Martyn, who made the call. We all agreed that he needed to keep his head down and grind out a big score, not only for the team but also to keep out of his captain's way for an hour or two.

The issue of substitutes is a tricky one. In the playing regulations, substitutes are only allowed in case of injury, or if the umpires give their approval. The habit of going off to change a shirt or make a phone call or have a rub down after a long spell of bowling has been going on for years. On the county circuit in the 1970s and 1980s it was known as 'doing a Z', after the great Pakistan and Gloucestershire batsman Zaheer Abbas, who did not enjoy fielding. The Australians were past masters at it, with Lillee and Thomson going off for a shower and a change of shirt whenever they felt they needed it. The West Indians in their great days did it too. It is simply a tactic to keep bowlers fresh and the best possible eleven fielders on the field.

As long as the umpires tolerate this practice, fielding captains will exploit it to the full, but it is not something that endears cricketers to the paying public. Ponting was right to complain about it, although it is not just England who are guilty. Added to the endless drinks breaks and twelfth men running on and off the pitch with bottles every time a wicket falls, the whole process makes a mockery of the stamina factor which is meant to be part of cricket.

It seems to me that there is a solution. If the playing conditions for Test matches were to state that a fielder can go off the field for any reason at any time, but that no substitute will be allowed for the first three overs of his absence, this would cut the shirt-changers down at a stroke. The Laws applying to when a player would be permitted to bat and bowl again after being off the field would continue as now. It might be unfair in the case of a genuine injury (as was the case with Simon Jones) but if it is invoked equally for both sides, then playing with ten men for three overs is a small price to pay for some return to sanity in the use of substitutes. I see no problem in scouring the countryside for your best fielder to act as substitute. That has always been the prerogative of selectors, but if we can keep the sub off the field except when one of the team is genuinely injured, it would help the image and the fairness of Test cricket. It might also force a few players to work on their fielding skills, but that is another issue. In this instance, even under my new proposal, Pratt would have been on for Jones, and Ponting would have been out, but we would not also have had Trevor Penney on for Flintoff, Pietersen and even Vaughan at one time. Do they all have weak bladders? Why do you never see a wicketkeeper who needs to take a break? Because substitute wicketkeepers are not allowed, that's why. The ten-men-for-three-overs rule has, in my view, much to commend it.

The rest of the day revolved first of all around Martyn snicking the ball to Geraint Jones just two overs later, when he had made only 13, and having to face his captain's wrath, poor chap. It was the over after Ian Bell came on to bowl. Vaughan was a bowler down and had seen what Ponting did to him in the first innings and wanted to see if Bell could do the same. I had the strong impression that Jones the Gloves had never seen Bell bowl before, as he stood up to him for several balls, before glancing over to the big screen and seeing his speed recorded at 74 miles per hour. He then retreated to a sensible distance behind the stumps. (To be fair, it might also have been something to do with Bell going round or over the wicket to the left- and right-handers).

Clarke and Katich found themselves back in the same pickle they had been in together 24 hours earlier, hanging on for the sake of Australia. They battled on to the 200, to the fifty partnership and eventually to the end of the day's play. Clarke was still there only because Jones missed a stumping chance – it was more than a chance really, it was a gift – on 212. When bad light stopped play a few overs early, the score was 222, double Nelson.

Day 3, Close of Play:

England 477 all out.

Australia 218 all out and, following on, 222 for four wickets in 67 overs (Clarke 39 not out, Katich 24 not out).

There seemed to be little doubt that the fourth day would be the final day of the Test. Even the Nottinghamshire committee were resigned to that. What's more, it looked as though England would canter home. After all, Australia were still 37 runs behind England with only six wickets in hand, and even with the decent track record of their lower order, Australia were unlikely to set a target of more than, say, 150, which would be easy pickings for England.

Michael Clarke and Simon Katich continued their overnight partnership with extreme caution. It was as though, after three and a half Tests of slugging it out at breakneck speed, the Australians suddenly realised that Test cricket is supposed to be played at 2, rather than 5, runs per over. The two men played every ball on its merits, or on the merits they feared in their worst nightmares it might possess. No chances were taken, no chances given. The score mounted slowly, but inexorably. Without Simon Jones, whose ankle injury was now seen to be something more than just an excuse to get a substitute on to the field, the attack lacked the bite it had in Australia's first innings, and the remaining bowlers were tiring. Twenty-nine overs were bowled before lunch, a very respectable rate, but only 48 runs were added. This was Test cricket at its most attritional, and Australia should have gone into lunch slightly happier, having knocked off the deficit and forced England to bat again. Unfortunately, they did not compile those 48 runs without losing a wicket, for Clarke wafted at a fairly innocuous delivery from Hoggard and nicked a catch through to Jones the Gloves a couple of overs before the interval. It was his only mistake. The pair had added exactly one hundred, and Clarke had made 56 from 170 balls, with only six fours, a very uncharacteristic Clarke innings. Adam Gilchrist came in determined to raise the scoring rate.

At lunch, Australia were 270 for five. Gilchrist came out after the break with his bat swinging, as usual, but also as usual in this series, he did not last long. Eleven runs in eleven balls was his lot, before Hoggard trapped him leg before. That left the innings in shreds, just 18 ahead with only four wickets remaining. Warne and Katich set about prolonging the agony. It was still slow going at Katich's end, as the dogged left-hander moved past his fifty, while at the other end Warne was following the Gilchrist method, and swinging his bat at almost everything. He hit Flintoff for three boundaries in one over, showing the full repertoire of cut, pull and drive. Warne's batting has improved so much he is virtually an all-rounder these days. It is bad luck for him and Australia that the batsmen are not making any runs above him, and that he is in the twilight of his career.

Opposite: Hoggard ends the stubborn partnership between Clarke and Gilchrist. Jones takes the catch behind.

One of the symptoms of Australia's plight was their poor running between the wickets. We had already seen Ponting run out, because of what was basically a poor call, and Clarke and Katich had a few close calls, especially when Flintoff missed a run-out chance that he probably would have taken seven times out of ten. Warne was also taking chances, and Katich was not reading his partner's mind very successfully.

Fielding all around the world has improved so much since the massive growth of one-day cricket, to the extent that run-out opportunities that fifty years ago would have been considered impossible, or flukes at best, are now seen as missed chances if the fielder does not hit. Similarly, fielders are getting their hands to catches they might have avoided in an earlier age: now people are accused of dropping catches which are no more than quarter chances. Is a missed run-out any less important than a dropped half-chance or a missed stumping?

Katich's fine knock was ended courtesy of the most dubious leg before decision of them all, when Aleem Dar adjudged that Harmison's delivery would have hit Katich's stumps. At least there was no bat involved, but the ball clearly pitched outside leg stump, and looked high. The TV replay confirmed that suspicion. Katich, one of the mildest men in world cricket, was livid when he saw the replay as he walked off the pitch. He launched a torrent of 'verbal abuse' at anybody within earshot as he stormed back to the pavilion, and forfeited a chunk of his match fee to referee Madugalle. It was a very poor decision, and Katich had reason to be angry, but not to show it. It was England's sixth lbw decision of the match, of which three were shown to be doubtful with the benefit of slow-motion replays. It might have been the decision that won the match.

Brett Lee, smiling as ever, came in and was dropped second ball by Geraint Jones, diving in front of Trescothick at first slip. Oh dear. Ashley Giles was brought back into the attack at the Radcliffe Road End, and Shane Warne hit his first ball for six over long-on, and the third ball for four more. Before the over was out, Giles had had a big leg before appeal turned down, and while everybody was engrossed in what looked like a good shout, the ball ricocheted out to Strauss at backward point and Lee and Warne set off for a run. Strauss threw well at the stumps, but Jones, still looking at umpire Bucknor for the lbw appeal, suddenly realised that the ball was homing in on him and as he went to take it, his glove broke the stumps. Lee scraped home. The umpires at first called for the third umpire to check the incident, but Jones, to his credit, went straight to the umpires and explained that he had not made the run-out. In fact, the miss was much less significant than it appeared. The throw from Strauss would not have hit the stumps directly anyway, so Lee would have been home. That did not stop some of the more vindictive cricket writers having yet another go at Jones the next morning.

The pace of progress by the Australians picked up. Warne flat-batted Giles for another six, but perished two balls later. He was stumped by Jones, a smart if routine piece of work. Kasprowicz came in and laid about him from the word go, so Giles' over was eventually worth one for 16. It had taken only 51 balls to get from 300 to 350. At 373 for eight, Pietersen dropped Kasprowicz at midwicket. This was Pietersen's sixth dropped catch out of six in the series, an amazing statistic for a man who is a very good fielder. He made a good run-out at Lord's, but otherwise had proved a liability in the field. Every time he stopped the ball, it seemed to involve falling over.

That particular drop was not expensive. A couple of balls later, Kasper edged one to Jones, and he was gone for 19. Tait, the new man, had added 43 with Lee in the first innings, but he showed no inclination whatsoever to get into line against Harmison. The pair played with luck for a few more overs – Flintoff hit Lee's stumps, but yet again the bails did not fall, and Tait got four through the slips from a very fast Harmison delivery. Tait's dismissal, clean bowled walking rapidly towards point, was comical, but it was another wicket for Harmy. Australia all out 387, and England needed 129 to win.

The England camp must have thought it was straightforward. But of course it would prove otherwise.

We were treated to about 25 minutes of free and easy strokeplay from Trescothick, who obviously imagined he could win it on his own. Kasprowicz went for 19 in two overs and Lee was hardly more economical. So Ponting did the only thing he could – he brought Shane Warne into the attack after just four overs. And of course the ploy worked. With his first ball,

Pietersen dives to make his crease.

he had Trescothick caught by the captain himself for 27, and England were 32 for one. Well, that was a quarter of the way to the target, so no cause for panic.

Michael Vaughan chose this moment not to play a captain's innings. Before he was off the mark, he tried to turn a Warne leg-break to leg, and it took the edge of his bat to give Hayden at slip an easy catch. 36 for two. Ian Bell came in, and with Strauss he tried to make steady progress towards their target. In six overs they added another 21 runs, but then Strauss tried to clip Warne to leg, but only hit it to Clarke, who took a very low catch. Strauss waited until a replay showed the ball had carried, having decided not to take the fielder's word for it. In both innings, Strauss had managed subtly to dispute his dismissal, but both times accepted the final decision without demur. Fifty-seven for three, with Warne having all three wickets for 7 runs in five overs.

Bell did not outlast his partner by much. He swatted the first ball of the next over, from Lee, to backward square leg, where Kasprowicz took the catch gratefully. Now it was 57 for four. Bell had had a bad game, despite his four catches. Why was Thorpe not in the side? England were still only 44 per cent of the way to victory, with 40 per cent of the wickets gone. Surely Australia could not win? At home, people started hiding behind sofas or going off to do the washing up, rather than watch the drama unfold on television. Over eight million tuned in to those final overs, the biggest audience Channel Four had ever known for cricket, and bigger even than their *Big Brother* viewing figures. This was reality television at its most real.

Pietersen and Flintoff were now at the wicket, so surely all would be well. KP played with a lot of bottom hand, as always. Huge cheers greeted Flintoff, as always. He edged his second ball through gully for four. After sixteen overs, the score was up to 65, and Lee, who had bowled eight overs on the trot, was rested. Tait took his place at the Radcliffe Road End, and went for 8 runs in his first over, including a Pietersen four over Gilchrist's head. Every shot was now being greeted with an 'ooh' from the crowd, and shouts of 'catch it' from the Australian fielders, even the shots that went all along the ground. Warne was tying up one end success-fully, but Tait could not prevent Flintoff and Pietersen bringing England closer to their target. Warne had one good leg before appeal against Flintoff turned down by Aleem Dar, which Flintoff reacted to by promptly hitting Warne for a big four over long-on. There was a tricky moment as the third umpire was consulted when Katich's throw hit the stumps at the bowler's end, but Pietersen was in. The tension mounted, and Freddie called for another drink. Tait had gone for 24 in four overs. It was a haemorrhage too far for Australia. The Barmy Army stepped up their singing: they knew the match was won.

Pietersen had other ideas. He had made 23, and added 46 with Flintoff, but had never really looked secure. It will be interesting to see whether KP has what it takes for a long career in Test cricket, because on the evidence of his first summer in the team, he does not cope with pres-sure very well. He has a huge natural talent, but on this occasion he was playing sweeps and missing, aiming at Lee outside off stump with equal lack of accuracy and generally abandoning common sense. One should not quibble with a man who makes a fifth of the runs required, but he gave the impression of a balloon about to burst with every ball. Twenty-three was

Lee and Flintoff gave each other no quarter on the pitch. Lee bowls Flintoff here with a lightning off-cutter.

obviously his limit, because as soon as Lee came back into the attack, Pietersen was gone, edging the first ball to Gilchrist. One hundred and three for five, and the nerves were back. A drinks break did not help the watching millions settle their nerves. It was now 5.45 p.m. Would the game not be over today after all? A friend rang to say he was cleaning up dog mess in his garden rather than watch the cricket: displacement activity was resulting in clean homes and gardens all around Britain.

Lee bowled a rocket at the new batsman, Jones, which was timed at 96 miles per hour. Yet there were no slips, so perhaps Jones should have edged it rather than left it. The discussions between overs got progressively longer. England were still 18 short of their goal when the score reached 111. Tactics be damned, it was the curse of Nelson that helped Australia at this point, as Lee bowled an absolute peach to take Flintoff's off stump. The hope of England gone for 26! A hundred and eleven for six: a breathless hush as the next man came in, Ashley Giles, not only the King of Spain but also Warne's bunny. What hope for England now? The tension had risen beyond even Old Trafford levels, although whether it had reached the heart-attack heights of Edgbaston was debatable. The only calm people seemed to be on the pitch. They at least had some control over their own destinies: we spectators did not.

Lee's first ball to Giles is a no-ball: the dreaded Nelson is passed with only one victim. Jones has to face Warne next over, and takes a single off the second ball. Runs are welcome, but can Giles keep out Warne? The fifth ball is a full toss, and Giles gratefully accepts a single. Off the sixth ball, Jones, bravely or foolishly depending on your opinion of him, tries to hit Warne for four over mid-on, but does not middle it, and is caught on the boundary by Kasprowicz. A hundred and sixteen for seven! Still 13 to win and we are thoroughly into the tail. Word goes round that Simon Jones, with his foot in traction or a jar of ice or plaster or something, will definitely bat. If Jones has to bat, we are dead. But he is probably padded up already.

Cometh the hour, cometh Hoggy. The happy smile was there, as ever, hiding no doubt a turmoil of emotions. The first delivery from Lee came at him at 93 miles per hour (Lee's slower ball?), but the second was hit for 2 through extra cover. The fourth ball heralded another huge leg before appeal from all the Australians, but Bucknor was unmoved. Replays showed the ball was going down leg. Then another no-ball, another run to the total. Two dot balls and the score was 119 for seven when Warne took the ball to bowl to Giles again. The batsman defended dourly, with soft hands and his bat in front of the pads as often as possible. Apart from the third ball, which he knocked for 2 runs through midwicket. England needed only 8 more runs to win.

Brett Lee's twelfth over decided the game in England's favour. A match which should have been won from early on the second day, and in which England never relinquished the lead, was finally secured by good old Hoggy, who ducked two bouncers and a yorker, before hitting the fourth ball, a full toss, through extra cover for four. The release of tension was immense. The crowd cheered as though we had won a war. When he followed it up by hitting 2 off the final ball of the over, England were just 1 run behind, with three wickets in hand.

And Warne still to bowl. So far he had taken four wickets for 29 runs in thirteen overs, and almost single-handedly had kept Australia in the match. Could he do it again? A hat-trick was not beyond him, at least in the minds of England's nervous supporters, now appearing from behind the furniture. But it was not to be one of Warne's greatest overs – perhaps he is human after all and tiredness had finally got to him. The first two balls were safely kept out, and the third, a full toss on leg stump, should have finished the game. Giles hit it hard, but straight at Katich at short square leg. It hit him on the body, and without Katich knowing anything about it apart from the pain, he saved the winning runs. But two balls later, Katich was not in the way. Giles clipped another leg-side delivery through midwicket, and England were home. A victory by three wickets, far too close for comfort, but a win nevertheless.

Andrew Flintoff was named Man of the Match. No surprise there, then.

Oh, and England's women won the Ashes, too. Chasing just 74 runs to win the deciding Test against Australia at New Road, Worcester, they made it with six wickets to spare. It was a good day for English cricket all round.

England v. Australia, Fourth Test Match

At Trent Bridge, Nottingham

25, 26, 27, 28 August 2005

Result: England won by 3 wickets

Toss: England

England

ME Trescothick b Tait	65	c Ponting b Warne	27
AJ Strauss c Hayden b Warne	35	c Clarke b Warne	23
*MP Vaughan c Gilchrist b Ponting	58	c Hayden b Warne	0
IR Bell c Gilchrist b Tait	3	c Kasprowicz b Lee	3
KP Pietersen c Gilchrist b Lee	45	c Gilchrist b Lee	23
A Flintoff lbw b Tait	102	b Lee	26
+GO Jones c & b Kasprowicz	85	c Kasprowicz b Warne	3
AF Giles lbw b Warne	15	not out	7
MJ Hoggard c Gilchrist b Warne	10	not out	8
SJ Harmison st Gilchrist b Warne	2		
SP Jones not out	15		
Extras (b 1, lb 15, w 1, nb 25)	42	(lb 4, nb 5)	9
Total (all out, 123.1 overs)	<u>477</u>	(7 wickets, 31.5 overs)	<u>129</u>

Fall of Wickets First Innings: 1-105 (Strauss), 2-137 (Trescothick), 3-146 (Bell), 4-213 (Vaughan), 5-241 (Pietersen), 6-418 (Flintoff), 7-450 (GO Jones), 8-450 (Giles), 9-454 (Harmison), 10-477 (Hoggard).

Fall of Wickets Second Innings: 1-32 (Trescothick), 2-36 (Vaughan), 3-57 (Strauss), 4-57 (Bell), 5-103 (Pietersen), 6-111 (Flintoff), 7-116 (GO Jones).

Bowling First Innings: Lee 32–2–131–1; Kasprowicz 32–3–122–1; Tait 24–4–97–3; Warne 29.1–4–102–4; Ponting 6–2–9–1

Bowling Second Innings: Lee 12–0–51–3; Kasprowicz 2–0–19–0; Warne 13.5–2–31–4; Tait 4–0–24–0

Australia

JL Langer c Bell b Hoggard	27	c Bell b Giles	61
ML Hayden lbw b Hoggard	7	c Giles b Flintoff	26
*RT Ponting lbw b SP Jones	1	run out (sub [GJ Pratt])	48
DR Martyn lbw b Hoggard	1	c GO Jones b Flintoff	13
MJ Clarke lbw b Harmison	36	c GO Jones b Hoggard	56
SM Katich c Strauss b SP Jones	45	lbw b Harmison	59
+AC Gilchrist c Strauss b Flintoff	27	lbw b Hoggard	11
SK Warne c Bell b SP Jones	0	st GO Jones b Giles	45
B Lee c Bell b SP Jones	47	not out	26
MS Kasprowicz b SP Jones	5	c GO Jones b Harmison	19
SW Tait not out	3	b Harmison	4
Extras (lb 2, w 1, nb 16)	19	b 1, lb 4, nb 14)	19
Total (all out, 49.1 overs)	218	(all out, 124 overs)	387

Fall of Wickets First Innings: 1-20 (Hayden), 2-21 (Ponting), 3-22 (Martyn), 4-58 (Langer), 5-99 (Clarke), 6-157 (Katich), 7-157 (Warne), 8-163 (Gilchrist), 9-175 (Kasprowicz), 10-218 (Lee).
Fall of Wickets Second Innings: 1-50 (Hayden), 2-129 (Langer), 3-155 (Ponting), 4-161 (Martyn), 5-261 (Clarke), 6-277 (Gilchrist), 7-314 (Katich), 8-342 (Warne), 9-373 (Kasprowicz), 10-387 (Tait).

Bowling First Innings: Harmison 9–1–48–1; Hoggard 15–3–70–3; SP Jones 14.1–4–44–5; Flintoff 11–1–54–1
Bowling Second Innings: Hoggard 27–7–72–2; SP Jones 4–0–15–0; Harmison 30–5–93–3; Flintoff 29–4–83–2; Giles 28–3–107–2; Bell 6–2–12–0

Umpires: Aleem Dar (Pakistan) and SA Bucknor (West Indies)

Man of the Match: A Flintoff

7

Satisfaction

The Fifth Test Match, The Oval

So, this breathtaking Ashes series was entering the final phase. England would take the field at the Oval one up in the rubber and as strong favourites to regain the trophy. Suddenly David Graveney's forecast of 2-1 to England, that had looked so ludicrously optimistic after the Lord's Test, might come true. Glenn McGrath's prediction of 5-0 to Australia, which had looked the likelier outcome as England slunk dejectedly away from Lord's, had been confined to the scrapheap reserved for other infamous predictions – an election victory for Neil Kinnock and a Wimbledon Singles crown for Tim Henman.

If England could avoid defeat in the Fifth and final Test, then the Ashes would be theirs. So win, draw or tie. Any one of those results would suffice and given the closely fought matches at Edgbaston, Old Trafford and Trent Bridge and the tensions and excitements endured by all concerned, the cricket gods might well decree that the Fifth Test should be tied. The thought of it is enough to set the pulses racing before the game has begun.

For those with an interest in cricket history, there were some heartening precedents. The last time that England had arrived at the Oval with a 2-1 lead and needing only to avoid defeat to regain the Ashes was in 1985. England won the toss, batted on a glorious August day, and when David Gower was out, the score was 371 for two. England totalled 464, and went on to saunter home by an innings and 94 runs.

For the first time in the summer, England had injury worries in their squad. Simon Jones' ankle was the prime cause for concern, and different options for cover for Jones were being discussed.

In many ways, Jones' improved bowling had been one of the major factors that gave England the edge over Australia. Just as in McGrath's absence Australia were not the force they used to be, so England without Jones had struggled to bowl Australia out in their second innings at Trent Bridge. To face them again over five days without Jones, one of the key members of the dominant bowling attack, was a worrying thought. The options were plentiful: the names of old warhorses like Darren Gough (retired from Test cricket, and injured), Andy Caddick (shin splints), and Martin Bicknell (bound to have something wrong with him) were bandied around, along with the names of younger men such as James Kirtley (doubts over action still unresolved), Jon Lewis (er . . . no), James Anderson (has he got it back yet?), Alex

Wharf (bang on form at present, but playing for Glamorgan, who were in whatever a stronger word for 'slump' is), Ryan Sidebottom (what – and break the statistical purity of he and his dad Arnie both being one-Test wonders?) and even Glen Chapple (good bat) who were suggested at one time or another, along with the twelfth man in residence, Chris Tremlett. Then there was always the option of Simon Jones making a recovery in time for the Oval. The Sunday papers before the game were full of optimistic reports of his recovery.

When the squad was finally announced, a couple of hours later than David Graveney had promised only the day before, the man given the job of covering for Jones was Lancashire's Jimmy Anderson. He had not played a Test since his disappointing tour of South Africa nine months earlier, but he had 51 wickets in the 2005 season, and, in the words of Graveney, 'James had "big match" experience with England.' To keep their options open, England also picked Michael Vaughan's close friend Paul Collingwood in a squad of thirteen. Collingwood was enjoying a great season, having scored over 1,000 runs and taken 20 wickets for Durham. He is also one of the best fielders in England. Collingwood was perhaps picked partly in case Ian Bell did not recover from the very bad case of cramp he suffered in the C&G Final at Lord's on the Saturday before the teams were announced, although he scored a good fifty in a losing cause for Warwickshire. However, there was no room for Chris Tremlett, who perhaps let himself down in that same C&G Final. Although his team, Hampshire, won the trophy, Tremlett did not bowl particularly well. Graveney said that he thought Tremlett was 'not at the top of his game at the moment', which must to a great extent be because he had not played much cricket thanks to his incessant England twelfth man duties. This was what had happened to James Anderson a few months before: being twelfth man for England is a great honour, but if it happens too often it will not do much for your immediate Test prospects, especially if you are a quick bowler.

The England squad as named was:

M.P. Vaughan (Yorkshire, captain), M.E. Trescothick (Somerset), A.J. Strauss (Middlesex), I.R. Bell (Warwickshire), K.P. Pietersen (Hampshire), A. Flintoff (Lancashire), G.O. Jones (Kent, wicketkeeper), A.F. Giles (Warwickshire), M.J. Hoggard (Yorkshire), S.J. Harmison (Durham), S.P. Jones (Glamorgan), J.M. Anderson (Lancashire) and P.D. Collingwood (Durham).

Two days later, though, Jones failed a fitness test, and had to drop out, meaning that England would not be able to field an unchanged eleven throughout a series for the first time since 1884/85, one of the more obscure statistics that this series threw up. The final place was between Anderson and Collingwood.

Compared with Australia, on the other hand, England were sitting pretty. Their tour had gone from bad to unexpectedly good (at Lord's) to very much worse, and after three Tests on the receiving end of a hiding, they had only their stubbornness and the brilliance of Shane

Warne to thank for the fact that it was still possible for them to retain the Ashes. Injuries had robbed them of Glenn McGrath for the two Tests they had lost, and only Brett Lee had bowled at anywhere near a threatening level at the English batsmen. The other three, Gillespie, Kasprowicz and Tait, had a combined bowling analysis of ten wickets for 671 runs, in 147 overs, a rate of 4.5 runs an over, compared with the rest of the bowling attack, who had conceded only 3.6 runs an over, and taken 63 wickets at 24 runs each. Even with McGrath back in the side at the Oval, which he was confidently predicting, and fully fit, which he clearly was not at Old Trafford, that gap in the attack would remain.

The Australian batsmen were all fully fit, which did little to solve the selectors' problems. If only Hayden or Martyn could have picked up an injury, then they could have brought in Hodge or Hussey without attracting any attention, but now they were committed to the batting line-up that had served them faithfully and well for so long. Until the summer of 2005, at least. In the first four Tests of the summer, Hayden, Martyn and Gilchrist, their numbers 1, 4 and 7, had totalled 506 runs for 23 times out, at an average of exactly 22, and a top score between them of 65. England's numbers 1, 4 and 7, not the most successful trio in the line-up, had made 729 runs at 31.70, with every one of them making 65 at least once. They even caught one more catch between them – 26 against 25 – than the Australian trio. In every phase of in the game, Australia were being outplayed. If a composite team were being selected of the two sides after four matches, only Ponting, Warne and, probably, Lee of the Australians would be sure of their places in the eleven. It was an unbelievable turnaround from seven weeks earlier.

However, the most dangerous opponent is one who is almost beaten. The Australians knew that a win at the Oval would allow them to retain the Ashes, and that any other result would mean the trophy was lost. So attack was the only option. Defeat by an innings was no worse than a tense draw. They had one two-day game against Essex, not first-class, over the weekend before the final Test to put a few plans into place. It did not quite work: Essex scored 502 for four on the first day, which included 214 from Alastair Cook, the 20-year-old newly crowned as 'Young Cricketer Of The Year', while the Australian bowlers, minus McGrath and Warne, toiled in the hot sun. The best analysis was Tait's two for 72 in fifteen overs, and Stuart MacGill, hoping to be included in the Oval squad, ended up with no wicket for 128 in 24 overs. Australia's coach inadvertently confirmed a common view that Australia were punch drunk by saying, 'Generally, I thought we bowled and fielded well. This was a day of opportunities for bowlers to press their claims for next Thursday's final Test and during the course of the day there were positives from all of them. The reality is that we would have liked them to score fewer runs.' This from the man who shoved quotations from Sun Tzu's *Art Of War* under the hotel bedroom doors of his players in 2001.

When Australia batted the next day, Hayden hit 151 in 118 balls, with 18 fours and seven sixes, before retiring, but all this proved was that he was still able to make a big score against lesser attacks, not that he could cope with England's bowling battery.

All in all, it was most unsatisfactory for Australia. The veracity of Buchanan's statements about the way his bowlers had performed at Chelmsford, and the veracity of Glenn McGrath's widely reported opinion that he would be fit for the Oval, was put into doubt when the Australian selectors called up Stuart Clark, the 29-year-old medium-fast bowler from New South Wales currently playing with Middlesex, as 'like for like' cover for Glenn McGrath. If he really had been like for like, he would have been in the Australian eleven a few seasons ago, and not awaiting his first Test cap. He had briefly joined the party before the Old Trafford Test, but McGrath had surprised everybody by making a miraculous recovery, so he went back to the county circuit. By the time of the Oval Test, his call-up meant that Gillespie and Kasprowicz had dropped out of the reckoning, and that only Lee and Tait were certain starters.

And what if the weather turned bad? Apart from Manchester, the Tests had been largely unaffected by the brief periods of bad weather that had occurred, but in early to mid-September, a downpour was a distinct possibility. One acquaintance, armed with a ticket for the first day's play at the Oval, declared that he wanted bright sunshine on the Thursday, and ideally England would win the toss, bat, and progress in a stately manner to 386 for two. He then stipulated that the heavens should open and four days of heavy rain follow. The match would be drawn and the Ashes would be England's. Although most people were maintaining stoutly that if England were to win the Ashes, they should be won fair and square without the help of the weather, there was a large body of opinion which secretly espoused my friend's cause. The weather forecasters in the day leading up to the Test seemed to agree that some rain was bound to fall, although there was disagreement about whether it would be enough to affect the result of the match.

By this stage in the series, cricket had taken hold of the public imagination in a way that nobody could have imagined, nor anyone from the ECB could have dared to hope for in his wildest dreams. It was not just the reports of the Tests that were given much more space than was usual: all media were finding cricket angles to the most banal stories. The business news was suddenly filled with the story of Woodworm Bats, the tiny firm that signed up Flintoff and Pietersen and found themselves sitting on a goldmine. Vicars interrupted their Sunday morning sermons to update parishioners on the score. Female columnists who usually wrote about au pairs and useless husbands were suddenly converted to the slinky good looks of Michael Vaughan and the open grin of Andrew Strauss. Simon Jones was modelling clothes in every magazine you cared to open. *Private Eye* managed to squeeze Christopher Martin-Jenkins into 'Pseuds' Corner'. Sports writers who had ignored cricket for years were suddenly trying to prove their willow credentials, and the BBC, who had not even bid for television coverage when the new contracts had been handed out a year before, suddenly realised that cricket was the new football. The old football was suffering from a hapless defeat in Denmark while the Test series was still in full swing, and league football was all of a sudden relegated to the inside pages. Who would have thought that Flintoff would be upstaging Rooney in September? Few people outside cricket had even heard of Flintoff six months ago, and now he was the front-runner for BBC Television's 'Sports Personality of the Year'.

That was part of the BBC's dilemma. In recent years, it almost seemed as though the corporation had no interest in any sport apart from football. They took the drastic, and foolish, step of announcing a complete relocation of BBC Sport to Manchester, despite the fact that at the time of the announcement London was bidding for the Olympic Games, and despite the fact that virtually every major sport has its headquarters in or near London, not Manchester. There was clearly no leadership nor logic in BBC Sport, and there is a strong case for believing that even if they had bid for Test cricket from 2006, they would not have won the bidding. They would not have deserved it, even though they have their digitals channels Three and Four, which do not start broadcasting until 7.00 p.m., available for cricket all day. So it was all the more bizarre that, with the success of the England team, Tessa Jowell MP, Minister for all sorts of things including sports, and who had never previously shown any sign of being able to tell her Vaughan from her Warne, suddenly started making noises to the effect that Test cricket probably ought, after all, to have been included among the sporting 'crown jewels' that have to be reserved for terrestrial television. She had obviously not seen any of the England v. Bangladesh Tests, or she might have held a different view. Whether a renegotiation of the contract was legal, possible or likely before 2010 was another matter, but if there are votes in cricket, you can trust the politicians to make for the boundary ropes. What has always been seen as a naturally Conservative sport was suddenly attracting New Labour's attention.

There was a strong danger that the brouhaha was getting all too much. Three days before the game even began, it was announced that the Greater London Authority had offered the ECB the use of Trafalgar Square for a victory rally if the Ashes were secured. If ever there was a case of counting your chickens, this was it. The ECB said that things like this have to be planned in advance, so it makes sense to work out the details before even knowing whether it would happen, but other people just shook their heads at this combination of arrogance and tempting of the fates. It gave the Australians an extra spur, if they needed one, to beat the Poms and hold on to the urn. After all, remember a previous sporting victory parade in Trafalgar Square on 8 December 2003. And why was that held? Answer: To honour England's World Cup winning rugby team. And whom had they beaten? Answer: The Australians. One huge sporting defeat hurts an Aussie; two would be cataclysmic. If there was even the slightest chance of spoiling the party, the Australians were going to make sure they took it.

But back to reality. The morning of the final Test dawned bright and clear. Well before ten o'clock the captains went out to toss, and there was a huge cheer from the massive crowd already gathered when it was announced that England had won the toss and would bat. This was the third consecutive toss Michael Vaughan had won, and the fourth Test in a row in which England had batted first. So far in the series, the side batting first had won three and drawn one, a good omen. The final place in the England eleven went to Collingwood rather than Anderson, so England, having relied on a five-pronged bowling attack all summer, would now make do with only four prongs, plus Collingwood, Bell, Vaughan and anybody else who fancied a bowl. Australia announced that McGrath was fit again, so their final eleven was:

R.T. Ponting (Tasmania, captain), M.L. Hayden (Queensland), J.L. Langer (Western Australia), D.R. Martyn (Western Australia), M.J. Clarke (New South Wales), S.M. Katich (New South Wales), A.C. Gilchrist (Western Australia, wicketkeeper), S.K. Warne (Victoria), B. Lee (New South Wales), S.W. Tait (South Australia) and G.D. McGrath (New South Wales).

Half an hour after this announcement, the media hype was confirmed by the playing of 'Jerusalem' for the crowd all to join in, and give the England team a boost. Maybe it was because I was sitting with an Aussie, but I got the impression that the singing was sparse at best. There are certain things that true cricket fans will not do voluntarily, and singing 'Jerusalem' at the start of a Test match is one of them. The people in the ground were all hardened cricket fans, who had bought their tickets the previous October or November, not the Johnny-Come-Latelys who had suddenly discovered that cricket is fashionable. They will have to wait until 2006 to join the Barmy Army. There may by then be an even bigger number of converts to the summer game, given that the England football team went down ignominiously to defeat against Northern Ireland the night before the Fifth Test began. The difference between the cultures of football and cricket was the one point on which all commentators agreed, and they also resolved that cricket should not follow the route that England's football has taken, the path lined with fifty pound notes all the way to the night clubs and the tabloids and the *Footballers' Wives*.

This was the first time that the Oval had hosted a Test match since the new Vauxhall End Stand – the OCS Stand – had been built, seemingly in about eight weeks using pieces of Lego. I had been at the Oval the previous summer and had seen the Stand being built at a remarkable rate. To see it now full to bursting on a sunny September morning was a great thing for English cricket, and for Surrey County Cricket Club, but I must admit I do not think it makes a great contribution to London's architectural heritage. It is rather better from the back side, where at last there is a sense of space at that end of the ground, and some rather jungly sorts of creepers hanging down from the Stand to appease the green lobby. The first time I ever came to the Kennington Oval, as it was then rather quaintly known, was in 1956 for the second day of the Fifth Test against Australia. England had already retained the Ashes, and we boys sat on the outer edge of the playing area, square on to the wicket, watching enthralled as Tyson bowled and Harvey and Miller batted and Tony Lock caught anything that moved: his catch to remove Colin McDonald off Tyson at his fastest stays in my memory almost fifty years on. Maybe I am curmudgeonly about change at this wonderful ground, but I do not think the OCS Stand has added much except capacity.

The Press Box is in that Stand too, and it gets the full glare of the morning sun, making the journalists squint to watch the cricket, and also very hot. I am glad I was in the Lower Lock Stand, well shaded and with a glass of lager in my hand, rather than up in that oversubscribed box with the working press.

There was no surprise when Lee and McGrath opened the bowling, Lee from the Vauxhall End and McGrath at the Pavilion End. Trescothick's single off McGrath's fifth ball, the first run

Previous pages: Joy unconfined as the Ashes return.

of the match, was greeted with a huge cheer from the full house, already geared up for five days of tension and nervousness. The first few overs were negotiated safely by the two openers, who have built themselves very quickly into one of the most solid opening partnerships in world cricket, with a very good understanding of each other's game. The way Trescothick plays the ball softly into the off side and calls for a quick single is well known to all England's opponents, but he and Strauss still continually get away with the run because their timing is so good. Trescothick also has the power, while Strauss relies more on placing the ball. Both men have fierce square cuts, a feature of all good left-handers' play, and both enjoy batting together. When Trescothick hit consecutive balls from Lee to the boundary in only the sixth over, Strauss seemed to enjoy the shots just as much as Banger did, if not quite as much as the baying crowd, becoming over-excited with every piece of action throughout the day. The fifty partnership came up in only 70 balls, courtesy of a square drive for four by Strauss off McGrath.

It was clearly a benign batting wicket, and England were setting out their stall for a score of 500 or so. Anything under would be too few for this mighty Australian team. It was fascinating to note how the English supporters, despite getting the upper hand over the Australians after outplaying them in three consecutive Tests, were still as nervous as rabbits on a crocodile farm about the prospect of Australia firing at full power for once. The reality was that England had played so well over the course of the past three Tests, at least, that Australia could not perform at their peak – so why should we expect that to change at the Oval? The answer was because England fans could not really believe that the Ashes were within their grasp, after being out of reach for so long.

The England team, on the other hand, did believe it. They knew they could recapture the Ashes. The Australian team, especially after losing the toss on such a helpful batting surface, seemed to begin to accept the inevitable – with one notable exception. Shane Warne, 'the pie chucker' as my Aussie mate calls him, came into the attack after just thirteen overs, when the score was 61 for no wicket. There was nothing in the pitch to help him, and the fact that he was bowling so soon on the first morning showed how scant the Australian bowling resources were, but he immediately put doubt into English minds. This man is without doubt the greatest spinner who has ever lived. Bowling wrist-spin is a tough business and to be at the top of the tree in this most physically stressful art for fifteen years is a feat of stamina as much as a feat of skill. Anybody who has been lucky enough to see him play cricket, even once, can tell his or her grandchildren in forty years' time that they saw Shane Warne bowl, just as my father used to say to me that he saw Bradman bat. Warne has become probably the only wrist-spinner who has ever been capable not only of taking wickets but also acting as a restraint on the run scoring. His control of flight, length and turn is so absolute that loose balls, certainly during the first thirty overs of any spell, are rare indeed. Throughout the summer, he was able to keep England to around 3 runs an over, compared with the 4 or 5 runs an over that all the other bowlers, with the honourable exception of McGrath, leaked to England. None of the England batsmen was ever comfortable against him, and his skills seemed only to increase with his workload. Add to his bowling the occasional brilliance of his batting and his safe hands at slip, and Englishmen were drawn to the conclusion that without Warne the Ashes would have come home a month earlier.

Ricky Ponting, like the man he so resembles, President George Bush, was in trouble when the drinks interval came along at 70 for no wicket after fourteen overs. It was not Hurricane Katrina that was flattening his world, but he was nevertheless 'up to his arse in stinking gumbo' as the chap sitting next to me so poetically put it. But Ponting had Warne, for whom there is no equivalent in America to help President Bush, nor anywhere else in the world. And of course he wrought his magic pretty quickly. In his third over, on this bland surface, he bowled the kind of ball that only he can deliver, and Trescothick, who had made a faultless and undisturbed 43, edged a ball that had been tossed up a little more than usual into the safe hands of Hayden at slip – a good low catch, the type of grab that kept Hayden in the Test side long after his batting had lost its value.

Michael Vaughan came in, determined to continue carrying the attack to Australia, hitting Warne himself for two fours in an over, one a rank long-hop pulled for four through midwicket, the other his signature shot, a lovely flowing cover-drive. That shot is one of the sights of world cricket, and worth the price of admission alone. The first hundred came up in the 23rd over, the same way that the fifty came up. Strauss square-cut McGrath for four. So far so good for the England assault on the Ashes, but they had to build on this good start, and turn a promising position into a winning one.

That is not how England's cricket works. Just when the hapless spectators sitting around the boundary think that they can relax, call for another round of drinks and crack open the sandwich box, England's batsmen find ways of increasing the stress levels. At 102, Vaughan played a very lazy shot to a Warne leg-break, and simply placed it into the hands of Clarke at short midwicket. Clarke is a very safe fielder, and this was absolutely routine for him. Then 102 for two wickets became 104 for three, as Bell played no shot to a Warne straight-onner and was absolutely plumb lbw. Ian Bell's summer has been a difficult one. It began very well with his taking the place of Robert Key (who is still scoring runs freely for Kent in the Championship) in the England side and then piling up the runs against Bangladesh. However, his performance against Australia was less successful. Apart from his two fifties at Old Trafford, he had looked out of his depth, but on the other hand, he had resisted Warne more successfully than some of his team-mates, having been out to him only twice before in the series. He also took some very good catches under the helmet at short leg, and his bowling had come into play once, at Trent Bridge. This duck would not help his cause, nor England's, but it certainly excited the Australians in the crowd. The English voice was hushed and the first few bars of 'Advance Australia Fair' could be heard amid the general hubbub.

Pietersen, our no-nonsense South African chum, was the next man in. Well, he is my chum now. He hit two fours off Tait in the only over he faced before lunch, to bring the score to 115 for three at the break. That meant I won the sweepstake we had organised for the lunchtime score, which was looking a very long shot at the beginning of the over. He may be a show pony with a dead skunk on his head, but if he plays like that when there is a sweepstake to be won, he can stay in my England team as long as he likes. All the same, with a match to be won, I would rather have been in Australian than English boots at lunchtime.

The afternoon session began badly. Strauss was all but bowled by the very first delivery after lunch, aiming a big hit at a ball that turned enough to pass between bat and pad, but it missed everything on its way through to Gilchrist. He survived to reach his fifty a few overs later, once again by virtue of his square cut, this time off Brett Lee, for four. Shortly after this milestone, Warne, who had by now bowled ten overs on the trot on a surface which could hardly have been less helpful, induced a rash stroke from his Hampshire team-mate Pietersen, who tried one of his bottom-hand whip shots across the line to quite the wrong ball. The dead skunk departed, bowled for 14, and Warne had four wickets for 32 runs in a total of 131 for four. This was a superb spell, keeping Australia in the game, and indeed on top, single-handed.

None of the other Australian bowlers, McGrath included, had troubled the English batsmen. Lee was bowling very fast, as a 93.4 miles per hour bouncer will testify, smashing into Flintoff's helmet and thence to the boundary for four leg-byes. The next ball was timed at 96.2 miles per hour. Lee has always been a quick bowler, but not necessarily an effective bowler. When he came into Test cricket, his strike-rate was phenomenal but nowadays he is a very fast bowler who occasionally picks up expensive wickets, He has many merits, and overall performed much better for Australia in this series than many Australian doubters expected, but all the same, a final bowling average for the series of over 40, and an economy rate of around 4.5, is not what Australia needed in the absence of McGrath and any other back-up fast bowlers. His batting average was better than either Gilchrist's or Martyn's, but that is not why he was picked for the tour.

Warne realised the responsibility that was being placed on his broad but increasingly rickety shoulders: he bowled a googly to Strauss, the first one he has bowled in years. It did not get Strauss' wicket, but it gave him something else to think about. Strauss was playing Lee very early, hitting him forward of square even when he was bowling at 92 mph and more, so Warne had to fish something extra out of the bag. When drinks were taken, at 161 for four after 41 overs (in the Lower Lock Stand drinks were being taken on a rather more regular basis), England were still racing along at four an over, but we needed a decent partnership to bring us back from the ignominy of a first-innings total under 300 on a pitch like this. At this point we set up our sweepstake for the total number of runs scored in the day: the guesses ranged from 322 at the bottom end (our optimistic Aussie) to 352 at the upper end. Even that looked low if Flintoff made a score. He did.

As the afternoon wore on, the pair looked ever more secure. Australia had to turn to Katich and his left-arm wrist-spin for a few overs, but that served no useful purpose other than to give England a few more runs. The 200 came up just before 3 o'clock, with Flintoff on 38 and Strauss 88. Tait and Katich were bowling, and it seemed no more testing than a net session with the bowling machine set to 'trundler'. A few balls later Flintoff played Tait through extra cover for four, a shot that was the high mark of his innings – the ball was caressed to the boundary. And so to tea, at 213 for four. After the alarms of the morning session, Strauss and Flintoff had steadied the ship, and although there was no real advantage to either side, England were certainly not losing their grip on the Ashes quite yet. The sun was getting brighter and the denizens of the Lower Lock Stand getting merrier, and all was well with the world.

After tea, Warne came back into the attack straight away, bowling as ever from the Vauxhall End. In Warne's first over, Flintoff hit him for one four, and in his second over, Flintoff hit him for three consecutive boundaries, the second of which brought up his fifty, his third of the series to go with his century at Trent Bridge. They were all three deliberate hits, two to the leg-side boundary, between square leg and fine leg, and the third a full blooded straight drive that wisely no fielder attempted to stop. With that the hundred partnership came up, and the chants of 'Freddie, Freddie' drowned out all other conversation. He is a very good cricketer, this Andrew Flintoff. Even the Australians knew that by this stage in the summer. By this stage, incidentally, Warne had bowled 20 of the 58 overs sent down at the English batsmen, so it was not surprising that he was a little tired.

Lee, bowling his twelfth over, was operating from the Pavilion End, and Strauss took advantage of a half-volley on his toes to clip Lee through midwicket for four, to bring up his hundred. Despite a slow start to the series, Strauss emerged to become the only man on either side to score two centuries in the series, and although he is one of the quieter members of the England side, the Oval crowd made sure that he knew how much they appreciated his innings. The century had taken 150 balls and was the nub of England's innings. He raised his bat to the crowds, proving that he had survived the bear hug his partner Flintoff gave him as the ball crossed the boundary ropes.

Soon the 250 came up, a streaky cut over point by Flintoff, and when the score had cantered along to 261 came the first strong appeal for quite some time. Strauss appeared to nick one from Lee through to Gilchrist, and although Lee bellowed as loud as ever, neither Gilchrist nor Warne at slip made much of an appeal. Strauss was given not out. It was only when the Snickometer was shown on the television that we realised that Strauss had indeed nicked it, and got away with it once again. In truth, Lee did not deserve much, given the pretty uncontrolled way he was bowling, but bad balls take wickets, as Ian Botham and hordes of village cricketers will confirm, and Lee was done out of a wicket there. Strauss is not a walker: he hates to leave the crease for any reason other than the total destruction of his wicket, or possibly an earthquake in South London, so there was no chance he would do anything other than wait for the umpire's decision. That's the way Test cricket is played these days, and he was perfectly within his rights to stay.

In the next over, Flintoff hit Warne for the first six of the day, and when drinks came an over later, England were, at 268 for four, firmly on top for the first time since Trescothick had been out. Warne had then bowled 24 out of 67 overs. My Aussie mate muttered, 'There's not a hope in hell you'll lose the Ashes.' I wished I could have agreed with him, but England have always had the knack of making hopes in hell come true. He then added, somewhat sourly, 'We'll never get any wickets with a South African and a Kiwi umpire.' I offered him another sandwich.

Pigeon McGrath returned to the fray at this time. I was reliably informed that he was called Pigeon not because of the skinniness of his legs, the normal explanation, but because he was such a pest. Well, if that is the reason, he lived up to his pestilential qualifications by getting rid of Flintoff for 72, with the score on 274. A little wobble as the ball went past the bat, and Flintoff caught the edge. So did Warne at slip. This was the fifth wicket to fall, four to Warne, and one caught by Warne. Is there anybody else out there playing for Australia?

Collingwood, the extra batsman, was Flintoff's replacement. It must have been a huge step for him to find himself in the side, barely ten days after he, along with the rest of England, was hiding behind the sofa as England made such hard work of winning at Nottingham. He also had the hardest job of the day, that of replacing Flintoff at the crease. He took some runs off Warne, and then after only a three-over spell, in which he took one wicket for 4 runs, McGrath was rested. Was he fully fit? After Warne, he was Australia's only effective bowler, and to bowl him so sparingly as England established control in Australia's Last Chance Saloon seemed like a very strange piece of captaincy, unless (as we all suspected) he was not fit. Or, possibly, an inspired piece of captaincy as Tait, his replacement, trapped Collingwood leg before with a fast inswinger that hit Collingwood on the toe. Replays showed that he might just have been out-side the line, but there had been one or two doubtful lbw decisions during the summer, and this was by no means one of the worst. Now England stood at 289 for six, and Australia's hopes were rising out of hell.

They rose a little more when Strauss finally fell. Just two balls before the second new ball was due, Strauss, on 129, could not avoid a well flighted delivery outside off stump which caught bat, then pad, then Katich, diving forward from short leg to take a very good catch indeed. The Australian close fielding had generally been very good throughout the summer, with Hayden, Warne and Katich all taking some very good catches. In the outfield, Lee and Clarke in particular had been brilliant. The standard of Australian fielding had not slipped, even if their batting and bowling had been showing signs of age all summer.

England were now on 297 with seven men gone, and Warne had his five wickets. This was certainly a below par score on this wicket, despite a fine century from Andrew Strauss and a belligerent 72 from Flintoff. Most of the other batsmen had failed to contribute. The low end of the sweepstake looked like taking the money. You could argue that all the matches in this series were comparatively low scoring, and that no side had ever looked dominant with the bat against very fine bowling, but even if that is so, the area in which England need to make further improvements is in the solidity of their middle order and the consistency of their batsmen in building big scores. England can put out a side with Test cen-tury makers batting down to number seven, but all too often only one or two of these proven batsmen get among the runs. The result is that England regularly make reasonable scores, but rarely make the sort of crushing total that wipes out the opposition at a blow – unless the opposition is Bangladesh, of course.

Geraint Jones was batting now, with Ashley Giles. The Spanish flags were out for the King of Spain, of course, but it was Jones, the burger king, who was taking the opportunity to put a few runs on the board before the end of the day. In his teenage days Geraint Jones used to flip burgers at the Brisbane Broncos stadium on match days. 'Most of them hit the ground', according to my Aussie mate.

The day ended in some confusion. There was a near run-out, which Billy Bowden referred to the third umpire, but which nobody on the ground, including the Australian players, really thought was out, and it was not. There was confusion as to why Ponting did not take the new ball straight away, but waited until the 86th over – a question nobody properly answered. And there was confusion over the state of Shane Warne's wrist. After bowling 34 overs in the day, he looked to have strained his wrist as he fielded out the final two overs of the day. Ice packs overnight was the general prescription. There were even differing opinions on which side had had the better of the day. It was generally accepted that the Australians had their noses in front in playing terms, but not such an advantage as would affect the fate of the Ashes. England's one-handed grip on the urn had not really been loosened by play on the first day. No confusion on who won the sweepstake – my optimistic Aussie mate with his guess of 322.

Day 1, Close of Play:

England 319 for 7 wickets after 88 overs (G. Jones 21 not out, Giles 5 not out).

The second day, in retrospect, decided the match and the destination of the Ashes. England needed to add at least one hundred more runs to their overnight total to have a realistic hope of warding off the rampant Australian batsmen (if they were to be rampant for the first time this series), and Australia needed to go hell for leather for a first-innings lead and a chance to make England sweat in the third innings, chasing a big Australian total. Neither event occurred. England did pretty well, adding 54 runs before being all out, but it was generally accepted that this was not nearly enough to keep Australia at bay. But then, much more surprisingly, the Australians did not attack from the outset, to build the big score quickly that they needed to win the match and retain the Ashes. They scored 112 for no wicket, but at a rate of barely three an over, slower than the complete England innings.

The factor that nobody got quite right was the weather. The two sides did not quite get it right, and the weather forecasters did not quite get it right. It was not surprising, because the weather was at its most fickle. Lord's, a couple of miles away to the north, was drenched by a massive downpour from about 3.30 p.m. that afternoon. The Queen's Club, no further away to the west, was flooded out. All over London there were reports of thunderstorms causing havoc, but at the Oval it was merely gloomy. The gloom limited play to a mere fifty overs during the day, and the loss of playing time was the crucial factor. Australia needed to play for as long as possible, but they could not.

The morning, gloomy but not threatening rain, was long enough to dispose of England. Jones was out to the ninth ball of the morning, bowled by a good one from Lee which took his off stump while he was playing down another line – 325 for eight. Hoggard came in, and survived for the 36 balls he manages to stay every time he bats. He scored about as many runs as usual, too, just a lucky edge off McGrath past Ponting at slip and an easy push to the leg side off Warne for two singles, not to mention a snick through to the 'keeper that everybody on the ground except Rudi Koertzen heard, before he was deceived by McGrath's slower ball and lobbed a simple catch to Martyn at short cover – 345 for nine. Giles was, meanwhile, progressing carefully but well towards a reasonable score. He survived one confident shout for caught behind, but otherwise seemed quite serene, unlike the England supporters who were getting more frantic with every run. Harmison joined Giles and for 25 minutes they wrought last-wicket havoc to bring the total up to something that would give the Australians pause for thought, at least. Harmison took a particular liking to the bowling of Brett Lee, whose return to the attack in the 105th over was greeted with three cracking fours. The first was a really good shot by Harmison, who put his front foot down the pitch and smashed the ball back past the bowler to the long-off boundary for four. Lee, who is predictable if nothing else, followed up this insult with a bouncer, which Harmison swished at, but barely got any bat on it. The ball flew over Gilchrist's head for four. The next ball, the last of the over, was yet another bouncer and Harmison, having had the sighter the previous ball, got much more bat on this and hooked it well down to fine leg for another four. Lee was most unhappy.

He never had the chance to get at Harmison again, because Warne captured his sixth wicket, that of Giles, in the next over. Giles had turned down an easy single off the second ball of the over, only to be caught leg before to the straight one the very next ball. Hawkeye implied that the ball would have missed off stump, but not by much. England were all out for 373, and Warne had taken six for 122 in 37.3 overs. He had bowled two immense spells of eighteen and sixteen overs on the first day, and just three and a half overs on the next day, to wrap up the innings. He bowled only three balls fewer than Lee and Tait combined, who between them took two wickets for 155. Warne is indeed worth any two other bowlers.

When Langer and Hayden opened the batting for Australia, the instructions must have been to make your runs as quickly as is reasonably possible. In theory there was a great deal of time left in the game, almost four days, and a score of 600 built up over two days would give Australia an almost impregnable position from which to force the victory they needed. But there was also the issue of the weather: on the Friday it was clearly not going to be good at any stage, and the chance of rain or bad light was very high. If it were only bad light, then the Australian batsmen could choose to stay on and play on, but if it rained, there was no choice but to lose some time. The forecast for Saturday was poor and for Sunday not much better. In a match likely to be severely curtailed by the weather, quick runs must surely have been the goal.

Justin Langer seemed to have got the message, but the terminally out-of-form Hayden did not. There was not long before lunch, so it was quite reasonable that the score should be no more than 19 by then, after seven overs. Langer had already taken another hit on the elbow from Harmison, something he seems to do with masochistic regularity, but with two fours off Hoggard and one off Harmison, 16 of those 19 runs were to Langer's name and only 2 to Hayden, who had by then been almost shredded by one over from Hoggard, who was bowling very well.

It took the Australian openers eighteen overs to reach the 50 partnership for only the third time in the series. The failure of this normally prolific partnership to give any sort of kick-start to the Australian innings had been one of the big losses for the Australians in 2005. Langer had batted well enough, and would by the end of the series be Australia's leading run-scorer and top of the averages, but Hayden had looked like a lost soul under the helmet all summer. Oddly enough, his failures with the bat had not affected his close catching, which was still in a class of its own: Shane Warne would have been much less effective without the towering menace of Matty Hayden at slip to disconcert every England batsman. But he is employed to score runs, and he had not been doing so. Everybody had written that his place in the side was in danger. Now Hayden had one last chance to make a big score. On the Friday he was playing as though he knew it.

Langer, on the other hand, was playing for his side. When Giles came on, at the Pavilion End rather than the Vauxhall End so recently occupied by Warne, Langer greeted him with two big sixes. He is only a little man, but he can hit the ball a long way. The smaller Oval ground, reduced by several yards since the building of the OCS Stand, made it even easier for him to clear the ropes, over long-on and midwicket, but it was a misfield by Flintoff, of all people, on the last ball of the over, that enabled Langer to come back for the second run that brought him his fifty. At this stage, Australia's total was 66, and Hayden had scored 13. Langer had scored more than that in Giles' first over.

There was some slight alarm when Langer flashed hard at Collingwood, having his first bowl of the game just after the drinks interval, but although Trescothick at slip got his hand to it, it was moving very fast and did not stick. A chance, certainly, but a very difficult one. Collingwood bowled well but without luck in his four-over spell. He reached speeds in the low eighties, comparable to Hoggard but without the blond flowing locks, much to the surprise of Jones The Gloves, and troubled both Langer and Hayden, but he could not make the break-through. But then neither could Harmison, Flintoff, Hoggard or Giles, so he did no worse than England's main bowlers.

At tea, the score was 112 for no wicket, with Langer on 75 and Hayden on 32 after 96 balls faced. It seemed as though Australia were in a position to press on after tea and build a foundation for a major assault on the England bowling the next day. But during tea the light deteriorated and no sooner had the batsmen come out again than the umpires offered them the light. Much to the amazement of all concerned, they took it, and marched back into the pavilion. Maybe Langer had not finished his slice of lemon drizzle cake, or Hayden wanted another cup of tea, but whatever the reason, they decided against scoring any more runs. It was a weird decision, and however much the Australian camp tried to explain it, it still sounded odd. 'It was very dark, and Andrew Flintoff was reverse-swinging the ball before tea,' said Langer. When the rain set in a little later and play was abandoned for the day, it sounded even odder. 'We were not expecting to lose as much time as we did, but the way the series has played out, most of the Tests have been decided inside four days.' He then made the remark that certainly showed the muddled thinking around the Australian dressing- room. 'We have got the opportunity to score heavily tomorrow or the next day, whenever the weather allows.' Whenever the weather allows! They only had four days in which to win the game and keep those Ashes, and yet they were willing to come off at the first hint of darkness and resign to staying indoors until whenever the weather allows. English morale must have been hugely boosted by this chicken-hearted decision by the Australians, a decision that certainly contributed to their ultimate downfall.

Day 2, Close of Play:

England: 373 all out.
Australia: 112 for no wicket in 33 overs (Langer 75 not out, Hayden 32 not out).

Play started late on the Saturday, because there had been early morning rain. Even at 10.30, it looked pretty hopeless, but the ground staff did a great job, and only half an hour was lost. The England fans were quite happy to sit in the rain or the gloom, as long as the cricket petered out towards a draw, but the cricketers clearly wanted to get on with it. The forecast was for more rain before the day was out. Hoggard's very first ball of the day was a full, swinging delivery that hit Langer low down on the pad. It seemed absolutely out – there was no hint of an inside edge, no question of Langer's foot being too far down the track, and no thought of the ball pitching outside the line of stump to stump – but Billy Bowden said no, and England were thereby condemned to a day of bowling at Langer.

The play continued for half an hour, with Langer playing confidently and Hayden treating the ball as though it were a hand grenade wrapped in a cowpat. His footwork was not at all that of the belligerent forward player of old, and his bat was not coming down straight. It almost seemed as though it would be kinder to put the man out of his misery than let him linger on, but no Australian ever gives up his wicket easily, and Hayden was at least proving capable of occupying the crease. He almost engineered his own downfall with an appalling running mix-up when the ball had gone to Collingwood, of all people, and a direct hit from the fielder would have done for Langer. But there was no direct hit. At 138 for no wicket, with a thundery light rain falling through the murk, the players came off again. By five minutes past midday, they were on again. Nobody seemed to know what significance this would have on the number of overs to be bowled in the day, nor on the hours of play, but such discussion was largely academic: the weather was going to dictate the day's proceedings.

The Australian batsmen played with rather more fluency until lunch, helped by some poor balls from Harmison and Hoggard. A single off Flintoff brought Hayden his half-century, which he greeted with only a slight wave of his bat in acknowledgement of the applause from the Australian balcony, and elsewhere around the ground. A few balls later the 150 came up, and by lunch, taken at 12.30 despite the interruptions, Australia were on 157 for no wicket. This was by some distance the biggest opening stand of the series, for either side, and things were beginning to look ominous for England. It was obvious that 373 was at least 100 runs too few. The many spectators in the crowd wearing 'Let It Rain' T-shirts knew what the winning strategy had to be.

After lunch, Langer and Hayden treated themselves to some careful runs off Giles and Harmison, but they did not force the pace as much as the England supporters feared. It was as though the Australians were assuming that England in early September has to have weather good enough to allow a Test match to reach an honest conclusion, and the murky cloud and warm drizzle were mere figments of their imagination. There could be no other obvious reason why they were taking their time, and most of England's too. Langer reached his second consecutive Oval Test hundred with a four to third man off Harmison. He had taken 144 balls to reach the landmark, while Hayden at the other end had faced 30 more balls and scored 30 fewer runs. Two balls later, another boundary off Harmison brought Langer's 7,000th run in Tests, going past Sir Donald Bradman's 6,996 in 41 more Tests. Two balls later he was out, playing on to Harmison, for 105. The opening partnership of 185 was a monumental affair, but it had taken all but 53 overs, and had spread over a full day's play. At this point, Australia looked well set for the 500 they needed to put pressure on England, but only if they could make the remaining 315 runs quickly, if at all.

Ricky Ponting came out, but had hardly got on to the playing area when the rain began, and play was suspended for what amounted to practically two hours. They went off at 1.40 and did not reappear until 3.30, by which time tea had been taken and the sun was shining. It was at this point that the Australians must have realised that the runs had to come quickly, or the Ashes would be lost.

Hayden and Ponting brought up the 200 with few alarms, and pressed on towards 250 and beyond. Giles was bowling a good probing spell from the Vauxhall End, which induced a very streaky four between 'keeper and slip for Hayden, and an even luckier escape for Ponting when an appeal for a bat–pad catch to Bell at silly mid-off was turned down by Billy Bowden on the grounds that there was no bat involved. Television replays showed there was some bat in it, but as Giles got away with a blatant snick through to Gilchrist earlier, he had to be philosophical about Ponting's slice of luck. It was at the end of the 65th over, with the total on 241, that Hayden struck the four off Flintoff that brought up his century. Flintoff was among the first to congratulate him, although he did not hug him quite as profusely as Ricky Ponting did. It had taken him 218 balls and he looked increasingly sure of himself as time passed. All the same, in the context of the game, it had been a slow innings, one more designed to protect Hayden's Test place than to win the game for Australia. The general view was that unless he stepped up the pace and went on to a double-century, his Test place was still as much in jeopardy as it had been before the match began. But five balls later, before Hayden had had time to show us his intentions, the rain came down again, the crowd burst out singing, and the players went off. And that was it until 5.30.

There was no real sign of any acceleration by the Australians. Rain breaks are usually a help to the fielding side, who can get refreshed, take a shower and put their feet up, but for the batsmen it is a break in their concentration and they have to start their innings all over again, so the kind of stop–start day that the Oval gave us on the Saturday should have helped England in the field. It helped them in terms of the match situation, because when all you need in a draw, the best thing is not to play at all, but this series deserved a more dramatic climax than a washout. Luckily, the weather relented enough to allow that to happen.

At the start of the 73rd over, with Australia on 264 for one wicket, Andrew Flintoff came back into the attack. With his second ball he removed Ponting. The ball was short of a length outside the off stump, but it bounced rather more than Ponting expected, and he could only fend it off to gully, where Strauss made a good catch, diving forward. The score now stood at 264 for two, and the captain had gone for 35, in a comparatively brisk 56 balls. He was replaced by Martyn, whose place in the side was even more precarious than Hayden's. Martyn hit the second ball he received for four, and then went back into his shell.

All the time the weather was getting worse, the skies were getting darker and the English fans were getting out their umbrellas. It could not be much longer before the umpires got together and discussed the light. When they did, after four balls of a Flintoff (fast-medium!) over, they looked at their light meters and offered the light to the batsmen. Without any hesitation they walked off. The England team hesitated a little. They could not believe that the Australians, with only two days to play and still 100 runs behind in the first innings, would willingly give up a chunk of play in a game they had to win. But they did. Half the day's play had been lost to the weather.

Day 3, Close of Play:

England 373.
Australia 277 for two wickets in 78.4 overs (Hayden 110 not out, Martyn 9 not out).

The fourth day, Sunday, was hardly better than Saturday. The skies were overcast, the light was no better than average and the threat of rain was never far away. Despite this, there was a huge crowd. For all five days, every ticket had been sold, and every seat seemed to be filled. The tel-

evision cameras spent time picking out celebrities: over the five days well known cricket lovers like Sir John Major, Sir Trevor McDonald, Stephen Fry, Hugh Grant and several pop stars (Tom Chaplin of Keane, Johnny Borrell of Razorlight) were joined by many household names whose love of cricket had been kept well hidden until now – Jonathan Ross, Frank Skinner and Dame Kelly Holmes among others. Cricket was embracing a whole new audience and this can only be good news for the game.

The expectations of the English fans, old and new, at this stage were not great: a lot of rain would help, but the prospect of Australia batting all day for a total of 550 plus, and then getting Shane Warne to run through England in two sessions on the final day was too worrying to think about. The Australians might have considered another option if the light had not been so poor – they could have declared at their overnight total 100 or so behind, and aimed at getting England out for another 150, and then scored the 250 needed to win on the Monday. The one thing that seemed sure was that the weather on Monday would be back to the sunshine of the Thursday, but if Australia declared early on the fourth day, England's batsmen would accept the light as soon as it was offered, and the best part of another day would be lost. Then it would not matter what tricks Shane Warne could employ; there still would not be enough time to force a win.

So batting on, rapidly and successfully, seemed the best option for Australia. Flintoff, who had two balls left in his over from the night before, began the session with a no-ball, but that proved to be about the only foot he put wrong all day. The crowd roared him on with every ball. Giles at the other end was keeping the Australians at bay, and Flintoff made the break-through. In his second over of the morning, he got one to lift on Martyn, who could only lob it up to midwicket, where Collingwood, running in, took a simple catch. Australia at 281 for three, with Martyn gone for 10, now exposed what some wags in the crowd called the tail. Little did they realise how right they were.

Flintoff got the first of several huge ovations that would come his way as he reached his fielding position on the boundary after that over, as Giles wheeled away. The new ball was due, but was not taken for a couple of overs, and when it did come, it at first caused the runs to flow a little quicker. Flintoff kept going, of course, and Hoggard partnered him, partly because Harmison was off the field at the time, his place being taken by one of the world's great fielders, Trevor Penney. Something has to be done about the abuse of the substitution rule.

The light was offered to the Australians with the score on 287, but they decided to stay on the field. This was the cue for Stuart MacGill, the Australian twelfth man, to come on with a message for the batsmen. He made no attempt to disguise his mission by bringing out new gloves or anything, and this is a further minor abuse of playing regulations. For what reason and under what authority was MacGill allowed on to the playing area? The question also arises as to why the Australian batsmen needed advice from the dressing-room after only six overs of play. Had they not discussed their tactics endlessly over dinner and breakfast? Or were they too

Opposite: Vaughan kept a calm head throughout the fraught series – most agreed he had the edge over Ponting in the captaincy stakes.

busy reading the works of Sun Tzu, or some other philosopher's works photocopied at midnight by coach John Buchanan?

A few balls later, Flintoff, in the slips, dropped a straightforward chance offered by Clarke, who was then on 3. Hoggard was not amused. At 11.15, it started to drizzle. The England supporters all put up their umbrellas, while the Australians in the crowd took off their shirts and pretended to catch a few rays. The English fielders had great difficulty in sighting the ball against the background of crowds and dark skies, but the Australians still saw no point in coming off. They stayed on for drinks, which were taken at 323 for four, with Hayden grinding on at 137, and Clarke on 11.

Once again, a wicket fell immediately after the drinks break. This time it was Hayden, undone by a brilliant delivery from Flintoff, which pitched on off slanting across the batsman, but straightened and hit his pad. Finally, the stubborn defiance of Hayden was broken. Australia may not have needed stubborn defiance, but they got it in spades from Hayden. To compile 138 in 303 balls may have been a monumental effort, but it might also have proved an Ashes-losing innings, taking far too long. Still, as he left the pitch, he had the good grace to say to Flintoff, 'well bowled,' and Flintoff nodded a 'well batted' back. The spirit in which the series was played survived even its tense death throes, even when it was by no means certain whose hopes were going to be dashed. England now had Australia at 323 for four, still fifty runs behind their first-innings score, but probably marginally ahead in terms of the match situation.

By the time Flintoff had removed Katich for 1, with a very similar delivery to the one that got Hayden, the score of 329 for five probably meant England's nose was ahead. But the awful thought arose – do England want to get Australia all out? Do England want to bat in this light, on this wicket against *that* bowler? Wouldn't they just fall apart, or could they be certain of being offered the light? Of course, England had to get past Clarke and Gilchrist first, and the Australian wicketkeeper, despite the thin time he had with the bat in the first four Tests, played his usual hand. Two fours in his first over, facing Hoggard, signalled his intentions. Hoggard was not bowling that badly, and his figures at this stage of the innings, 0 for 84 in 19 overs, certainly did not reflect his true worth. But he kept at it, as he always does. At the other end, Flintoff kept at it all morning. The bowling spell that had begun the previous afternoon was still going strong, and nobody was able to take liberties with him. As ever, it was a great performance, but Freddie knew that if he could be in the team that won the Ashes, no effort was too much. And Michael Vaughan knew he would bowl until he dropped if he was asked to (and quite probably even if he was not).

On the stroke of lunch, it was Hoggard who made another breakthrough, and who tipped the session firmly in England's favour. Gilchrist was trapped by a big swinging ball which he tried to clip through the leg-side field, only to miss, almost topple over and end up very lbw. Yet another cameo, 23 in 20 balls including four boundaries, but no big innings from Gilchrist all summer. Controlling Gilchrist was one of the keys to England's hopes of success, and they did it well throughout. Lunch was taken with Australia on 356 for six, and English fans the happier.

Geraint Jones did not help his cause in the first over after lunch by dropping Clarke, who edged a ball from the unfortunate Hoggard towards first slip. Jones dived for it, got a glove to it, but could not hold it. Clarke seems to have been the main beneficiary of England's fielding lapses throughout the summer, but, with the exception of Lord's, has not really gone on to punish England for their mistakes. This time he added only 1 more run before Hoggard, in his next over, earned his third lbw of the day, and none of them was a doubtful decision. Now the score read 359 for seven, and Clarke was gone for 25, put together over two hours.

Warne and Lee, whose batting all summer had been a revelation, came back to earth at the Oval. Warne found it difficult to get off the mark, and after ten balls his patience was exhausted. He tried to hit Flintoff over mid-on or midwicket, but got the ball too high on the bat and merely spooned it to mid-on, where Vaughan held the catch at the second attempt – 363 for eight. So Warne was gone for a duck in what was beginning to look like his final Ashes innings. He got a huge ovation as he walked back to the pavilion, but perhaps not quite as big as the ovation for Flintoff, who had thus picked up his first five-wicket haul of the series.

McGrath, who had not yet lost his wicket in the series, now marched to the middle with his 'X-Factor 61' branded bat, which commemorated his highest Test score in more than 120 innings. Six balls later, McGrath was marching back to the pavilion, still carrying his 'X-Factor 61' branded bat, which was still correctly recording his highest Test score. He had at least now been dismissed in the series, so he had a batting average which at 36 was higher than all his team-mates except Langer, Ponting and Clarke – 363 for nine. Shaun Tait was the last man in. He has yet to perfect his technique against the quicker bowlers, but had little for time that as Brett Lee who was soon out, wonderfully caught on the long-on boundary by Ashley Giles as he attempted to hit Hoggard out of the ground. Australia were all out for 367, and trailed England by 6 runs. Eight wickets had fallen for 90 runs in the day, and Flintoff had bowled unchanged from the Pavilion End for eighteen overs since the previous evening. He took five for 38 in that spell, five for 78 in the innings. Hoggard, an able number two, took four for 4 in 3.1 overs at the death, to give respectability to figures that had previously read 21-1-93-0, and now England were well and truly on top.

So it was crunch time and the destination of Ashes would be decided by a one-innings match. There were 160 overs still left in the game, and England would have to bat for 100 of them to make the game safe. To take ten English wickets Australia had Shane Warne, and the not quite fit McGrath, along with Lee and Tait, two men who leak runs more readily than a Downing Street source leaks memos. If England collapsed against Warne yet again, the Ashes could be lost. England had enjoyed a very good first half of the day but that had not lessened the nervous tension amongst the England supporters. If anything the tension was even greater now that the finish line was in sight. No room for errors, no time to make up for mistakes. Do not rely on the weather to bale you out. Just do it!

McGrath took the new ball in poor light. As England began their innings, the Barmy Army trumpeter, a chap called Bill Cooper, began playing 'Jerusalem', and a good proportion of the crowd joined in – at least as many as sang along with the official tenor on the first morning. Trescothick's first run, a single off the fifth ball of the first over, was greeted with huge cheers from the crowd. The battle lines were drawn. Lee, at the other end, was bowling ten miles per hour faster than McGrath, and at the end of his first over, the umpires got together to talk about the light, but did not yet offer it to the batsmen. All the same, Ponting got the message and after just one over of Lee, gave Warne the ball to carry on where he left off at the Vauxhall End. The light was fading, but we cannot give all the credit to Mother Nature for Warne's first wicket. It was a big leg-break that Strauss tried to cover, playing with soft hands with bat and pad deliberately apart to minimise the chance of a bat pad catch, but Warne was too good. The ball ripped even more than Strauss was expecting, and took the edge of his bat, then the pad and into Katich's safe hands at forward short leg. England were 2 for one, and the jitters came rushing back like Indians circling the settlers' wagons.

Vaughan came out, clearly expecting play to be suspended very shortly, but McGrath was allowed to continue for one more over in the worst of the light. One ball almost sliced Vaughan in half, but still the play continued. Billy Bowden signalled to Ponting at the end of the over that if the Aussies wanted to stay on, they would need to have spinners at both ends, but it was during Warne's second over that the umpires conferred again, and this time decided to offer

Warne was thrown the ball at every opportunity, and consistently made the breakthrough. Strauss is bamboozled again by a fierce leg-break, and Katich completes the dismissal.

the light to Vaughan and Trescothick. They took it, and the huge crowd roared its approval. It was 2.30 p.m. The players took an early tea, and were back on the field by 3.20. The cheering was far more muted for their re-entry than it had been for their departure fifty minutes before, partly because the Australians when they came out were all wearing dark glasses.

But the light had not really improved, and twenty minutes later the option to leave the field was again offered to England's batsmen, despite their facing a bowling attack of Shane Warne and Michael Clarke, who bowls slow-medium left-arm spin, like Derek Underwood but less effective. Enland accepted the offer of bad light, and that was it for the day. At 34 for one wicket, England faced the prospect of having to survive most of the day to make the game, and therefore the Ashes, absolutely safe. It was a daunting prospect.

Day 4, Close of Play:
England 373 and 34 for one wicket in 13.2 overs (Trescothick 14 not out, Vaughan 19 not out). Australia 367.

England's task was a straightforward one. There were 98 overs to go in the series, and the weather for this last act was bright and sunny, with no prospect of rain, mist or snow to stop play. England had to prevent Shane Warne from running through them so quickly that Australia had time to make the runs required to win. It was an equation involving runs and overs, and at the start of the day, if it had not been such a crucial Test, then the draw would have been the expected outcome, and nobody would have been particularly concerned about it. But it was a crucial Test, and the career prospects of almost everybody involved hung on this day's work. The nerve ends of millions of Englishmen, those which had not already been shredded, were jangling as they prepared to be squeezed through the mangle one last time.

How do you start a day as momentous as this if you are England captain and batting? Answer – you hit Warne's second ball of the day for four. The cheers for Vaughan's on-drive from the huge crowd were deafening, and the noise levels continued unabated all day. Later in the day, dot balls were being cheered uproariously, as was any ball that did not take a wicket, and therefore took England closer to the Ashes. Trescothick and Vaughan played sensibly where they had to, and hit the loose balls as they were offered. In any other circumstances it might have been dull, but this is where cricket scores over many other sports, when circumstance is everything. Circumstances, in this case, decreed that Shane Warne would bowl all day if necessary. Ponting did give him a brief rest to allow Brett Lee to bowl a couple of overs as England reached 50, but all that did was give the England batsmen a short respite before Warne came back into the attack. Warne rested for just five overs, which accentuated the dearth of bowling resources at Ponting's disposal. In the whole day's play he only gave Tait five overs, which is hardly likely to build the confidence of a young fast bowler new to Test cricket. But Ponting would argue, rightly, that retaining the Ashes was more important than Tait's confidence. It begged the qustion was to why Tait was in the team? To which the answer was he was considered the best of a mediocre selection of support bowlers. Australia were operating with three bowlers in the Oval Test and had done so throughout the series.

It was McGrath who made the next breakthrough. Vaughan, who had been middling the ball all morning and who had made 45 in only 65 balls, got a thick edge to one of the best balls McGrath had bowled all summer, and Gilchrist took a quite magnificent catch, diving one-handed to his right – 67 for two and the captain gone, and 89 overs still to go. This meant that Ian Bell, who had a first-innings duck, ought to have been the next person to walk on to the pitch, but he was not. Two streakers, one of each gender, chose this moment to invade the ground and find their own way of joining in the cricket. It did not last long, as both were soon rounded up and led away, but it must have added to Bell's nervousness when he finally made it to the middle. Whatever the reason, Bell did not look settled at any stage of his innings: not when he took guard, not when he looked around at the field settings, not when he edged the first ball he received to Warne at slip, and not as he walked back to the pavilion. Now it was 67 for three and English hearts began to sink.

Kevin Pietersen was the next man in, show pony all summer, the man with too much talent but also too many advertising contracts, the man who dropped six catches and held none. If ever there was a time to prove his talent was matched by his application, that time was now. McGrath's first ball to the new man, the hat-trick ball, was a snorter that rose from just short of a length. Pietersen managed to get both bat and gloves out of its path, but it hit him on the right shoulder and bounced to slip. There was a massive appeal from all the Australians, but Bowden called it right – not out. Pietersen lived again, by the skin of his teeth.

The battle now began for survival until lunch, or at least until drinks. The tension in the ground was mounting by the minute, as it seemed that England might just crumble under the pressure as they closed in on cricket's ultimate prize. The gents around the ground started filling up with those who could not bear to watch, and the Aussies in the crowd started believing the impossible just might happen. When Warne dropped Pietersen in the slips off Lee when he had made just 15, a fairly simple chance, it was merely poetic justice for the time when Pietersen dropped Warne at Old Trafford. But even though Pietersen's drop was one reason why England did not force victory at Old Trafford, Warne's drop proved far more dev-astating. Mistakes made on the final day of a 25-day series cannot be avenged. 'Warnie's dropped the Ashes' was the chant all round the ground for the rest of the day. It was an unfair taunt, because without Warne the Australians would have lost the Ashes at least one Test ear-lier, if not two. But today it was true: that dropped catch cost Australia any chance of retaining the little urn.

Trescothick meanwhile was playing determinedly and well, although he was almost undone by a ball from Warne that pitched way outside the off stump and turned almost square to hit the Somerset man on the pad. Umpire Koertzen, probably quite rightly, adjudged that the ball turned too much to hit anything wooden, either bat or stumps. Pietersen had his own way of playing Warne, which involved hitting hard against the spin. This is dangerous unless you connect really well, which Pietersen usually did. In one over, he hit two big sixes into the leg-side crowds, but missed another big swipe completely. He brought up the England 100, and raised our hearts from our boots to our mouths, but what we really wanted was for them to be in the right place, and beating normally. But Pietersen was out to show Australia, and the English doubters, what he could do. But then Warne struck. Trescothick played and missed, Warne hit his pad, and the finger was raised. Trescothick's 33 had taken him 84 balls and contained only one four, a most untypical innings, but a very useful one in the context. Now, however, England were on 109 for four, and there were 78 overs to go. This was not good: Australians all around the ground were taking the opportunity to sing again, and an Australian singing is not a pretty sound or sight.

Of course, Flintoff was the next man in. Flintoff the hero, Freddie the saviour of England, so now it all depended on him. But for once he was not able to deliver. Given his staggering bowling performance of the day before, it was fairly amazing that he could even stand up, but we expect miracles from him every time, and he cannot always deliver. After hitting Shane Warne through the covers for four, he misjudged a slightly more flighted ball and hit the ball back low to Warne, who took a good return catch. Now England were tottering at 126 for five,

Pietersen takes a risky run to Clarke, and just beats his throw.

and Collingwood, the 'extra' batsman, had to hold the fort with KP. There were still 70 overs to be bowled, and Australia now looked to be firmly in charge. Lunchtime came with England at 127 for five. The mood around the ground was gloomy. The tension was worse than at any other ground (with the possible exception of Edgbaston that final morning) because this was the last chance. Squander it and England have to wait another eighteen months for a chance to beat these ageing champions. Nobody ate much at lunchtime.

Matches can turn round quickly, and this one turned more quickly than I can remember in a major encounter. Whatever Pietersen had for lunch, he should be encouraged to share it with the rest of the team, please, because it works. In Lee's first over after the break, Pietersen seized the initiative by taking two 2s and then smacking the ball over midwicket for six. It was all bottom hand and across the line, of course, but he has such a good eye that the outcome was never in doubt. Suddenly he was approaching his fifty, which he achieved in the next over from Warne, with a trademark clip through midwicket for 2. The crowd applauded long and hard, but we all knew that there was a lot more work to be done before the game was safe. Luckily, Pietersen knew it too. One big over for England is fine, but two in a row off the same bowler changed the course of the game. Two runs came off the second ball, a clever little run down to third man; the third ball, a bouncer, was hit for six well into the stands backward of square; the fourth ball, another attempted bouncer, was pulled backward of square, where Tait made a despairing dive in an attempt to catch it – four runs; the fifth ball, timed at 96.7 mph, also found its way to the deep backward square boundary for four more and Pietersen had taken 27 runs off two overs from Lee. England's total raced up to 160 for five, and the possibility of escape to victory had become more of a probability for England. Pietersen only faced the last two balls of Lee's next over, but he hit both for four to take Lee's analysis to the horrors of 11-0-66-0. That was enough for Ponting. McGrath came back into the attack.

Meanwhile at the other end Collingwood was not scoring many runs, but playing an important anchor role to Pietersen who had 'caught fire'. Collingwood smashed one ball into the shoulder of Katich, fielding at forward short leg, which surely hurt, but otherwise was leaving the belligerence to his partner. Pietersen was playing the innings of his life. He had another escape on 78, when he hit a ball from Warne on to the ground and/or his foot, and thence into the hands of slip, but after some conferring, the umpires decided it was not out. Television replays subsequently confirmed the correctness of this decision.

McGrath slowed the scoring rate somewhat, but failed to make the breakthrough. Every dot ball was being cheered to the rafters (although the brand new OCS Stand would not have anything as old-fashioned as rafters) and the number of overs remaining was beginning to assume a crucial significance. At drinks, England stood at 182 for five, but there were still almost 60 overs possible that day if the weather and light held. Once again, the drinks break was followed by the fall of a wicket. This time the diving close fielder was Ponting, but the bowler as ever

Opposite: The power of Pietersen.

was Warne. The victim was Collingwood, but his 10 runs were worth at least double that in the context of the game. With Pietersen he had added 60 runs, and English hearts, while still fluttering, were beginning nurture real hope.

Geraint Jones was the next man in, but he did not last long. McGrath gave way to Tait, for his first bowl of the day, and after Pietersen had smacked him for two fours to welcome him into the attack, he got a ball to reverse swing and keep low, and that was enough to see off Jones the Gloves – 199 for seven, and still 55 overs possible. England had taken 57 overs to get this far, so there was certainly a need for another fifty or sixty runs if England were to feel safe. Another wicket now, and we would all be reaching for the Valium. But a wicket did not fall. It Pietersen took another six overs to creep through the nineties to his hundred, but when he got there, with a fine extra-cover-drive off Tait in the over before tea, the Oval erupted yet again. In a day of over-excitement verging on panic, there was plenty of noise from the crowd all day, but this reception was perhaps the biggest of all.

After tea, there was a sense that we had got there. English people in the crowd were smiling at first, then laughing and hugging each other and, inevitably, singing. Giles and Pietersen carried on batting, and soon it was clear that England would not lose the game. Pietersen hit both Lee and Warne for further sixes, in the process breaking the record for most sixes in an Ashes innings, and by the time the score had reached 272, with only 36 overs left to play, the game was completely safe. The rest of the innings was perhaps an anti-climax: a series where the tension had begun with the second ball bowled by Harmison at Langer at Lord's on 21 July was now free of tension again, with barely two hours left of the summer, on 12 September. Now there was just exhilaration – Pietersen's 150, brought up with a six and a four off successive balls from Warne, and Giles' highest ever Test score, 59. Only 2 more and he can borrow McGrath's bat. The Australians were interacting with the crowd all afternoon. At third man, the crowd were chanting 'Five-nil, five-nil' to McGrath, who was signalling back to them with his fingers. I assume the message was 'two-two', for how else can you interpret two fingers on each hand waved vigorously at the crowd? Shane Warne got a massive ovation almost every time he moved. Everyone on the ground knew that, although he was going to be on the losing side, this was one of the great cricketers of all time, and they would not see him in a Test match in England again. (You could always pop down to Southampton and see him there, though).

For the record, Pietersen was finally out, bowled by McGrath for 158, just as Richie Benaud was saying his farewells on Channel Four. The publicity surrounding Benaud's final broadcast on UK television had at one stage threatened even to surpass the press over-reaction to the summer's Test series, but Benaud himself made sure that he was not the centre of attraction and that the cricket was. It was in many ways fitting that Benaud, the great master of understatement, who only ever said anything if he could add to the understanding or pleasure of the viewer, should depart at exactly the same time as Pietersen, who has yet to learn the meaning of understatement. One has been a giant of the game as player and broadcaster for fifty years: the other has the potential to do so if he can build on this stupendous innings, one of the very best innings seen in the 128 years of England v. Australia Tests. KP's 158 is exactly the same score that another South African Brit made in an Oval Test to help beat the Aussies – Basil D'Oliveira in 1968. The only differences were firstly that D'Oliveira's innings helped merely to tie a series, and secondly that there was no doubt about Pietersen's being picked for the winter tours. Giles became Warne's fifth victim of the innings when he was bowled round his legs by the blond bombshell. He and Pietersen had added 109 for the eighth wicket in 26 overs. Harmison became Warne's final Test victim in England by edging his second ball to Hayden at slip, and Hayden as ever took a good catch. England were 335 all out, (Warne six for 124) and Australia needed 342 to win in eighteen overs, a rate of exactly 19 an over.

Under ICC regulations, both teams had to return to play out most of the rest of the session. Conveniently, the light had begun to fade and the sunshine that had bathed the England cricketers and the crowds for most of the day disappeared. Harmison bowled four balls at poor Justin Langer at the fastest pace he could muster. The fourth ball pinged off his helmet for four leg-byes and the umpires offered the light. The Australians eagerly accepted, and everybody marched off the field. From this point on, the crowd had no idea what was happening. Was the match over? Were the Ashes officially England's? They knew that ICC regulations demanded the full day's play unless play was definitely impossible, but light can always improve, even if neither side wants to play on. What the crowd did not know was that the umpires and the match referee, Ranjan Madugalle of Sri Lanka, were meeting in the pavilion to decide what to do next. Fortunately common sense prevailed, and Billy Bowden and Rudi Koertzen, in a final act of pure theatre, marched out to the middle of the ground and formally removed the bails and knocked out a stump. With that, the match was over and the Ashes were England's. After sixteen years, for the first time since Allan Border snaffled them in 1989, the Ashes were England's again.

There were no surprises in the presentations. Kevin Pietersen was Man of the Match for his astonishing 158; Shane Warne was Australia's Man of The Series; and Andrew Flintoff was both England's Man of the Series and also the first winner of the Compton-Miller Medal for the Player of the Series. And so the celebrations began, and the Trafalgar Square parade could go ahead.

England v. Australia, Fifth Test Match

At the Oval, Kennington

8, 9, 10, 11, 12 September 2005

Result: Match Drawn

Toss: England

England

ME Trescothick c Hayden b Warne	43	lbw b Warne	33
AJ Strauss c Katich b Warne	129	c Katich b Warne	1
*MP Vaughan c Clarke b Warne	11	c Gilchrist b McGrath	45
IR Bell lbw b Warne	0	c Warne b McGrath	0
KP Pietersen b Warne	14	b McGrath	158
A Flintoff c Warne b McGrath	72	c & b Warne	8
PD Collingwood lbw b Tait	7	c Ponting b Warne	10
+GO Jones b Lee	25	b Tait	1
AF Giles lbw b Warne	32	b Warne	59
MJ Hoggard c Martyn b McGrath	2	not out	4
SJ Harmison not out	20	c Hayden b Warne	0
Extras (b 4, lb 6, w 1, nb 7)	18	(b 4, w 7, nb 5)	16
Total (all out, 105.3 overs)	373	(all out, 91.3 overs)	335

Fall of Wickets First Innings: 1-82 (Trescothick), 2-102 (Vaughan), 3-104 (Bell), 4-131 (Pietersen), 5-274 (Flintoff), 6-289 (Collingwood), 7-297 (Strauss), 8-325 (Jones), 9-345 (Hoggard), 10-373 (Giles).

Fall of Wickets Second Innings: 1-2 (Strauss), 2-67 (Vaughan), 3-67 (Bell), 4-109 (Trescothick), 5-126 (Flintoff), 6-186 (Collingwood), 7-199 (Jones), 8-308 (Pietersen), 9-335 (Giles), 10-335 (Harmison).

Bowling First Innings: McGrath 27–5–72–2; Lee 23–3–94–1; Tait 15–1–61–1; Warne 37.3–5–122–6; Katich 3–0–14–0

Bowling Second Innings: McGrath 26–3–85–3; Lee 20–4–88–0; Warne 38.3–3–124–6; Clarke 2–0–6–0; Tait 5–0–28–1

Australia

JL Langer b Harmison	105	not out	0
ML Hayden lbw b Flintoff	138	not out	0
*RT Ponting c Strauss b Flintoff	35		
DR Martyn c Collingwood b Flintoff	10		
MJ Clarke lbw b Hoggard	25		
SM Katich lbw b Flintoff	1		
+AC Gilchrist lbw b Hoggard	23		
SK Warne c Vaughan b Flintoff	0		
B Lee c Giles b Hoggard	6		
GD McGrath c Strauss b Hoggard	0		
SW Tait not out	1		
Extras (b 4, lb 8, w 2, nb 9)	23	(lb 4)	4
Total (all out, 107.1 overs)	367	(0 wickets, 0.4 overs)	4

Fall of Wickets First Innings: 1-185 (Langer), 2-264 (Ponting), 3-281 (Martyn), 4-323 (Hayden), 5-329 (Katich), 6-356 (Gilchrist), 7-359 (Clarke), 8-363 (Warne), 9-363 (McGrath), 10-367 (Lee).

Bowling First Innings: Harmison 22–2–87–1; Hoggard 24.1–2–97–4; Flintoff 34–10–78–5; Giles 23–1–76–0; Collingwood 4–0–17–0
Bowling Second Innings: Harmison 0.4–0–0–0

Umpires: BF Bowden (New Zealand) and RE Koertzen (South Africa)

Man of the Match: KP Pietersen

Players of the Series: A Flintoff and SK Warne

8

Not Fade Away

An email from an Australian friend in Melbourne: 'Don't say anything.'

I didn't need to: the England team said it all. In Andrew Flintoff, England possessed the best all-rounder in the world for the first time since Ian Botham's heyday. In the fast bowling quartet, England have the strongest attack since Trueman, Statham, Tyson, Loader and Moss were operating in the 1950s, and in Trescothick and Strauss probably the best opening partnership since Boycott and Edrich. Michael Vaughan has proved himself a captain equal to anybody in the world, and without question our most successful captain since Michael Brearley. There are still weaknesses in the side, notably at numbers four and seven, and Ashley Giles, though a key member of the side, is not the match-winning spinner that Warne, or Muralitharan or Mushtaq Ahmed or Anil Kumble or even Daniel Vettori can be. The strength is in the whole. The England team is a team, and greater than the sum of the parts. No other side in the world, with the possible exception of New Zealand, can fairly claim that.

The general view at the end of the series was that Michael Vaughan had easily won the battle of the captains, and that he had outwitted and outflanked Ricky Ponting at almost every turn. Well, he led the side that won the Ashes, so he got the main thing right – the winning – but how far ahead was he in the other areas of captaincy?

Frankly, it is quite difficult to tell, even though Ponting has not yet established himself as anything other than an ordinary captain at the helm of an extraordinary side. Ponting made one, or possibly two, big mistakes. Firstly, he put England in to bat at Edgbaston in the Second Test, even though his main strike bowler McGrath had just withdrawn from the game with an ankle injury, and thereby lost the match. Secondly, he allowed his batsmen to take the light not once but twice at the Oval, in a match they had to win, and not even Shane Warne could pull the game out of the bag for his captain from there. But these are decisions that look bad in retrospect because they were both unorthodox and failed. If they had worked, which the Edgbaston one very nearly did, Ponting would have been called a brilliant strategist. If he had done the orthodox thing and batted at Edgbaston, his captaincy would not have been questioned even had the Australians lost.

Michael Vaughan, on the other hand, made no really obviously brilliant decisions, and in many ways was comparatively unadventurous on the field. His bowling changes, for example, were fairly predictable, although he was willing to chop and change more than most captains would in an attempt to find the right bowler for the right end in any situation. His success as

a captain was based around two main strengths: his unflappable nature which allowed him to keep a firm control on the game where lesser men might have felt the rising tide of panic within them, and his endless capacity for planning. He had a firm belief in all eleven players on the field, and in their ability to carry out the plans that had been worked out to attack each Australian in turn.

But that begs the question – where does Duncan Fletcher's input end and Michael Vaughan's begin? The strategic field settings for certain batsmen, the round-the-wicket attack on Gilchrist and the hectic assault on the Australian bowling by Marcus Trescothick and others at Edgbaston were just three examples of ideas that grew from discussions before the Ashes series began, and not with flashes of inspiration on the field. These discussions were usually begun by Fletcher, although the ideas that were put into practice might have originated from anybody in the team. There is no doubt, however, that Duncan Fletcher's tactical nous was an essential part of the winning of the Ashes. As Nasser Hussain said to Duncan Fletcher on his retirement, 'Thank you for making me look a better captain than I was.'

Vaughan's real edge over Ponting was that he was able consistently to get the best out of all his players whenever he needed it. During the summer, every England cricketer made at least one major contribution to the team's unexpected victory, and it was clear that whoever was scoring the runs or taking the wickets, the rest of the England side got genuine enjoyment from sharing their successes. They all knew the jobs they had to do and they all did them well. This was Vaughan's contribution. By contrast, Ponting was unable to get his squad working so efficiently as a unit – the one area in which touring teams usually have the edge over the home side – and the Australians merely looked more and more bedraggled as the summer wore on. England caught Australia on the hop by playing them at their own game of applying pressure fast and consistently, and not even Warne's sustained brilliance, nor Ponting's best efforts at captaincy, could paper over the cracks.

In the end, Vaughan was Napoleon's lucky general, and Ponting was not.

If you were to speak to the players on both sides, the overwhelming view would be that the umpiring during the summer was of a high standard. There were some awful mistakes – lbws that pitched outside leg or took a thick inside-edge, for example – but there were also a much higher number of excellent decisions. These were mainly 'not out' decisions, and as such get forgotten quickly, but when eleven hungry men are appealing for a bat–pad catch, it is often difficult to get the decision right in the heat of the moment, especially if the batsman has actually hit the ball.

But would more electronic aids help? We already have run-outs and stumpings referred routinely to the third umpire (who has to justify his presence somehow), and many would say that lbws and catches should be judged electronically too. Hawkeye, Channel Four's remark-

Previous pages: Unashamed patriotic fervour in Trafalgar Square.

able cartoon duplicator of every ball bowled, appears to tell us when a ball would or would not have hit the stumps, and television can certainly confirm when a ball has pitched outside leg stump. However, the present technology, being two dimensional, cannot absolutely identify whether a catch has carried, anymore than the fielder sometimes can, and to use the third umpire in these cases would only slow down the action still further without making the quality of the decisions any better.

There is only one case in which I believe television technology can and should make a difference now, and that is with the calling of no-balls. No-balls are a line call, and television can be used entirely accurately to determine whether a bowler has overstepped the line in delivering the ball. It is, on the other hand, very hard for umpires to have to look down for the possible no-ball and then up again for the potential lbw or bat–pad decisions that will come a split second later. It is even more difficult for an umpire to spot the bowler overstepping the return crease (as Law 24 says, for a ball to be fair 'the bowler's back foot must land within and not touching the return crease') and even though Shane Warne, for one, regularly contravenes this part of the Law, he was never no-balled for this infringement during the series. If no-balls were to be confirmed by the third umpire, there could be two advantages: firstly, that the call would always be correct, and secondly, that the bowler's umpire would be able to concentrate on the batsman receiving the ball from an earlier moment. It is true that a cry of 'No ball' might sometimes be retrospective via the third umpire and the bowler's umpire's earpiece, but few batsmen are able to take advantage of the no-ball call anyway. It would also do away with the ludicrous situation, which occurred at Trent Bridge in 2001 for instance, when the bowler's umpire referred a close decision to the third umpire, who gave the batsman (Trescothick) out even though the replay also showed that the delivery was a no-ball which the umpire had missed. The third umpire is only allowed to answer the question asked – a silly situation.

Some say the umpire's job would be easier if batsmen 'walked' when they knew they were out. After all, in the good old days, batsmen were honest and if they knew they were out, they headed back to the pavilion, honour more intact than their wicket, didn't they? Actually, that is somewhat of a myth. And the only fair way to approach this issue is to leave it to the umpires, as they did in 2005. Even in this series of very good relations between the teams, nobody – not even Adam Gilchrist – walked until the umpire's finger went up. This is a good thing. The umpire's decision must be final, and to subject him to extra psychological pressure when, maybe, a known 'walker' does not walk when there is a questionable appeal, is unfair. It means that batsmen must subject themselves to occasional poor decisions, but over a professional career, the good and bad decisions tend to even themselves out. Keep the umpire firmly in control: do not encourage batsmen to walk, nor to dispute any umpire's decision.

The press have a role to play in this. Unless an umpire is clearly incompetent, they should not highlight poor decisions without also mentioning the good ones, which tend to be less newsworthy as they bring with them no 'what ifs'. Umpires do sometimes bring troubles on themselves when they have an eye on their public image, seemingly competing to be as renowned as the players, and a high profile merely makes you a bigger and easier target. If the players are famous enough to be ripe for criticism, then perhaps the high-profile umpires should be too. However, most of the eccentric umpires of recent times – and Brent 'Billy' Bowden is the obvious example in 2005 – are easily good enough at their job to avoid being targets for press sniping. All the same, an umpire should really be like a vicar at a wedding; he is vital to the success of the whole day, but he should never distract the congregation from the central characters.

Among the targets of criticism for the press throughout the summer were Ashley Giles and Geraint Jones. Well, in a summer of success, the press had to have some stories of English incompetence or they would have suffered acute withdrawal symptoms, and they hovered around the England numbers seven and eight like hungry vultures over a healthy herd of cows. After the Lord's Test they were all gunning for Giles (no runs, no wickets, no good) and when he began to show why he had been selected with a fine performance at Edgbaston, the attention turned on Geraint Jones. Mind you, he did take the match-winning catch, so it took a little while for the sniping remarks to turn into a full blooded hail of bullets. Some of the criticism, of Jones especially, was vindictive and unpleasant, and yet by the end of the series Jones had better statistics than his world-class counterpart Adam Gilchrist. Sometimes the press seem to get something into their heads and refuse to let go. 'Chris Read is the better wicketkeeper, so Chris Read should play for England' was the cry. Nobody is really disputing the idea that Read is a better 'keeper, but Jones is without doubt the better bat, and England have decided that their 'keeper needs to be an all-rounder. The selectors are not going to change their minds on policy (as the selection of Matt Prior of Sussex as number two 'keeper for the winter shows), and there is solidarity in the England ranks. Jones himself would admit that he made mistakes during the summer, and that there is work to be done to raise the standard of his glovework, but he is a fixture in the England side. Prompted by a journalist's observation that 'Geraint Jones has taken a lot of criticism,' Andrew Flintoff responded immediately and pertinently: 'Not in our dressing-room, he hasn't.' Ashley Giles is not a great mystery spinner like Warne or Murali or Saqlain, but then which English bowler is? Alex Loudon and his new-found 'doosra'? I think not. Loudon may well be an England player before long, but it will be as a batsman who bowls, not the other way around. If we had a great spinner in England, Giles' place might be in jeopardy, but at the moment he is the best we have, a wholehearted team man and a useful batsman and fielder to boot. The press will have to turn their feeding frenzy elsewhere.

If Giles were to lose his place, it would be a sad loss to the England supporters. Few men have been taken to the crowd's hearts as quickly and as completely as Ashley Giles, King of Spain. They cheered his every move at every ground, as they did the other talismanic members of the England side, Flintoff, Harmison and Hoggard. The Australian fielders, especially those on the boundary within earshot of the more raucous sections of the crowd, were not always so lucky. Justin Langer, who took on the Barmy Army in 2002/03 and lost, was one target, as was Damien Martyn (who tripped over himself in the outfield almost as often as Pietersen did), and all the fast bowlers, notably McGrath, Lee and Gillespie. Lee took it all with a smile, but Gillespie even went so far as to complain that he suffered verbal abuse from the crowds. Well, playing like he did, he left himself open to ridicule. I suspect the verbal abuse came as much from his own supporters as from the Barmy Army. It did not seem to me, as a member of those crowds (although not part of the Barmy Army strongholds) that the cries from the crowd were anything other than good humoured shouts, and certainly when the Australian players responded in kind – as Shane Warne or Glenn McGrath sometimes did – they became firm favourites with the crowds. It helped that they played well too. There was no chance of slagging off Shane Warne when he played all summer like a god (apart from the seminal moment when he dropped Pietersen at the Oval: it seemed to me that he was still thinking of his long conversation with Ponting the ball before and had not refocused his concentration on the moment). If Warne was a god, Gillespie looked and played like the minor prophet Ezekiel down on his luck, and then launched into lamentations of which Job would have been proud. The crowds knew and liked their cricket, so if you play well, they treat you well: play like a drain and they will flush you away. The interaction between the players and the spectators throughout the summer was good humoured and, mainly, enjoyable. It was only when extreme drunkenness or extreme nudity took over that spectators found themselves justifiably ejected from the ground.

The England and Wales Cricket Board set out a few seasons ago to create an England team that would be the best in the world by 2007. At the time, the aim was mocked by one and all, because England had a poor side then, and anyway such grandiose targets are somehow un-English. But who is laughing now? The England Test side shows every sign of taking over the number one spot from the ageing Australians, and there are no other international sides coming up on the rails to pip them at the post. Number one in 2007 looks all but certain now. To be the number one one-day team in the world is a much more difficult task. Until international managers realise that the skills required for one-day success are very different, at the highest level, from the skills required for Test success. A wonderful Test side can only go so far in one-day cricket, and vice versa. It would be astonishing if the England one-day side as it is in 2005 can be the best by 2007, simply because there are too few performers in that side who really understand the game. It's like clay court to hard court to grass court tennis: some people, the Roger Federers of this world, who are geniuses, can succeed on any court, but the majority of merely extremely good players become expert at one surface or another, and merely chance their luck on their less favoured surfaces. The national cricket sides who concentrate more seriously on one-day cricket, as Sri Lanka did in the late 1990s, will be the best, however hard our very fine Test side tries.

Four years ago, when I wrote about the 2001 series, I noted that the first intake of the Academy was to include Andrew Strauss, Stephen Harmison, Simon Jones, Ian Bell, Rob Key and Chris

Tremlett, among others. I wrote, 'They are a motley if talented crew who will no doubt benefit from their winter in the Adelaide sun, but was their selection really part of a long-term policy rather than a quick fix?' I can answer that question now – it was indeed a long-term policy. This is where the strength of England's present set-up lies. Once a player's talent has been identified, there is a long-term effort to turn him into a world-beater. Of course, it does not always work (the youthful promise of Derek Kenway, Chris Schofield and Nicky Peng, for example, has not developed as hoped) but when the long-term policy works, as it has done with half a dozen of that intake of four years ago, then it means that players coming into the Test side already have a degree of familiarity with the set-up and an understanding of the team ethic, which makes the transition from county to Test player less daunting. Of the twelve players who won back the Ashes, only Kevin Pietersen and Geraint Jones largely by-passed the A team and Academy route to the side, but these are both men whose early cricket careers were spent overseas. The Academy works, central contracts work and even though there is undoubtedly an effect on County Championship cricket, in both quality and crowd appeal, there is no real opposition to the idea of subordinating all local interests to the success of the England side. Because the success of the England side means more money for the game, more money for the counties, and – in an ideal world – more money at grassroots level for the development of future generations of cricketers.

What lasting impact on the game and the followers of the game will England's success have? The early indications are mixed. The fact that all sorts of people who are not cricket lovers are now talking about cricket is a good thing. The fact that politicians are falling over themselves, like Pietersen in the outfield, to be part of the Ashes success is all good, especially if it gives the British public a cynical laugh at the expense of our politicians. Open-top bus celebrations in Trafalgar Square are all very well, but they hide the true cause of our joy this summer: the England team has been so awful for the best part of two decades, and this victory is long overdue. Winning the Ashes is not like winning the rugby World Cup or a gold medal at the Olympics. It is something that ought to happen regularly, and there is a danger that the huge media interest in the summer's cricket will produce a backlash if, for example, England fail to win the World Cup in 2007. The fact that cricket is fashionable again is fine while it lasts, but there is nothing as uninteresting as yesterday's big thing. Cricket needs to hold on to current levels of interest. Just because we have not won the Ashes for almost twenty years, there should not be any greater celebration of our victory than if we had not lost them for twenty years.

The England players have a big responsibility in this. Vaughan, Flintoff, Harmison, Strauss and the rest have just begun to realise what it means to be a sports star as opposed to a successful sportsman. The press will hang around outside their houses, hoping for a candid photo

Previous pages: Vaughan displays the prize urn – the dark glasses hide the evidence of the excesses of the night before.

NOT FADE AWAY • 193

of almost anything. They will be asked to model clothes (which Simon Jones has already taken to with a will), to comment on any sporting matter, and no doubt also to choose their favourite recipes, their favourite holiday destinations and their eight desert island discs. At some stage it will all turn sour. Yet they need to show that not all sports heroes are vapid nightclub devotees in their off-duty hours. They need to show that being a professional cricketer is fun, healthy and – heaven forbid – cool. If cricket is to flourish in the 21st century, it needs role models and it needs to grab the public imagination at all levels and in all age groups.

The Channel Four viewing figures for the Ashes series in 2005 make interesting reading. Those figures of seven and eight million viewers are exciting, if a little sad for the channel that was showing its final summer of Test cricket, but the demographics of those viewing figures show that the people who watched spellbound were largely the same people that have always watched cricket – the over 35s. Terrestrial television is becoming an older person's playground, but the breakdown of those millions of viewers shows that the lure of cricket has yet to spread to the young. Only 6 per cent of the viewers were under fourteen, even though the lateness of the series meant that it took place in the school holidays; another 16 per cent were aged between 15 and 35, 20 per cent were aged 35 to 55, 17 per cent between 55 and 65 and a whopping 35 per cent were over 65. I suppose that usually Channel Four relies on its over-65s every afternoon, but if over half those eight million viewers are over 55, the reach of cricket into the younger generation has a long way still to go. If we compare these viewing figures with those for football on both terrestrial and satellite TV, the age profile is almost completely the opposite. Football fans want to go out clubbing with their heroes; cricket fans want to mother them. It is worth noting that when Nottinghamshire won the County Championship a week after the Ashes triumph, BBC's Ceefax service listed this achievement as about the fifth sports headline, well below Chelsea's sixth Premiership victory of the new season (only 32 more games to go). Cricket does not yet even start to challenge football's popularity, and it would be a foolish person who thought otherwise.

All the same, my expectation is that the England cricket team will be the best in the world at Test cricket for some years to come. This statement represents a huge turnaround in four years since the previous Australian tour of England, but it is realistic. Barring injury or illness, the England team will contain, until 2010 at least, four or five of the best players in the world. As the Australians, as well as greats like Brian Lara, Sachin Tendulkar and Muttiah Muralitharan approach the end of their brilliant careers, most of the England side are new boys. With the retirement of Graham Thorpe, nobody in the side has played more than 66 Tests, which is Marcus Trescothick's total, and the five-man bowling attack, the hub of England's success, has a total of just 200 Test caps between them. There is a lot of power still to come. While Warne, McGrath, Gilchrist and the rest fade gracefully into the Australian sunset, hoping to take Richie Benaud's place in the commentary box or Rod Marsh's slot in the Academy, the revitalised England under Michael Vaughan ought to be able to take on allcomers for a few seasons, and beat them.

There is no magic formula for world domination at any sport. These things go in cycles, and it is cricket's turn to bask in the sunshine for a few years. However, the biggest challenge to English cricket in the foreseeable future is not likely to come from another cricketing country, but from Britain itself, or to be more precise, from London. The awarding of the Olympic Games to London in 2012 will divert attention away from practically everything else of a sporting nature, and cricket, not being an Olympic sport, may well suffer. Cricket should not be an Olympic sport (nor should ice dancing and synchronised diving, in my view) any more than tennis or rugby should, because the ultimate challenge for a cricketer comes in Test matches, not in Olympic competition. All the same, if we are to live through several years of building up hopes and expectations of Olympic medals in a whole variety of sports and several other musical or athletic pastimes, then the sports pages and the attention of the sports public will be diverted from cricket. Even Andrew Flintoff may struggle to compete for column inches with 2012's equivalent of Kelly Holmes, Steve Redgrave or Paula Radcliffe, or all the yachtsmen, boxers and cyclists who briefly grab the headlines in any Olympic year. In the build-up to 2012, there is a danger that government money for sport, such as it is, will be concentrated on producing Olympic champions, so that the grassroots of cricket, so sincerely praised by the politicians in the wake of this Ashes victory, may well be ignored. That is the challenge for cricket's administrators now.

All in all, it has been a wonderful summer of unforgettable Tests. England have shown what we did not dare to hope – that their cricket team are indeed world beaters, and they showed it in one of the greatest Test series ever played. Everybody who followed the Tests, whether live or on television or radio, would have been gripped by the sheer excitement of the games. This five-match, twenty-five day series was decided at around teatime on the final day. Until that moment, the result could have gone either way, and within each game, with the possible exception of the First Test, there were whole sessions during which the emotions swung from hope to despair and back to exhilaration, whichever team you supported, or if you supported neither. The cricket was wonderful, and the tension unbearable. At least two new world stars appeared on the scene, in Flintoff and Simon Jones, and several more confirmed their status – none more so than the incredible and indomitable Shane Warne. There may have been less great batting than in many series, although Ricky Ponting at Old Trafford and Kevin Pietersen at the Oval produced innings of prolonged brilliance, but that was in part because the bowling was so good.

There were moments of pure joy – Brett Lee's smile when he hit Steve Harmison into the gardens across the road from Trent Bridge; McGrath and Lee dancing on the pitch when the Old Trafford Test was saved; the purity of Flintoff's back-foot straight drives and the dazzling brilliance of Shane Warne bowling to the left-handers. There were moments of sadness – watching Gillespie's career end in ignominy; seeing Gilchrist as only half the player he was four years earlier and feeling for Ian Bell as he struggled for runs in the later Tests. For me, though, the sustaining memory is of the spirit in which the game was played.

A small cameo of the respect the teams had for each other and for the game was seen at Old Trafford on the third day. Brad Hodge, fielding substitute for Michael Clarke, made a brave attempt to catch Vaughan in the second innings. He immediately signalled that the ball did not carry, and Vaughan, who had made a big hundred in the first innings and was likely to do the same this time round, batted on. In the event, it did not cost Australia many runs, but the absolute honesty with which the games were played was, to the players and all concerned with the series, more important than fiddling out the opposition captain. There were many more examples of this spirit throughout the summer, and it was for me the happiest feature of the series. Cricket is not only once again ruled by England, but also by sportsmen for whom the game is bigger than the result.

We could not hope for a better outcome to the summer than that.

Averages

England

Batting

	M	I	NO	Runs	HS	Avge	SR	Ct	St
KP Pietersen	5	10	1	473	158	52.55	71.45		
ME Trescothick	5	10	0	431	90	43.10	60.27	3	
A Flintoff	5	10	0	402	102	40.20	74.16	3	
AJ Strauss	5	10	0	393	129	39.30	57.79	6	
SP Jones	4	6	4	66	20*	33.00	67.34	1	
MP Vaughan	5	10	0	326	166	32.60	60.82	2	
GO Jones	5	10	1	229	85	25.44	57.97	15	1
AF Giles	5	10	2	155	59	19.37	50.65	5	
IR Bell	5	10	0	171	65	17.10	45.35	8	
SJ Harmison	5	8	2	60	20*	10.00	84.50	1	
PD Collingwood	1	2	0	17	10	8.50	22.07	1	
MJ Hoggard	5	9	2	45	16	6.42	19.65		

Bowling

	O	M	R	W	Avge	Best	SR	Econ
SP Jones	102	17	378	18	21.00	6-53	34.0	3.70
A Flintoff	194	32	655	24	27.29	5-78	48.5	3.37
MJ Hoggard	122.1	15	473	16	29.56	4-97	45.8	3.87
SJ Harmison	161.1	22	549	17	32.29	5-43	56.8	3.40
AF Giles	160	18	578	10	57.80	3-78	96.0	3.61
PD Collingwood	4	0	17	0	–	–	–	4.25
IR Bell	7	2	20	0	–	–	–	2.85
MP Vaughan	5	0	21	0	–	–	–	4.20

Australia

Batting

	M	I	NO	Runs	HS	Avge	SR	Ct	St
JL Langer	5	10	1	394	105	43.77	58.63	2	
RT Ponting	5	9	0	359	156	39.88	59.63	4	
MJ Clarke	5	9	0	335	91	37.22	54.38	2	
GD McGrath	3	5	4	36	20*	36.00	63.15	1	
ML Hayden	5	10	1	318	138	35.33	46.97	10	
SK Warne	5	9	0	249	90	27.66	70.53	5	
SM Katich	5	9	0	248	67	27.55	46.79	4	
B Lee	5	9	3	158	47	26.33	65.02	2	
AC Gilchrist	5	9	1	181	49*	22.62	71.82	18	1
DR Martyn	5	9	0	178	65	19.77	53.13	4	
MS Kaprowicz	2	4	0	44	20	11.00	67.69	3	
SW Tait	2	3	2	8	4	8.00	29.62		
JN Gillespie	3	6	0	47	26	7.83	21.55	1	

Bowling

	O	M	R	W	Avge	Best	SR	Econ
RT Ponting	6	2	9	1	9.00	1-9	36.0	1.50
SK Warne	252.5	37	797	40	19.92	6-46	37.9	3.15
GD McGrath	134	22	440	19	23.15	5-53	42.3	3.28
B Lee	191.1	25	822	20	41.10	4-82	57.3	4.29
SW Tait	48	5	210	5	42.00	3-97	57.6	4.37
SM Katich	12	1	50	1	50.00	1-36	72.0	4.16
MS Kasprowicz	52	6	250	4	62.50	3-80	78.0	4.80
JN Gillespie	67	6	300	3	100.00	2-91	134.0	4.47
MJ Clarke	2	0	6	0	–	–	–	3.00